PRIMARY COMMODITY CONTROL

PRIMARY COMMODITY CONTROL

C. P. BROWN

KUALA LUMPUR
OXFORD UNIVERSITY PRESS
LONDON NEW YORK MELBOURNE
1975

Oxford University Press, Ely House, London W. 1

GLASGOW NEW YORK TORONTO MELBOURNE WELLINGTON
CAPE TOWN IBADAN NAIROBI DAR ES SALAAM LUSAKA ADDIS ABABA
DELHI BOMBAY CALCUTTA MADRAS KARACHI LAHORE DACCA
KUALA LUMPUR SINGAPORE JAKARTA HONG KONG TOKYO

Bangunan Loke Yew, Kuala Lumpur
● *Oxford University Press 1975*

Printed in Malaysia by
ART PRINTING WORKS, KUALA LUMPUR

To
Katharine and Harry

Preface

THIS book suggests lines of reasoning with which to analyse primary commodity control. It may provoke the reader to become more critical of often simplistic approaches to control frequently found in the reasoning of committees of 'experts', government officials administering national devices and negotiators of international commodity agreements. Not all the answers are provided here, however, and where all the ramifications of a particular argument would be tedious without necessarily being edifying, these have not been followed through. Related topics such as the pattern of international primary commodity trade and the possible effects of fluctuations in export earnings on growth and the distribution of income are not treated as thoroughly as they might be in a volume on international or development economics. Historical aspects of control are introduced only where these might indicate the type of agreements to expect in the future or provide pertinent lessons from past control of trade. The reader can find many important aspects of the subject matter related to the material of this book, but not duplicated here, in Rowe's *Primary Commodities in International Trade*. There is little in the main part of this volume beyond the reach of those acquainted with the fundamentals of economics. Virtually all of the mathematics has been confined to the appendices and the geometric diagrams in the text are no more sophisticated than those found in introductory texts. Each chapter is concluded with an extended summary designed primarily for those who want to avoid the more involved discussion and the diagrams that precede but who wish, nevertheless, to grasp the underlying arguments and the conclusions. Those who read the main body of the text may choose to by-pass these summaries.

Much of the first chapter is devoted to a rather thorough, descriptive explanation of those factors which are likely to lead to instability in primary commodity markets—a subject unlikely to have been intensively covered in normal introductory readings in related fields of study. An understanding of these factors is essential for the later analysis of control since application of the analysis is predicated upon some knowledge of the more fundamental market parameters. The rough *ad hoc* method of estimating these provided should prove particularly useful to those who are intimidated by constructing and testing complicated market models, but wish to use the techniques of analysis suggested. A little useful knowledge of parameters and analytical techniques is better than none at all in the undoubtedly frequent situations requiring policy makers to rely on intelligent guesses when they do not have access to an expert who has the time and resources to study the problem in depth. For the ambitious reader, the appendices provide illustrations of more elegant approaches.

For the most part, the discussion of control in succeeding chapters has been limited to those commonly found devices whose popularity implies their workability and acceptability in a world in which decisions are not made by economists alone. When covering international devices attention is focused particularly on those formal devices that conform to the egalitarian spirit of the Havana Accords and GATT and the general view taken throughout is that of the developing country exporting to developed countries. Although conventional devices used individually may bring undesirable effects as well as those sought, combinations of such devices can be used to neutralize these effects. The historical popularity of these devices and combinations makes discussion of them more relevant than consideration of hypothetical possibilities which might find little acceptance or understanding among those who make the final decisions on their use. However, limited discussions of untried devices are given throughout. These untried devices have been selected either to illustrate the range of plausible possibilities or because their serious consideration at policy levels becomes likely as they are more widely understood. After the number of decades over which they have been discussed, some of these no longer appear unconventional.

The questionable advantages, the high costs of implementation and the difficulty of negotiating international control devices have caused efforts to be directed toward national control devices in recent years. Considerable stress is placed here on these national efforts. This is not intended to deny the current and future role of international devices, especially in conjunction with carefully chosen national devices. However emphasis in those areas where, through wisdom or folly, most effort is being expended should bring the greatest returns to the reader.

At present no introductory text is devoted entirely to the analysis of commodity control by conventional devices. Without reliable antecedents in the form of axioms of commodity control the writer is obviously more open to censure. A tendency to retreat into abstract generality which allows some ambiguity and latitude of interpretation is tempting. However, a concerted effort has been made here to be specific and to encourage, so far as possible, the relating of theory to fact, particularly through the testing of alternative control methods in specific sets of circumstances. Where this relationship seems obscure in the text because of the limitations imposed by a non-mathematical medium, some compensation is made in the appendices.

Sections of the book have appeared elsewhere in shorter or expanded and different form. A number of the ideas presented were developed in a D. Phil. dissertation for the University of Oxford in 1968. Some of these were subsequently elaborated in articles appearing in the *Journal of Development Studies* (1970 and 1974), *Eastern Africa Economic Review* (1970), *African Social Research* (1971), *Malayan Economic Review* (1972) and *Developing Economies* (1973).

Kuala Lumpur,   C.P. BROWN
August 1973

Acknowledgements

THE preparation of this book and the period of study of which it is a culmination have left me indebted to numerous individuals. In particular I am grateful to Miss P. Ady and Mr. R. Bacon for supervising my initial efforts while at Oxford, Professor A.I. MacBean for suggesting the need for a text in the field, Mr. R. Thillainathan for detailed remarks on Chapter 5, and the Commodities Division of UNCTAD for a number of helpful comments on Appendix 4. I am especially thankful for the patience my students in the Universities of Malawi and Malaya have shown through several drafts of the text in its formative stages and for their comments on its clarity. Appreciation for my wife's painstaking editing efforts is best not expressed in the printed word. As a non-economist, her comprehension of the main body of the text was a measure of its readability. The tedious job of typing and retyping the several drafts fell to Miss See Koy Yon who deserves special recognition for perseverance beyond the call of duty. Finally, I wish to release all those associated with the book of any responsibility for its shortcomings. I alone am accountable for these.

Contents

IV. PRICE CONTROL SIMULATION

Figures

Graph

Chart

Tables

I
Causes of Instability
in Primary Commodity Markets

1. INTRODUCTION

DURING the post-war period the proportion of primary producers in developing countries affected by international and particularly national efforts to control trade in their products has steadily increased. Nearly every primary commodity of importance as an export or domestic staple in developing countries has either come under some degree of control or been considered for control recurrently during this period. The production of primary commodities in these countries frequently occupies most of the land resource and economically active population, and individually or as a group may make the largest single contribution to the total value of economic activity. Those that are exported frequently provide a major source of foreign exchange earnings and government revenue. The importance of primary commodities as a source of employment, savings and foreign exchange and the evidence of steadily increasing control, warrants consideration of the possible effects of the various control measures being adopted.

The discussion here presupposes a market environment: an exchange relationship in which trading parties exercise a range of choice with respect to their selection of primary commodities, prices, quantities and trading partners. Control under completely centralized co-ordination systems, where the scope of individual action and choice is severely limited, is not prevalent in developing countries because of the cost of providing an administrative substitute for the market. The skills, social habits and essential information necessary for such an administrative system to be viable are generally lacking. Under the more typical condition of private ownership, control over markets is intended to bring the activities of private owners into conformity with basic development goals. This may be effected by control aimed at the volume and prices of primary commodities, their quality and the distribution of transactions among potential sellers and buyers.

The present chapter, by way of introduction, defines the terms 'primary commodity' and 'stability' and briefly reviews the patterns of world trade in primary commodities. Its bulk is devoted to an illustration of lines of inferential reasoning which can be used to determine the kind of market in which a prospective control device is to operate. For meaningful application of the techniques of analysis suggested in the following chapters, some knowledge of likely supply and demand elasticities and shift characteristics is essential. For those seeking a more sophisticated approach to the estimation of market parameters and who have access to a computer, Appendix 1 demonstrates the construction of a market model for a tree crop. The general principles involved are readily transferable to annuals and minerals.

2. DEFINITION OF PRIMARY COMMODITIES

All products of the land whether they are extracted from the land (minerals), grown on the land (crops, including timber), or raised on the land (cattle) are considered to be primary commodities while they remain in an unprocessed or partly processed state. Products which are harvested or fished from bodies of water (e.g. shell fish, plants, salt, and water itself) are also primary commodities until they have undergone a 'substantial' transformation or combination with other inputs. The point in processing at which products are no longer considered to be in a primary state is ambiguous, largely a problem of semantics, and perhaps best illustrated with a few examples. Raw cotton remains a primary commodity after ginning but is no longer considered so after it has been spun and woven into a textile. Cocoa and coffee remain in the primary category after drying, sorting, grading and baking. Most natural rubber on world markets has been combined with chemicals that gell and preserve it. In this state it is more processed than the raw latex from which it is derived but it remains a primary commodity because these are minor inputs, which do not alter its essential characteristics. When it is combined as an input, however important, with other inputs in a manufactured product such as a tyre, the tyre is not considered to be simply rubber in a more elaborate form, it is a manufactured product. Cane sugar remains a primary commodity through increasing degrees of refinement but is no longer considered so when it becomes confectionery. Tin retains the primary status through cleaning, smelting and refining.

Most primary commodities on the market are semi-processed, either by the original producers, as in the case of rubber which is smoked by the smallhold producer, or by a separate processor as in the case of tin smelting. The above examples indicate that the general terms used to describe primary commodities, such as 'natural rubber' and 'cane sugar', in fact refer to groups of products at different levels of processing. These groups are further subdivided according to types and qualities. There are, for instance, hundreds of types and qualities of rice each with its own price and nomenclature. Types of rice are generally distinguished by grain length, circumference, and cooking characteristics while quality is based on the degree of mixed, broken, immature, empty, or diseased grains and the amount of dirt and straw in a given quantity of rice. At any point in time each of these types and qualities may be found on the market at various levels distinguished by dryness, milling, polish, and par-boiling.

3. THE IMPORTANCE AND PATTERN OF PRIMARY COMMODITY TRADE

Table 1.1 illustrates, using rough orders of magnitude, the relative importance of primary commodities in international trade. Primary

TABLE 1.1

THE COMPOSITION OF WORLD TRADE

(by value)

	World Trade in all Commodities	World Trade in Primary Commodities	Exports of Developing Countries	Exports of Developing Countries Excluding Fuels	Primary Commodities from Developing Countries
	(1)	(2)	(3)	(4)	(5)
Agricultural	30%	60%	50%	75%	85%
Minerals (excluding fuels)	10%	10%	10%	10%	15%
Fuels	10%	30%	30%	Excluded	Excluded
Manufactures	50%	Excluded	10%	15%	Excluded
	100%	100%	100%	100%	100%

commodities represent about 50 per cent of the value of world trade in all products (Column 1). Within the category of primary commodities, about 60 per cent of the value of those traded is agricultural produce (food, raw materials, timber and animal products) and about 40 per cent mined products (Column 2). Exports from the developing countries (Column 3) indicate a pronounced dependence on agricultural exports for foreign exchange earnings. Primary agricultural exports from a number of developing countries account for as much as 90 per cent of the value of total merchandise exports and frequently this dependence is concentrated in one or two agricultural commodities. Despite the importance of agricultural exports to developing countries individually and as a group, they export only 35 per cent in value of total world agricultural exports. Similarly, manufactures from developing countries, accounting for ten per cent of total export earnings, represent only five per cent of world trade in manufactures. The bulk of trade in primary commodities occurs between developed countries.

If we exclude fuels from our figures on the grounds that fuel is exported by only a handful, though a growing handful, of developing countries, the more representative figures (Columns 4 & 5) show an increased predominance of agricultural exports and an improved position for manufactures over the aggregated figures. Fuel is the single category of exports shown for which developing countries account for a majority of world exports.

While the exports of developing countries tend to be concentrated on agricultural products and frequently a limited range of agricultural products, the absorption of their primary exports tends to be highly concentrated in the developed countries. Over 90 per cent of the petroleum, tea, cocoa, rubber and sugar exported by developing countries is consumed by the developed countries. In some cases one region or country accounts for a pronounced proportion of total demand. This is true for Western Europe as the largest importer of tea, wheat, cotton and cocoa, and the United States as the largest single importer of tin, coffee, cane sugar and natural rubber. Each of these areas absorbs over one-third by value of the world imports of these commodities. In contrast to this pattern of trade, rice is traded primarily between the developing countries of Asia.

4. DEFINITIONS OF STABILITY

'Instability' is a major factor giving rise to primary commodity control. In the context of primary commodity trade, 'instability' normally

refers to variation in prices, quantum, incomes, profits or export earnings and is ascertained by the amplitude of changes in these variables
and the frequency of change. These two criteria assume meaning in an
objective sense only when there is comparison with other economic
or social phenomena. That is, a particular fluctuation is seen to be excessive only in comparison with more stable phenomena such as a past
period in the same time series, retail prices, gross national product, or
world wholesale prices for manufactures. A less objective standard
may be provided by specifying a range within which fluctuations are
considered normal and necessary to adjust supply and demand. Intra-
seasonal fluctuations would be excessive, for instance, if they had no
functional significance in the efficient and smooth allocation of resources.
High prices normally create incentives and attract resources. But 'excessively' high prices may attract more resources into a particular economic activity than the longer run equilibrium price would justify. An
excessive flow of resources to an industry increases the likelihood of
dislocated resources when prices return to normal and resources are
forced to leave the industry. The price is seen to be excessive because it
may dislocate or misallocate resources. Large and frequent fluctuations
increase the costs of adjustment of factors. If resources flow smoothly
in and out of an industry simultaneously with changes in price without dislocating resources, or creating hardship by upsetting the balance
of payments or export tax receipts or affecting demand, etc. no amplitude or frequency of price movement would be considered excessive
in this sense.

   A given price change could be considered excessive if, due to an inability of supply to respond more than a limited degree in the short or long
run, a lesser price change would achieve the same response. Alternatively,
supply may be too responsive to price such that the overreaction brings
cycles of glut and scarcity in the familiar cobweb pattern. Price fluctuations of single primary commodities might be considered excessive if
they have unfavourable secondary effects on attitudes of those producing other exports or contemplating irreversible forms of substitution
on the demand side of the market. Short-term income instability is
considered undesirable (excessive) for the above reasons when producers look to income in determining their investment pattern. Such
instability also creates a climate of insecurity among producers and
those from whom they purchase goods and services. Inter-seasonal (day-
to-day or month-to-month) fluctuations in prices would be considered
excessive when they leave producers no coherent basis for making short
run allocations of their resources and when they tempt producers and

intermediaries to concentrate on speculation rather than productive pursuits.

The period used for measuring instability will depend on the problem under consideration. If you are interested in controlling short run speculation on an organized commodity market, comparison of average day-to-day prices may be made. If an attempt is being made to relate the price of a seasonally harvested crop to its costs of storage over time, a comparison of average monthly prices rather than daily prices may be useful because they mask day-to-day fluctuations which are not of interest in this case. Year-to-year comparisons are commonly used for export earnings, profits, producer income, and export tax revenue over time since these comparisons mask daily and seasonal variations that may obscure the longer term variations.

In drawing a comparison between yearly averages to determine the degree of fluctuation, a distinction should be made between fluctuations due to trend movement and those due to fluctuations around the trend. This distinction is particularly important in periodically establishing a controlled price when the control authorities wish to avoid influencing the trend of prices. Without adjusting for trend movement, an exaggerated impression of the magnitude of the fluctuation may be obtained, leading to an overestimate of the resources required to control the fluctuation. If an annual time series develops 90, 95, 100, 105, 110, for instance, an instability of about five per cent a year is indicated. After adjusting for the smooth upward trend development, however, there is no yearly fluctuation. In the series 90, 85, 100, 95, 110, 105 we have the same trend development but in this case it must be sorted out from fluctuations around the trend. If it is not, the impression will be that the control device must be very strong in order to control both the wide yearly fluctuations and support a ceiling price for a number of successive years. Such a false conclusion (in light of the intention not to control the trend) may discourage an attempt at control altogether or elicit an exceedingly wide price range that provides only limited support over widely spaced periods.

5. SUPPLY RESPONSE TO PRICE AND INCOME CHANGES

Instability in price, quantum or income and its importance is dependent upon shifts in the demand or supply schedule, or both, and their elasticities. Consider, for instance, Figure 1.1 where D, D_x and S denote, respectively, domestic demand for the exported primary com-

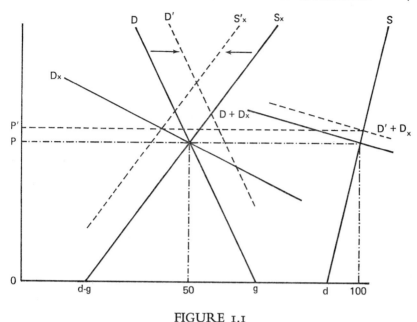

FIGURE 1.1

THE EFFECT OF DOMESTIC DEMAND ON EXPORT SUPPLY

modity, export demand and domestic supply. For simplicity it is assumed that at price P domestic consumers absorb half of total domestic output and the other half is exported. Exported supply, S_x, is derived by horizontal subtraction of domestic demand, D, from total domestic supply, S. Thus, export supply elasticity will be a function of domestic demand elasticity. Should D shift to the right to D', total demand, $D + D_x$, will shift by the same amount to $D' + D_x$. World price and domestic consumption will increase while export supply and export consumption will decrease. If exports decrease in the face of an elastic export demand, export earnings will decrease. The magnitude of the change will depend on the elasticities of D, D_x and S and the size of the shift in D. The necessary strength of stabilization devices and their possible favourable and detrimental effects will largely depend on whether the commodity under control is in a market in which instability is caused primarily by fluctuations in demand (a demand-shift market) or supply (a supply-shift market). Estimation of values of these parameters and the demand and supply elasticities for a commodity is facilitated by an understanding of the probable reasons for them assuming given values.

a. LONG RUN FACTORS AFFECTING CROPS

Fundamentally different factors influence the supply response of tree

crops, annuals and minerals to market forces over time. Production of
tree crops is likely to be unresponsive to recent upward price movements because current output is heavily dependent on the stock of
trees. Increases in output in a given period will be due to young trees
becoming, for the first time, economically harvestable. The current
yield change attributable to this will, in the case of rubber, for instance,
be a response to planting decisions made 5–8 years previously and, in
that of cocoa, 8–12 years. Changes in total cocoa production are further complicated by a two yield spurt growth pattern. In roughly the
eighth and twelfth years after planting, yields show a pronounced increase and may decline between these two periods. While current output of a tree crop will be responding to planting decisions taken some
years before, the decision to plant may have been based in part on
prices in periods previous to that in which the decision was made. A
lagged reaction of planting decisions to price changes is also common
with annuals for reasons discussed below.

Planting decisions will be based on the farmer's expectation of future
prices which may take into account recent past prices and the trend of
prices over a considerable past period. This subjective forecast will
enter into an *ad hoc* estimate of the discounted present value of the
future income stream he expects to receive from the tree crop. The
rate of discount and the anticipated net income stream will be influenced, respectively, by his time preference for income and by the proportion of prospective gross income which will be spent on variable
cash inputs. His costs of establishment may be sufficiently negligible
so that the risk of an incorrect projection does not deter him from
planting, especially if his own opportunity cost is very low. Actual
costs of establishment may be covered by the sale of timber from land
cleared. If a tree crop is interplanted with other crops of commercial
value these may help additionally to defray costs. In fact, the farmer
may not consider the costs of establishing a tree crop if the land must
be cleared for other crops he wishes to grow. If he is dependent on
the tree crop for an income, however, low costs of establishment suggest that he is likely to be responsive to increases in price and somewhat less responsive to decreases. Planting of annual or perennial crops
may be unresponsive to price changes if the nearest crop substitute is
not more remunerative at low prices than the crop in question. On
the other hand, if the ratio of the value of output of alternative crops
is similar to that of a given crop on a unit of land with the same human
and capital resources, a small change in the relative price will affect
the cropping pattern.

Returns from farm resources in different uses will depend on how specific the resources are to certain activities. If the farmer lacks knowledge of how to grow an alternative crop effectively, returns to effort devoted to growing the alternative crop will be low. Land and capital inputs may also be specific to certain uses, particularly farm capital in advanced agriculture. Specificity of resources reduces alternative returns and, as in all cases where returns are low or zero, resource use in the alternative employment will not respond readily to price increases. The possible specific nature of the human resource may increase the period of 'long run' for an annual crop to a period of time comparable to that for some tree crops. Under conditions of slow and inefficient acquisition of knowledge, it may take a farmer a number of years to learn to grow an alternative crop. Knowledge of the alternative may be acquired piecemeal, perhaps from his neighbours, until he feels sufficiently confident to plant. The initial incentive to acquire the knowledge, and the decision to plant, may be induced by relative price movements a number of years before the planting occurs.

The availability of land will influence not only cost of the land resource and thus the ease with which planting may occur, but in the case of perennials, the capital stock of trees during a severe price decline. Conditions of land abundance lessen the likelihood of uprooting trees during prolonged price declines for replacement by alternative crops. Thus, where trees have a long period of economical bearing, capacity may not decline with a decline in price. Some trees give an economical yield for upwards of thirty years and, in the case of cocoa, yield may never decline if the tree regenerates itself properly and the soil does not lose its nutrients. In land scarce multicrop agriculture the same total area of land may be reallocated between different crops in response to relative price changes, but total output may not change due to a general rise in prices since a response in aggregate output depends upon increasing productivity on existing land which, in turn, is dependent on the availability of additional labour and other variable inputs.

Yield from new planting will depend on the area of land planted, the amount of interplanting, the method of planting, the variety of plant used, the quality of the land and a number of shorter term factors which intervene between planting and initial bearing. The yield from new planting, as the planting itself, will depend on the farmer's responsiveness to price changes. However, once the costs of establishment have been incurred, the crop is likely to be harvested even at a low price if the price more than covers variable costs. Variable costs of harvesting are frequently negligible where harvesting is a semi-skilled labour intensive activity in a labour abundant economy. The farmer will harvest as long as he can cover the cost of his family's labour in terms of its short term alternative income.

The response of planting to changes in price may be a correlate outcome of public expenditure on research into improved inputs and extension education. Where smallholders face no competing alternative employment, planting could be dependent solely on the rate at which knowledge of the market for a crop is disseminated, the ease of reaching the market and the development and availability of improved inputs. Planting and the yield from new planting as a result of these factors may be influenced (with a lag) by world price if they are financed from an export tax on the commodity. (In areas which are isolated from markets by lack of communication and transport facilities, however, there will be no response to price change).

The planting of annuals may be unresponsive to price if farmers are near subsistence levels of income. Where the annual is a staple food, the farmer might avoid the risk of insufficient food by planting enough to meet his family's food needs in a poor year, devoting the remainder of his effort to an annual or perennial cash crop. Yield variability in this case increases production of the staple crop. In normal and good years he will produce a surplus of the staple crop that can be marketed. Although production is unrelated to price, the amount marketed may be, since the market price will influence the amount of the surplus consumed on the farm. Income from marketed food surplus is often needed to buy purchased household necessities if income from the cash crop is low. If income from the cash crop remains constant, the farmer may consume part of the surplus because his real income is higher in good years for the staple crop. Although he may not maximize his average cash income by devoting effort to a low return food crop, the cash loss may be seen as the price necessary to avoid the income risks involved in greater specialization. Specialization in the cash crop would make the farmer dependent on its income relative to the cost of the food he would have to purchase. Should the vagaries of the market place cause the latter to exceed the former, he could experience severe hardship. Furthermore, when he produces his subsistence food needs, he in effect pays the wholesale on-farm price. When he buys from the market he would pay a margin covering the cost of market functions. Loss here may exceed any gain acquired through specialization in the cash crop. Where effort and resources devoted to a food crop are fixed for the reasons cited here, response to an increase in the cash crop price will not involve a switch in farm resources between the two types of crops. Rather, the response will be an allocation of additional inputs to the cash crop, and thus total farm output will increase.

If the farmer's time horizon is sufficiently truncated or he has no experience with growing the crop in question, he will look at the price risk of a cash crop and discount the average price of the cash crop by the importance he attaches to this risk. If the discount is sufficiently large he will not switch to the cash crop as its price increases. However, a more sophisticated or experienced farmer may be interested in the income risk. If income is stable when price is unstable, because price varies inversely with output, the farmer may be encouraged to increase his specialization in the crop. Both price and income risk will become relatively less important in relation to average price and income as the farmer moves up the income scale. For this reason we could expect poorer farmers to respond more readily to efforts to stabilize price or income than rich farmers.

Poor farmers may not respond to changes in price and risks in the short or long run because they do not have savings or access to credit for investment in improved variable inputs or because they do not understand the use of or cannot afford to assume the risks attached to such innovations. Many technical innovations which offer the farmer an opportunity to respond to a price increase require added labour input at peak labour periods. If wage or unused family labour is not available, farmers will find it difficult to respond to a favourable movement in price. Wealthier farmers are better able to purchase labour saving equipment or wage labour in order to accommodate these innovations.

Material goods and services, bought with effort expended on the land, and leisure are subject to declining marginal utility. The low utility derived from continuous leisure suggests that primary producers can be expected to expend some effort on the land even at low returns. In societies where social prestige is attached to leisure or where social activities are time-consuming and important, the marginal happiness derived from additional material goods and services may diminish rapidly if these are acquired with time-consuming effort. Where producers possess a so-called 'target-income' mentality due to limited felt wants and rigid consumption patterns, work effort may decline as yield or price increases. As prices decline production will be unresponsive or perversely responsive if producers maintain or increase production to meet minimum purchased necessities. This reaction to an unfavourable price change is more likely in an area in which a decline in income from a primary product leads to a decline in the general level of economic activity and, thus, in alternative employment. Where wage employment opportunities are limited, however, farmers may turn to poultry-rearing, handicrafts and similar non-wage activities if these remain more remunerative than crops.

The primary producer's response to price is likely to be restricted where consumption incentives to increase effort are lacking. Even where felt wants for material goods have developed, incentive may be absent if attractive consumer items are not available or if they are in a cost category above the producer's reasonable income possibilities. Incentives in the form of productivity increasing modern inputs are limited in effect if the inputs are not available, or are available but not in the right location, form or time or, due to inferior marketing, only at a high cost to the producer which precludes opportunities for gain.

b. MEDIUM RUN FACTORS AFFECTING CROPS

Changes in current crop output will be a function of activities occurring between the period of planting and the present. The nearer the present these activities occur, the more likely they will increase supply response to current price, especially if reliable projections of market conditions can be made over their gestation periods. The reliability of forecasts tends to be in inverse proportion to the period of the forecast. Thus, farmers with knowledge of market projections are likely to respond increasingly, as the harvest date approaches, in a manner which will cause the harvest output to be responsive to market price at the time of harvest. Where farmers are not informed of market projections, they may still respond if the current price reflects anticipated harvest period prices. If harvest prices are expected to be low, for instance, those holding stocks from a previous season will place them on the market to avoid loss or further loss from accumulating storage costs. Consumers may delay purchases in expectation of lower prices in the future. Both reactions to an accepted bearish projection will reduce current price and discourage production increasing efforts even by farmers who are unaware of the market expectations.

The tendency for projections to become increasingly accurate as the period of the forecast is reduced is illustrated in Graph 1.1, showing F.A.O. cocoa production forecasts. Short term forecasting of cocoa production, as for some other tree crops, is usually based on data regarding the number of acres planted to the crop, sample surveys of the tree density per acre, age distribution of trees and the proportion of diseased or damaged trees. In the case of cocoa, six months elapse from the time the flower is fertilized to the ripening of the pod, two

GRAPH 1.1

FAO QUARTERLY FORECASTS OF WORLD COCOA PRODUCTION, 1958–1966

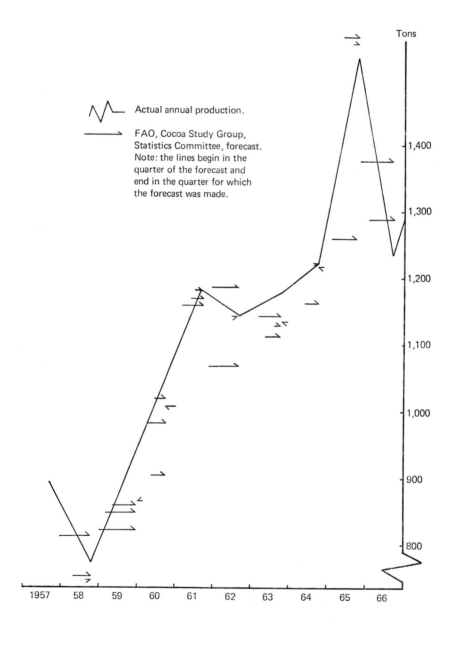

Source: FAO, *Cocoa Statistics*, Quarterly, 1958–1966.
Note: Forecasts are published each quarter. Quarterly forecasts which were not
         revised from previous quarters are not shown.

months of which is needed for the pod to reach maturity and three, to ripen. However it is not possible to determine yield accurately from the overt evidence during these six months. Though thousands of flowers blossom on the mature tree during the year and may be counted, there is no means of determining what proportion of these flowers will bear fruit. Of the fruit borne, only a small number reach maturity, since the pods in the first few months of growth are quite susceptible to diseases, pests and wilting. Other natural phenomena which intervene between a sample and harvest may also upset a projection. Heavy rains at flowering and/or two months after pod setting are considered harmful, while rains one month after setting are considered to be beneficial. As is often the case, very little has been proven about the effect of weather on yield and quality. Inability to predict the number of flowers that may bear fruit and the effects of nature on the fruit borne will cause price throughout most of the year to develop according to guesses of what the yield will be. This may contribute to price, and consequently, supply instability. Nearer the period of harvest, samples can be taken of the number of maturing pods, and the conditions of the pods noted along with the opinions of the cocoa farmers regarding the expected yield of their crops. Any weighing of these and other factors, however, would tend to be subjective. Although the number of pods and their condition can be determined shortly before harvest, yield per pod can not be. A conversion ratio may be devised from ripe pods picked before the main harvest, possibly increasing the accuracy of the very short run forecast. Attention to the pod on the tree takes into account the disease and pest control, weather, cultivation, husbandry and other production influencing intangibles. If the number of trees and their age distribution is known, as it is to some extent in the larger cocoa producing countries, knowledge of the conditions of the pods and the number on each tree alone may provide a reasonable three month forecast. If the sample size is substantial, as it is in Western Nigeria, the age distribution of the trees may not have to be considered as a separate variable for allowance for it will be included in the sample. Marketable output after harvest can be affected by weather through its influence on the quality of the fermenting and drying process which occurs at the local level, often under rather makeshift conditions. Thus, accurate forecasts of harvested production may not reflect market supply.

Where the cost of crop maintenance during the interim period between planting and harvest of a crop is high relative to expected returns and expected net returns are low relative to those from alternative uses of the resources, less effort and funds will be expended on weeding, thinning, cultivating, and applying fertilizers, insecticides, fungicides, herbicides and other plant protection measures. The action of fertilizers on a tree crop are often slow with the resultant changes in output occurring as much as six months to a year later. The effect on annuals, however, could be felt within one growing cycle or less. Where soils are not deficient in certain ingredients, crops may be unresponsive to fertilizer inputs. The irreversibility of the investment in fertilizers and their yield effect once applied to the crop will decrease supply responsiveness to unanticipated changes in the harvest price. Natural acts such as blights, fungi and viruses and damage by pests (birds, rats, worms) in this period can be controlled and, if control fluctuates with price, supply may become more elastic. The effect of weather, however, cannot be easily controlled. Heavy rains during certain periods of growth of the plant or its fruit and drought during other periods may be harmful. Humidity, cloud cover and other meteorological phenomena can appreciably affect yield during this interim period. Peak labour input periods, especially those of harvesting and planting, frequently occur during periods of climatic change that increase illness among the productive labour force; the extent of illness will be related to the severity of the change. Susceptibility to climatic variables for the reasons given here normally indicates a supply-shift market.

c. SHORT RUN FACTORS AFFECTING CROPS

In the short run supply may exhibit a limited response to price through the intensity of harvesting, sometimes with detrimental results. In the case of tea, intensive plucking could damage the plant. Intensive tapping of rubber trees is discouraged for this is likely to retard later growth, consume bark faster than the normal rate of replacement and lead to brown bast. When prices are low, plots difficult to reach may not be harvested. The more common it is for farmers to own plots some distance from their residence, especially those planted to tree crops that do not need close attention, the more pronounced would be the short run production response to price change. Crops for which the harvest period is not severely restricted will be more sensitive to price. Cassava, for instance, has no rigid harvest time; some varieties can be harvested any time from 6–48 months after planting.

Current price may also affect the quality of the harvest, and through this, output in different grade categories. High prices tend to increase the amount of unripe fruit harvested or the quality of tea through coarse plucking. When prices are low tea bushes and cocoa trees may be harvested less frequently so that a larger proportion of the product is not picked at the prime time. Cleaning, drying and sorting may be done carelessly. Careless drying, threshing, pounding and local storage of food grains by traditional techniques will cause loss of product as well as quality. To the extent that such factors operate, short run market supply elasticity will be increased.

Where production is relatively capital intensive, as is often the case on plantations, production may not be highly price responsive in the short run. Unless plantations have been operating at less than capacity, they might not respond to price changes because of the high ratio of fixed to variable inputs. Estates are generally believed to be more interested in maximizing long run returns and often have to maintain normal output at low prices because they are subsidiaries of fabricators or have long term contracts with buyers. Estate labour is frequently employed on long term contract and involves considerable expense in disbanding and recruiting anew, particularly where remoteness from population centres fixes labour supply. Large labour overhead in housing and social services on estates, representing a form of fixed payment for labour, could also discourage short run dispersing while overtime payments and bonuses may discourage more intensive use of existing labour.

Although the stock of mature trees of a tree crop cannot be expanded in the short run, trees may be uprooted for replanting during periods of high prices because of increased ability to invest in replanting and anticipation of continuing high prices. However, the stock is unlikely to be reduced in the very short run since replanting requires some planning and preparatory work. High prices could also act as a disincentive to replant because greater income is foregone than at low prices. Producers are not likely to uproot trees to grow alternative crops in areas where the tree crop grows on land of limited alternative use or if land abundance permits alternative crops to be easily grown on new land.

There are undoubtedly numerous qualifications and exceptions to these general observations. Rubber, for instance, provides at least one. A recently discovered yield stimulant, 2 chloroethyl phosphonic acid, increases yields of all clones tested by 100–150 per cent within two weeks of application. If discontinued, yield reverts to normal within two months. If more than one application is made in two months, later growth is affected through the drying up of the tree. Thus, although the very short run production response to an increasing price will initially be marked, production could be expected to decline in the face of price increases that continued for up to two months. That is, supply response to price would become perverse.

d. SUPPLY RESPONSE OF MINED PRODUCTS

Certain capital intensive forms of dredging and strip and lode mining tend to have long gestation periods and consequently are unresponsive to current price. As with tree crops, changes in current output may be a response to the price in some past period upon which decisions to invest in mining were made. Less capital and skill intensive mining, such as gravel pump mining, hydraulicing and panning, will exhibit shorter gestation periods and greater responsiveness to current price.

Capital intensive low variable cost mines will continue to operate at low prices so long as operating costs are being covered. Less capital intensive high variable cost mining may be more responsive to price. The normally lower level of skills in such operations would, however, suggest less alternative employment opportunities in labour abundant economies. On the other hand, labour and capital tend to be less specific than with more sophisticated mining techniques. Workers in small labour intensive mines may accept a reduction in wages in a price decline, while mines with high fixed-variable cost ratios may have the financial resources to allow production to continue, and will be likely to continue where they have contracts with buyers or are subsidiaries of fabricators. As with crops, remoteness from labour markets inhibits a positive response to a price increase and may discourage disbanding since hiring anew under such conditions is costly. A positive response to a short run price increase in mines with essential fixed inputs and easy access to variable inputs will depend on the possibility to use the existing capital stock more intensively. The high costs of reopening unused mines restricts production increases in periods of price increases and acts as a restraint on closing mines in a price decline. Complete closing may lead to flooding of the mine and dispersal of the specialized labour force. Thus, mines could be expected to operate at prices below variable costs as the cost of reopening increases and the expected time period over which these losses must be borne decreases. Once closed, prices must rise considerably and be expected to remain favourablebefore reopening is seen to be economical. It is not uncommon in some countries for mine proprietors to operate dependent ancillary enterprises, the profits of which are then available to operate the mine in a period of depressed prices. This could be expected to occur especially where the proprietor's other business, such as a store selling to miners or a credit facility, would suffer if the mining operation closed. If mining the product represents a substantial proportion of total economic activity, a price decline will lead to an overall contraction in the economy and to reduced alternative employment opportunities for resources attached to the mining industry, a factor which may induce both capital and labour to accept a lower return in mining.

Supply may be unresponsive to price if mines switch from rich to poor veins of ore in periods of rising prices and *vice versa*. Poor veins and trailings of earlier workings can be economically mined only at high prices while at low prices, mining of rich veins of ore remains profitable. Where minerals are co-occurent, more of one will be mined if, *ceteris paribus*, the price of the other rises sufficiently. Both these phenomena have the potential for creating perverse supply functions.

6. TRADER MONOPOLY-MONOPSONY

Whether a producer participates in the net increase in income which occurs with a relative change in the prices of his inputs, output and purchased consumption items will in part depend on the monopoly-monopsony power of the traders purchasing the producer's marketable surpluses, suppliers of farm inputs and household necessities, money-lenders and landlords with whom he deals and upon his control over his own consumption patterns. He may be unable to fully enjoy an increase in income if, for instance, additional income is by custom expected to be shared among an extended family, kinship group or village. Since man tends to be motivated by the prospect of personal acquisition, incentive for increased effort in the face of increased marginal returns is diminished if the benefits do not flow directly to the nuclear family unless status or power in the wider group is determined by one's contribution to it and this status or power is important to the individual. Thus, in societies where income is shared beyond the nuclear family, supply response to increased opportunities for income may be dampened. Landlords who increase rent with income may have similar disincentive effects.

In remote areas where the number of buyers, moneylenders and suppliers are limited or in areas where they collude to exploit the primary producer, supply may not respond to changes in nominal market prices because these market agents draw off the benefits of price increases for themselves. Market agents without monopoly or monopsony power can still exploit the producer through the fixing of scales, misgrading and incorrect accounting of items purchased from and sold to the producer. Such exploitation insulates the primary producer from fluctuations in main market prices and, consequently, reduces his supply response to these prices. Low market margins, however, do not necessarily indicate competition or efficiency in marketing. Rather, they may reflect low opportunity cost of resources used in marketing and limited services.

Exploitation of producers can be expected to be greater for primary commodities in inelastic supply. The monopsonist buyer (and indirectly the monopolist seller) in effect shifts downward the demand function facing the producer. A given shift in this function will cause a greater producer price decline if supply is inelastic than if it is less so. On the other hand, in the unusual case where the monopsonist faces a producer with a 'backward bending' supply function of greater elasticity than the monopsonist's demand function, a downward shift in the monopsonist's demand function would increase the producer's price. In remote areas the local market may be large enough to support only one market agent in each of the buying, moneylending and supplying activities and each may exercise market power. Their aggregate market power over the producer will be increased if through kinship ties, for instance, they act together as one buyer-moneylender-supplier. Where the market is extremely small, there will be economies of scale in combining these three related functions in a single enterprise. If the scale of output for lowest cost is considerable, monopoly-monopsony may exist where markets are not severely limited by low income and production and market deficiencies. In some instances the producer benefits from dealing with the monopoly-monopsony enterprise. As a monopsonist buyer an intermediary knows that the producer will continue to make deliveries in order to purchase inputs and household necessities. The consequent reduced risk of lending to him may be reflected in interest rates sufficiently low as to compensate for the low monopsonistic prices the producer receives for his primary produce and the high monopolistic prices he pays for supplies.

The exploitation of the producer is not normally prevalent in populated areas that will support a number of competing buyers, moneylenders and suppliers. Conditions of pronounced unemployment would argue for the existence of numerous undercapitalized petty traders engaging in these three activities. Their number will normally be great because their opportunity cost and financial resources are low.

Monopoly or monopsony will exist in areas that would support competing agents in these fields if there is one licensed buyer with exclusive legal rights to operate without competition, several licensed buyers who collude, coercion of producers to sell to particular buyers, collusion of traders who act together like a monopsonist or confine their activities to mutually exclusive areas, or if a market agent is threatened by other agents when he attempts to act in a competitive manner (e.g. through raising the producer price to obtain a greater share of the market). Monopsony will exist when a producer has a choice between buyers but does not choose to exercise it. Such a situation may arise if the producer is unaware of the existence or prices of alternative traders, if he feels obliged to sell for cultural reasons to a relative who takes advantage of his 'cultural power' over the producer by offering a monopsonist's price, or if he sells to a trader in order to maintain a friendly relationship because the trader is also a prospective source of credit.

7. MARKET SUPPLY

a. At the Farm Level

Actual output or ultimate consumer demand affects market price indirectly because prices ruling at various market strata between the producer and ultimate consumer are also a function of factors that intervene in the process of marketing. At the individual farm level, the responsiveness of market supply of food crops should be measured separately from that of output since the quantity of food surplus a farmer markets will depend partly on how much of the output is consumed on the farm. If the farmer has a perverse production function, the elasticity of his market supply will also be negative. Alternatively, the food surplus farmer may have a positive output response to price and a negative marketed supply response because on-farm consumption varies in the same direction and by a greater amount than output. A negative price elasticity of supply may be occasionally explained by the subsistence nature of foodcrop production. We could expect that as the poverty of a staple food producer increases, the chances of a negative price elasticity of marketed surplus also increases. Price increases reduce the volume of sales needed to satisfy given cash requirements allowing the poor farmer to enjoy a large diet of his staple food crop. In the frequent cases where a farmer has a fixed cash debt or rent to pay, a decrease in the price of a staple food crop would force him to sell more of his produce and eat less. Normally, however, the price elasticity of market supply is greater than the price elasticity of output. A price increase will encourage a farmer to sell seeds being held for sowing the next crop, reduce family consumption, or sell from stocks held for family consumption, gifts, rent or tax in kind in anticipation of buying back an equivalent amount of food nearer the period of its use.

Local shifts in export supply can be caused by switching of marketing channels. For instance, the very short run rubber export supply function in Malaysia shifts as labour resources move between different types of producing units in response to world price changes. Wages for tappers on estates are tied to prices lagged three months or move less than proportionately with current price, while medium sized holdings frequently use a 'bagi dua' (50–50 share) system of sharing income or yield with no lag. This leads to short run switching of labour between estates and medium holdings with a consequent shift in the export supply function since estate rubber is normally ready for export less than ten days after tapping while the lower quality of small and mediumhold production makes smoking and grading more time consuming. With the greater number of middlemen, it may take one month from mediumhold tapping until export, although this might be reduced if a favourable change in price is considered temporary. Thus, in a price rise the normally smooth flow of rubber from estates is reduced and a reverse shift occurs several weeks later when increased mediumhold production appears on the market. These export supply variations may occur in the face of fairly steady aggregate tapping. Increased thefts of rubber from estates during periods of high prices will have a similar effect on export supply since stolen rubber tends to be marketed through smallhold channels. Apparent supply may also be reduced if traders switch market channels. During periods of high cocoa prices, for instance, cocoa is smuggled from Ghana, where producer prices are net of a heavy export tax, to the Ivory Coast where they are more closely related to world price. This activity would tend to reduce apparent supply response of Ghanaian producers to price increases and increase that of Ivory Coast producers.

b. SPECULATION

Market supply may be influenced by speculative stockholdings at all levels. Speculation has the effect of increasing or decreasing the elasticity of market supply over the elasticity of output and will occur primarily with standardized seasonal products. Any commodity the bulk of whose supply comes on the market during a small portion of the year only but whose consumption is continuous throughout the year must be stored by someone on behalf of society. Such storage in the face of possible shifts in demand and supply inevitably involves an element of speculation. If speculators buy when price falls (as after a harvest) in anticipation of a profit if it increases, they dampen and possibly reverse the unfavourable price movement. If they sell when prices are rising, their action may prevent further increases. By storing in times of relative abundance and declining prices they reduce market supply and by selling in periods of scarcity and rising prices they increase it. When this occurs on the supply side of the market (e.g. in an exporting country) the effect is to increase export supply elasticity. Speculators on the demand side of the market can have similar stabilizing effects on prices. On the other hand, if the expectations of speculators are erroneous they may destabilize price. For instance, they may buy on a price decline in anticipation of a recovery. If price does not recover, they will dispose of their stocks on the market to avoid loss on accumulating storage costs, driving prices even lower. Speculators will destabilize market price if they buy on a price rise expecting prices to increase further or sell on a price decline in expectation of a further price decline. Their actions have the effect of driving prices higher and lower, respectively. Producers and merchants, though knowledgeable of market supply (output prospects and stocks) in their own area, may be unaware of overall conditions on the wider market in which prices are formed. Decisions regarding storage in these circumstances will be made with very incomplete market knowledge and, thus, will tend to increase price instability. Sales of a seasonal crop which is stored after harvest may be reduced in expectation of prices in the future being sufficiently high to cover initial purchase costs plus storage costs and offer a net return which is higher than the same market resources could obtain in their best alternative use. Where these conditions are not met, sales from stock will probably be increased. The cumulative cost of scarce marketing resources included in storage (special marketing skills, godowns, fumigation facilities etc.) will increase in a predictable manner over time. Possible windfall gains of speculative activity can be seen as useful and socially necessary if they occur in a competitive and well informed market. For instance, it is useful whenever supplies are scarce that the available stock be evenly distributed over the period of scarcity. Should there be an official attempt to force out stock by compulsory sales or artificially low price, the scarcity would become more acute at a later period.

Market supply or export supply response to price may be indeterminant because the elasticity of inventory accumulation is dependent not only on the price level but also upon an expectational variable— that is, upon the expectations of future prices, government policies and similar phenomena by the holders of stocks. A positive elasticity of inventory accumulation may give rise to a temporarily perverse export supply function. However, since stocks can neither be depleted nor accumulated indefinitely, the net effect over time is not likely to be significant in terms of gain or loss of foreign exchange for an exporting country. The price of seasonal crops is unlikely to continue rising sufficiently to justify storage for more than one growing cycle since a new crop will be injected into the market with the next harvest. Furthermore, demand may become elastic at high and low prices placing a limit on the width of price fluctuations. In the final analysis, actual production of the product will normally remain the most important factor influencing export supply.

c. Entrepot Trade

Export supply elasticity will be a function of the level of imports for countries which serve as entrepots. Where speculators are active and reexports compose a large proportion of total exports, net export earnings will decline with price if imports for speculative storage are greater than exports. In the absence of significant speculative stock accumulation, export supply will be closely related to the outflow of foreign exchange to purchase the commodity.

8. GEOGRAPHICAL CONCENTRATION OF SUPPLY

Local shifts in supply will affect aggregate world supply in relation to the amount of the shift and the proportion of total supply coming from the area. Geographical concentration of supply of a commodity subject to supply destabilizing factors suggests a supply-shift market. Short run supply shifts, a major source of price and income instability, will be caused by climatic variations, disease, pests, national political crises, wars, strikes and other similar phenomena. Climatic variations such as unusually heavy rains can significantly affect mining by flooding mines, and disrupting power, the movement of labour, material inputs and outputs. Variations of crop output due to weather may be random as for wheat or cyclical as for olives and coffee. Seasonal variations in output will occur for crops harvested only during certain periods of the year. Local or regional shifts in the supply functions will tend to influence aggregate supply instability in direct relation to the geographical concentration of production and the proportion produced in areas affected by similar destabilizing factors. Aggregate seasonal variations in output, on the other hand, will be limited where harvest occurs at different periods in several important producing areas.

9. DEMAND RESPONSE TO PRICE

Price elasticities of demand vary between commodities and markets. Demand elasticities tend to be lower for commodities without close substitutes (coffee, tea & cocoa) than for those with (sisal, jute, cotton, cane sugar & natural rubber). Where substitutes are available, demand elasticity may be high because buyers switch between the two similar products. Switching, however, could be limited in the short run even where wide price differentials develop because of technical difficulties, retooling costs, the need for new labour skills, and long term contracts with suppliers. Switching between types of the same commodity may be restricted because they are not perfect substitutes for one another. The cross elasticity of demand for various types of cocoa or coffee, for instance, is greater or less depending on the amount of substitution that is possible without perceptibly changing the flavour of a blend. A narrowing of price differentials between types will often switch demand toward more expensive blends and widening of differentials will have the opposite effect. Demand elasticity for a particular type becomes inelastic, however, when the flavour threshold of the blend is reached. Where synthetic rubber is not a perfect technical substitute for the natural product, a similar limitation is imposed on switching. In a sense, switching can occur between identical products. Switching to secondary tin recovered from tin scrap, an almost perfect substitute for the primary tin exported by developing countries and a major source of tin in times of scarcity, will increase the elasticity of demand for primary tin at high prices. Such a switch may be expected to occur even in the short run because it does not entail expensive changes in production processes.

In switching to a substitute the large consumer may reduce the differential upon which the decision to switch was made. Switching will tend to occur where the product represents a major input cost and processing qualities are similar. Where the product is a major input at the fabrication stage, manufacturers will tend to increase economies in the use of the product, reducing requirements for a given level of output. The manufacturer can effect economies through more efficient use, varying the input content of the end product or by varying the range of items placed before the consumer where, as with sugar in confectionery, there is similarity in a number of end products using the input. In the latter case, consumption can be influenced by the advertisement given to alternative end products. Such 'economies' are subject to technical and consumer taste limits.

Substitution may be limited by vertical integration of fabricating enterprises in consuming countries. If the consumers are also producers of the substitute product, a synthetic that has a natural counterpart, for instance, they will be reluctant to switch to the natural product for in doing so they would reduce the output of part of their vertically integrated enterprise. With low prices for the natural product, synthetic production itself might not be considered economical, but the loss on the synthetic product may be covered by profits at the end product level.

In the case of competition between synthetic and natural products, it can be argued that significant price differentials periodically develop because of stable nominal synthetic prices and fluctuating natural product prices. The apparent stability of synthetic prices has been attributed to manufacturers' policy of basing prices primarily upon production costs with little regard to market forces. Short run stability in the supply to customers is affected by inventory fluctuations. Stable nominal quotations for synthetics may, however, disguise variable discounts and offers of credit facilities which in effect cause the synthetic price to vary with that of the natural product. Such disguised variation is likely to occur where the break-even point of the synthetic industry is near full capacity and where there are considerable economies of scale, as is the case in synthetic rubber production. The synthetic price could be expected to move down with the natural product price to avoid loss of market and consequent low returns to resource inputs. Should considerable sympathetic movements in the price of synthetics exist, demand elasticity for the natural product would not increase appreciably with synthetic competition.

Where processing costs are high relative to the cost of the raw material or the raw material is used together with other more costly material inputs, the price to the ultimate consumer may be only marginally affected by wide swings in its price. When the price of the primary product experiences a pronounced increase, the price of the end product might still remain unchanged or rise by so little as to go unnoticed or to be disregarded by the consumer. The end product price will not change if the manufacturer allows his profit margin to absorb changes in total costs or if movements in other input costs neutralize the effect of a change in the primary product price. Conceivably the end product price might fall in the face of a primary input price increase if cost increases were exceeded by decreases. In the latter event, demand for the primary commodity would be expected to increase with price.

Tropical commodities like bananas, cocoa and coffee, which are still

considered a luxury in some developing and centrally planned economies, may have a higher income and price demand elasticity there than in
those developed countries where their consumption is near the saturation level. A saturated demand could be expected where consumers
have been long exposed to the product and the product is of minor
importance in household budgets.

The effect of a given degree of supply instability on a country's export earnings will depend on the elasticity of demand. The more elastic
an elastic demand is, for instance, the more pronounced is the effect
of a shift in supply on export earnings. The elasticity of demand facing
a single country or group of countries is influenced in part by the elasticity of total demand discussed above. An important factor, however,
is the country's share of the total world market. A country whose exports form only an insignificant part of aggregate supply is in the
position of a perfect competitor facing a perfectly elastic demand function, whereas a country whose exports form a large part of world supply will, *ceteris paribus*, be faced with a demand function of lesser elasticity. Supply fluctuations of a given magnitude can be expected to generate greater percentage fluctuations in export receipts from a commodity the smaller the country's share of total supply. A country or
group of countries supplying total world production of the commodity
will be confronted with the world demand function, which may be
elastic or inelastic depending on the time period and the factors considered above.

10. GEOGRAPHICAL, FABRICATOR AND END USE CONCENTRATION OF DEMAND

Some primary product markets are intrinsically more volatile than
others. To a large extent this is due to demand related factors. One of
the most important factors affecting the level and variability of demand
is consumers' income. The extent to which shifts in demand arise from
changes in consumer purchasing power will depend on the income
elasticity of demand for the end product to which the primary commodity is an input. End products with a relatively low income elasticity
experience less demand variability than those with higher. The saturated demand situation mentioned earlier would imply a low income
elasticity. On the other hand, income elasticity may be high and exceed
unity for consumer durables such as automobiles and home appliances.
Demand for tin, copper, rubber and other primary commodities used
in their manufacture will experience a variability greater than that of
income. Demand shifts can also arise from the development of substi-

tutes, technical innovations which economize on the amount of the commodity needed, labour disputes, political disturbances and changes in exchange rates, trade policies, defence expenditure, and strategic stocks. Trade policies influence international demand through preferential arrangements, tariffs, multiple exchange rate manipulations, import quotas, subsidy of domestic production in importing countries and the like. Stability in international demand will also be influenced by the purchasing policies of the centrally planned economies. Where their attempts to create an orderly flow of primary imports over time are limited, aggregate world demand may be destabilized.

The effect of fluctuations in these demand related variables on aggregate demand and world price instability is an increasing function of the geographical concentration of demand. Although the geographical origins of demand for most primary exports from developing countries are spreading with the industrialization and growth of developing consumer countries, demand, as previously illustrated, continues to originate primarily in North America, Western Europe and the Soviet Bloc. Changes in the macro-economic variables, trade policies and other demand related variables of one or two major consuming countries may have a noticeable influence on aggregate demand. The effect on demand stability can be aggravated if different markets are imperfect substitutes for one another as a result of trade preferences, bilateral trading arrangements and other impediments to free multilateral trade. On the other hand, where exports are well diversified among recipient countries unaffected by similar demand destabilizing factors, the international market is not likely to be characterized by demand-shift situations.

Demand for some primary commodities is further subject to instability through concentration in the hands of several fabricating enterprises in the main consuming countries. Shut-downs accompanying disputes at one or two of the major enterprises may cause important variations in total world demand for the commodity with consequent effect on prices and incomes of the primary product exporters. Where end use is limited, as for natural rubber in tyres and tin in tin plate for canned goods, disruption in the major end use market may produce a marked effect on total absorption. On the other hand, through processing some primary commodities can be separated into two or more distinct products which together experience a more stable demand because their markets are unrelated. The demand for palm oil used in margarine and cooking oils, for instance, is largely independent from that for oil palm kernel cake (a by-product of palm oil extraction used for cattle feed) and palm kernel oil (used by the chemical industry and in soaps and confectionery). The markets for cocoa cake and fat are somewhat less mutually independent.

An individual producer country is confronted by a net foreign demand function, based on aggregate demand and supply. A shift in either of these variables will alter the position of the net demand for that country. A downward shift in the export supply function of other countries will, *ceteris paribus*, cause the demand function facing a single exporter to shift upwards. Domestic demand in producing countries is affected by the same destabilizing factors as affect demand in importing countries. Instability in domestic demand for a product, given a stable supply, tends to produce instability in the export supply (the quantity offered abroad after domestic demand at the market price has been met—cf. p. 7). Fluctuations in the domestic demand will produce similar effects on world price and export earnings to domestic supply instability. In general, if the overall level of demand is stable, agricultural exports may be expected to experience greater fluctuations in price than manufactures or minerals because of the normally greater relative output variability among agricultural products. Some agricultural products may be an exception to this rule: timber, rubber, cattle, dairy products, poultry and other products similarly unaffected by production destabilizing factors. In contrast, if instability in price is the result of fluctuations in the general level of income, it will tend to affect most goods but will have greater impact on goods with high income elasticities.

II. SUMMARY

Despite the minor importance of developing country primary commodity exports in overall world trade in primary commodities, they represent important sources of foreign exchange, government revenue, employment and savings for many developing exporting countries. Export earnings of developing countries tend to be highly concentrated on primary commodities and in individual producing countries they are frequently concentrated on one or two commodities with the effect that total export earnings and related variables are strongly influenced by activities in one or two world markets. These markets tend to be volatile because of their susceptibility to demand changes in a few major recipient countries and the proportionately large supply coming from areas affected by similar destabilizing factors.

The degree of market instability for a primary commodity, and thus the necessary strength of control devices, will depend on the elasticities of domestic and export demand and domestic supply and the magnitude and frequency of shifts in the demand and supply functions. The favourable or unfavourable effects of particular control devices on the level and stability of producer income, world price, export earnings, government revenue and other similar variables and the importance of these effects will be related to whether the market in which they operate is one characterized by demand or supply shifts.

Supply shift markets can be expected where changes in current output are largely a response to investment decisions in a past period. The more distant this past period, the less likely the market situation which evoked the decision to invest will be closely related to the current one. Long gestation period tree crops and capital intensive mining are indicative of supply shift markets. Short run price responsiveness of supply is confined to variations in the utilization of the existing stock of capital through, for example, more intensive and careful harvesting and processing, and overtime employment of labour in mines. In the medium run supply response will be limited to the extent variable inputs such as labour, fertilizers, and insecticides may economically increase output of the fixed factor inputs. Mistakes in the use of these because of erroneous projections and variations in natural phenomena will cause short run supply conditions to be unrelated to those of demand. Aggregate world supply variability is related to the geographical concentration of supply and the degree to which different producing areas are subject to simultaneous supply-destabilizing factors. A country's export supply elasticity, in contrast to its elasticity of production, will be influenced by the importance and elasticity of domestic demand for the commodity and domestic speculative stock accumulation.

Demand shift markets are prevalent where the general level of economic activity in recipient countries varies appreciably and a high degree of geographic, fabricator and end use concentration of demand exists. Such concentration suggests that demand destabilizing factors such as political disturbances, labour disputes, and changes in macroeconomic variables in major consumer countries will exercise a noticeable effect on aggregate world demand. The demand facing the exporting producer will be less elastic where it is derived and more elastic where substitutes exist and significant differentials develop between the alternative products. The elasticity of demand facing the exporter will be a decreasing function of his share of the world market but will always be more than the elasticity of aggregate demand if he is not the sole supplier.

The lines of inferential reasoning adopted in the above paragraphs suggest that tree crops like coffee and cocoa which are exported to a limited number of relatively stable developed countries, where they are in income inelastic derived demand, will be in a market characterized by supply shift situations and price inelastic short run demand and supply. Products in more stable supply such as tin, copper and rubber will experience a price inelastic derived demand subject to appreciable shifts due to the income elastic nature of their end products. Short run supply elasticity of these primary products will depend in part on the average fixed-variable cost ratio while that of demand will be influenced by the existence and relative price stability of technical and economical substitutes. Rice, groundnuts and maize produced under conditions of marked yield uncertainty, in income inelastic demand, and sold primarily to economically volatile developing countries may be expected to be in markets where market functions are inelastic and fluctuating. Export supply will be more price responsive than that of production since domestic consumption in exporting countries is significant. Where their import demand is a residual of a fluctuating domestic production in importing countries, demand shifts may predominate.

Readings

Bauer, P.T. & Yamey, B.S., 'A Case Study of Response to Price in an Underdeveloped Country'. *Economic Journal*, Vol. 69, No. 276, December 1959, pp. 800–5.

————, & Yamey, B.S., 'Response to Price in an Underdeveloped Economy: A Rejoinder', *Economic Journal*, Vol. 70, December 1960, pp. 855–6.

Blau, G., & Music, D.A., 'Agricultural Commodity Trade and Development Prospects, Problems & Politics', *FAO Commodity Policy Series No. 17*, Rome, 1964.

Clayton, E.S., 'Small Scale Cash-Crop Production in a Developing Economy', *Economic Development and Cultural Change*, Vol. 9, No. 4, Part 1, July 1961, pp. 618–24

Coppock, J.D. *International Economic Instability*, New York, 1962.

Dean, E.R., 'Social Determinants of Price in Several African Markets', *Economic Development and Cultural Change*, Volume 11, No. 3, Part 1, April 1963, pp. 239–56.

Dubey, V., 'The Marketable Agricultural Surplus & Economic Growth in Underdeveloped Countries', *Economic Journal*, Vol. 73, December 1963, pp. 689–702.

Ezekiel, H., & Mathur, P.N., 'Marketable Surplus of Food & Price Fluctuations in a Developing Economy', *Kyklos*, Vol. 14, fasc. 3, 1961, pp. 396–406.

FAO, *Commodity Review*, annual.

——————, *Trade Yearbooks*.

Hogg, V.W., 'Response to Price in an Underdeveloped Economy', *Economic Journal*, Vol. 70, December 1960, pp. 852–5.

Horner, F.B., 'Elasticity of Demand for the Exports of a Single Country', *Review of Economics & Statistics*, Vol. 34, No. 4, November 1952, pp. 326–42.

Hussain, S.M., 'A Note on Farmer Response to Price in East Pakistan', *Pakistan Development Review*, Vol. 14, Spring 1964, pp. 93–106.

IMF, *International Financial Statistics*, quarterly.

Krishna, R., 'A Note on the Elasticity of Marketable Surplus of a Subsistence Crop', *Indian Journal of Agricultural Economics*, Vol. 17, No. 3, 1962.

Lipton, M., 'Should Reasonable Farmers Respond to Price Changes: a Review Article', *Modern Asian Studies* Vol. 1, 1966, pp. 95–9.

MacBean, A.I., 'Causes of Excessive Fluctuations in Export Proceeds of Underdeveloped Countries', *Bulletin of the University of Oxford Institute of Statistics*, Vol. 26, November 1964, pp. 322–41.

Madappa, P.P.,' Tea Price Fluctuations: Causes and Remedies', *Indian Journal of Agricultural Economics*, Vol. 23, No. 4, Oct.–Dec.1968, pp. 170–8.

Maizels, A., *Exports and Economic Growth of Developing Countries*, Cambridge University Press, 1968.

Massell, B.F., 'Export Concentration and Fluctuations in Export Earnings: A Cross-Section Analysis', *American Economic Review*, Vol. 54, No. 2, March 1964, pp. 47–63.

McHale, T.R., 'Changing Technology and Shifts in the Supply and Demand for Rubber, an Analytical History', *Malayan Economic Review*, Vol. 9, No. 2, October 1964, pp. 24–48.

————, 'The Competition between Synthetic and Natural Rubber', *Malayan Economic Review*, Vol. 6, No. 1, April 1961, pp. 23–31.

Mellor, J., *The Economics of Agricultural Development*, Cornell University Press, 1967, pp. 196–206.

Michael, M., *Concentration in International Trade*, Amsterdam, 1962.

Mohammed, G., 'Some Physical & Economic Determinants of Cotton Production in West Pakistan', *Pakistan Development Review*, Vol. 3, No. 4, 1963, pp. 491–526.

Porter, R.C., 'Risk, Incentive, & the Technique of the Low-Income Farmer', *Indian Economic Journal*, Vol. 7, No. 1, 1959, pp. 1–27.

Porter, R.S., 'Cotton and the Egyptian Economy', *Kyklos*, Vol. 11, 1958, pp. 231–43.

Rabbani, A.K.M. G., 'Economic Determinants of Jute Production in India and Pakistan', *Pakistan Development Review*, Vol, 5, No. 2, 1965, pp. 191–228

Rowe, J.W.P., *Primary Commodities in International Trade*, Cambridge University Press, 1965, pp. 1–55.

Stern, R.M., 'The Determinants of Cocoa Supply in West Africa', in Stewart, I.G., & Ord, H.W., eds., *African Primary Products & International Trade*, Edinburgh University Press, 1965, pp. 65–82.

————, 'Malayan Rubber Production, Inventory Holdings and the Elasticity of Export Supply', *Southern Economic Journal*, Vol. 31, April 1965, pp. 314–23.

————, 'The Price Responsiveness of Egyptian Cotton Producers', *Kyklos*, Vol. 12, 1959, pp. 375–84.

————, 'The Price Responsiveness of Primary Producers', *Review of Economics & Statistics*, Vol. 44, May 1962, pp. 202–7.

Tomek, W.G., & Robinson, K.L., *Agricultural Product Prices*, Cornell University Press, 1972.

UN, *Commodity Trade Statistics*, annual.

————, *Monthly Bulletin of Statistics*, monthly.

UNCTAD, *Commodity Problems & Policies*, TD/8/Supp.1, 14 November, 1967.

————, *Commodity Survey*, New York, 1969, JX 1977, A2TD/ B/C1.

Weymar, F.D., *The Dynamics of The World Cocoa Market*, M.I.T. Press, Cambridge, 1968.

Wharton, C.R., Jr., 'Marketing, Merchandising and Moneylending: A Note on Middleman Monopsony in Malaya', *Malayan Economic Review*, Vol. 7, October 1962, pp. 24–44.

————, 'Risk, Uncertainty, & the Subsistence Farmer: Technological Innovation & Resistance to Change in the Context of Survival', *Studies in Economic Anthropology*, AS7, 1971, pp. 151–78.

————, 'Rubber Supply Conditions: Some Policy Implications', in Silcock, T.H., & Fisk, E.K., *The Political Economy of Independent Malaya*, University of California Press, 1963, pp. 131–62.

Also see Appendix 1. Readings.

II
Commodity Market Problems

1. INTRODUCTION

THE present chapter puts forward a discussion of the more notable problems of national and international primary commodity markets. Consideration is given to the effects of market instability at the producer or microeconomic level as well as at the national level, for the usefulness of control is determined in both spheres. Attention is also directed to the political and social implications associated with the asymmetry in trade relations between the developing and developed countries. This dependent relationship in trade adds a sense of urgency to reform as it underlines the apparent inequities arising from trade restrictions, synthetic competition and secular declines in terms of trade. Finally, the most commonly sought objectives of international control are enumerated. The determination of which devices are most suited to meeting given objectives will be the subject of the succeeding chapters.

2. MARKET INSTABILITY

a. THE INDIVIDUAL PRODUCER

As indicated in Section 6 (p. 18) of the preceding chapter, the producer's real net income is a function of his output, the price of the output, and the price of production inputs and consumption items, including the price of credit to finance inputs or consumption. Fluctuation or stability in any of these variables may destabilize his real net income. For this reason it is important to know not only how successful a particular control device is in stabilizing price but also how successful it is in stabilizing relative prices and producers' incomes.

The primary commodity producing unit is exposed to three types of risk which may be subject to control: price, yield and income risk.

Of these three, the risk that prices for inputs, consumption items or output in relative or absolute terms will vary unexpectedly traditionally receives most attention because it is easiest to identify and control. Yield risk, or the risk that output from given resource inputs will vary unexpectedly, is identifiable but more difficult to control. Yield risk may be further delimited as the risk that essential inputs, such as improved seeds in agriculture and family or hired labour, will not be available in the right form, location and time needed. That is, the output and returns to a single resource, like land, will be uncertain because of variations in the supply or performance (production coefficients) of other resources. These include free resource inputs like rain, humidity and cloud cover where timing is important to output. Yield and price risks will be experienced through their influence on income, lending to income an uncertainty or income risk.

The low income producer will be especially interested in avoiding income risk since a period of low income may cause extreme hardship. If a certain product offers him a known average income over a period of years with fluctuations of an equal magnitude above and below the average, he will subjectively attach more importance to the possible shortfalls below the average than to increases of similar magnitude above it if the marginal utility of his income increases as income decreases. Although an increase in income in excess of the average may provide a high increment of utility at low levels of income, the disutility suffered by a shortfall in income, experienced as unmet necessities and important felt wants, would predominate. In allocating his resources between alternative uses the producer will discount the average price in relation to the amount by which the utility gained in a good year is exceeded by the disutility of a bad year. That is, the justification for risk exposure, a higher average income, is qualified by an instinct for survival expressed through risk aversion. This is generally true for given levels of income, although the primary producer's preoccupation with income risk will diminish as income increases, for at higher income levels he is more capable of absorbing fluctuations. At sufficiently high income strata wide fluctuations in income may be felt only through variations in savings, with consumption patterns remaining unchanged. In the absence of risk, or where risk assumes no importance, the primary producer's resources will normally be allocated to those activities which produce the highest average returns. As risk becomes a consideration, resources will not be allocated to maximize average returns. That is, risk aversion activities will distort the allocation of resources, in terms of average returns, away from risky endeavours. Reduction of risks may thus serve the twofold purpose of protecting the poor producer against periods of severe hardship and of correcting risk distorted patterns of investment.

The variable output producer will find his gross income destabilized if market price moves with his output or remains constant while output fluctuates. Differences in soil, methods of cultivation and climate between farms, local areas and regions may be expected to cause the yield fluctuations of some producers, possibly a large proportion, to be unrelated to price. For instance, yield variation may differ appreciably from average for the padi farmer whose crop ripens first for, being early, his harvest will suffer the most damage from birds. Some wet padi cultivators will periodically be unable to harvest because of flooding while others who cultivate land under a controlled water regime will not experience this hardship. Where all producers are subject to similar yield destabilizing factors, consumer demand may nevertheless shift so as to neutralize the normally income stabilizing effect of price movements. If output fluctuates without considerable changes in resource inputs, as would be the case with yield variations in crops due to weather with purchased seed and fertilizer inputs remaining constant, net income will be destabilized if price remains fixed. Net income instability can show less variability than gross income if total input costs vary with gross income or the price of the producer's output. This might be the case where a sector represents a large proportion of total economic activity in an area. A decline in price and income may lower the general level of economic activity, and thus the wage rate for those producers who hire labour. If a major primary product is produced on farms where income is shared, average income, or the 'institutional wage', will be reduced and, in turn, the cost of labour to other economic activities using hired labour will be lowered. On the other hand, if the wage rate is determined in marginal industry, rather than in the primary producing sector, unit costs of labour will be influenced by what is happening in that sector as well.

The above lines of reasoning suggest that some categories of producers and products warrant more attention than others from those concerned with the effects of market instability on welfare and resource distribution. For example, rich producers will probably be of less interest than poor producers and low yield risk producers than high yield risk producers. Staple food crops as wage goods may attract control because their price instability significantly affects the real incomes of those for whom food is a large item in the family budget. High food prices encourage undesirable switching to inferior forms of food or reduction in food consumption. Poor diets may increase irritability and apathy and adversely affect health, productivity and family and political stability. Moreover, dietary deficiencies at certain developmental stages during childhood will retard mental growth with consequent effects on long run productivity.

The special position of food as a wage good and an important source of income for a large part of the population in developing countries accounts for the current interest in many developing countries in controlling food markets. The effects of market instability may create severe hardship on surplus food producers (whose income is dependent upon their food product) and domestic non-food producing consumers. The low output risk non-food producer's real income will move with the price of food relative to the price of his output (or wage) while the high output risk producer's real income at any moment in time will also depend on the level of his fluctuating output. Price and yield variability will also affect the food deficit farmer who is both a producer and buyer of food. He may be in food deficit because his farm resources are not capable of producing enough food to meet needs or because he is specialized in a non-food crop. (The rationale behind the prevailing use of a kitchen garden among low income farmers has been considered in Chapter 1, Section 5a., p. 10.) If unplanned fluctuations in his food output are unrelated to market price, his real income may or may not be stabilized by food price fluctuations. The food deficit farmer could experience greater hardship than non-food producers who receive a constant wage if his yield tends to fluctuate in the same direction as national or world yield. In a low yield period for him and other producers in the market, on-farm food production declines and the price of purchased food increases. Unit fixed costs of food crop production of the food deficit farmer will increase with decreases in output causing reductions in net real unit income. He may seek off-farm employment to meet the decline in income but with low food harvests there is likely to be less opportunity for wage labour. Furthermore, wages may be low because other food deficit farmers are also looking for wage employment. Those food deficit farmers who produce other farm products, such as poultry, rubber, and pigs, could be expected to use resources devoted to these more intensively with consequent increases in gross income if demand is elastic. If efforts to increase income assume the form of premature slaughter of cattle or harvest of other crops grown, current income increases will cause longer run losses. Such activities will occur, however, if poor farmers attach a rather high discount to future income because their current well-being is threatened.

With food in inelastic demand, the food surplus farmer, affected by similar yield destabilizing factors as the food deficit farmer, may experience lower gross and net income in years of large yield. Wage rates for farm labour will increase since food deficit farmers will devote more time to harvesting their own large harvest and there will be greater demand for labour on food surplus farms. Also food deficit farmers and non-food producers will need less wage employment as food prices decline with the large yields and real incomes increase. The surplus producer, faced with increased labour costs, lower prices and lower gross incomes may harvest less intensively or increase on-farm consumption. The large harvest period is one of high incomes for the food deficit farmer for his off-farm wage is high, food crop large, and food price low. In contrast, with nominal fixed costs, the low yield period can be a high income period for the surplus farmer because his unit labour costs are low, harvest small, and price high. Food surplus farmers facing an elastic aggregate demand would experience less income variability because large harvest years would be years of high gross income as well as high labour costs, and conversely. They can, moreover spread income risks from crops affected by similar climatic variables by distributing farm resources between food crops in elastic and inelastic demand. Starchy staples in price inelastic demand may be combined with vegetables and fruit in elastic demand. A general decline in the yield of both will increase income from the former and decrease it from the latter, and conversely. The reduction in income as a result of reduced specialization can be seen as an acceptable price for reduced risk. Where costs attributable to purchased inputs other than labour (e.g. seed and fertilizer) are important, they may counteract the income destabilizing movements in labour costs since unit costs of these fixed inputs will move inversely with yield.

This common situation of price and yield risk and a price inelastic demand may create the greatest hardship, at a given level of income, among non-food producing agricultural and non-agricultural workers, since their food prices and wages are likely to move inversely. The food surplus farmer's income can be subject to variability because his labour costs and price move inversely. However, since he is in food surplus, his food supplies are not threatened. By supplying at least some of his own food requirements, the food deficit farmer enjoys an advantage over the non-food producer. As his self-sufficiency increases, he will be increasingly insulated from the vagaries of the markets for food and off-farm employment. The non-food producing employer of labour may be un-affected, for his food and labour costs move inversely. If he does not hire labour, he is nevertheless better off than non-food producers who work for wages. Although his opportunity cost may decline with the wage level, the wage he pays himself does not if his non-food product price does not decline. If the demand for food is income elastic, as it may be for fruits, vegetables, meat and dairy products, outlays for food by the non-food producing agricultural and non-agricultural worker will be stabilized relative to the latter case because his wage and ex-penditure on food will move together.

Where primary producing enterprises such as plantations and extrac-tive operations are foreign owned, changes in gross receipts will not be reflected in changes in returns to indigenous factors if fluctuations in demand are met by variation in foreign funded inventories rather than in the level of operation. Returns to labour will remain unchanged where changes in receipts are absorbed by profit margins, stock options, and management bonuses. Instability will be exported through fluctu-ations in remitted profits and salaries of foreign management and the high propensity to import of those whose salaries do fluctuate with the success of the enterprise.

b. Savings and Investment

Fluctuations in the income from a primary product will cause the total value of economic activity to fluctuate where resources are not easily and rapidly readjusted between alternative uses. Under such con-ditions, fluctuations in price may cause dislocation or underemploy-ment of resources and may be expected to lead to parallel fluctuations in the amount of savings and, thus, investment. Declines in aggregate income and savings will be restricted if resources flow rapidly into alternative fields of activity that offer a return approximating that of the original activity before returns to factors in that activity declined. A lag between a change in income or price and the reallocation of a resource will occur where the process of decision-making is not in-stantaneous, holders of resources are unaware of profitable alternatives, and resources are specific to certain uses or tied to a function, area or village for cultural reasons. Fluctuations in aggregate savings available for investment will not be as great as that in domestic savings if there are offsetting autonomous fluctuations in capital inflow from abroad. A high level of savings during a period of high income, moreover, may be superfluous in a fully employed economy since the use of addi-tional savings for investment purposes will be limited.

Instability in primary producers' incomes may increase savings and, thus, resources available for investment if the marginal propensity to save above the level of assured income is high. Producers may believe they are assured of a given level of income in all periods equal to the income received in the lowest income years experienced; periodical fluctuations above this permanent income could be seen as transitory. If consumption patterns are rigid and based on permanent income, additional income will be saved. The lower the permanent income the higher savings will be and, thus, wide income fluctuations around a mean, by lowering permanent income, will increase savings. Those who do not have opportunities to use savings profitably, because of low marginal returns to additional investment in their primary producing unit, will be less likely to save. Where consumption patterns are not rigid and income above the permanent level is seen as windfall gain, transitory income may be used for conspicuous consumption if the recipient's time horizon is sufficiently truncated or if the general display of wealth and expenditure on activities associated with birth, marriage and death are likely to provide long run social returns.

Those producers at the other extreme, who have rigid consumption patterns based on income in high income periods, will attempt to maintain their standard of living during periods of low income by saving less or dissaving. In contrast to the permanent income case, this attitude would tend to reduce total savings with income fluctuations. Those who base expenditure on average income, on the other hand, will save enough during periods of high income to support average consumption in periods of low income. Because the reserve of savings for a period of low income would not exist if income did not fluctuate, income fluctuations increase savings, but not by as much as for those whose consumption is based on permanent income.

While the permanent income case may not be typical of the family producing unit, it may be representative of larger enterprises that allow profits to absorb income changes; the marginal propensity to save out of profits is normally higher than the average propensity. A cautious dividend policy would relate dividends to what is seen as permanent profits, while profits above this level are reinvested in the enterprise. Where the marginal propensity to save out of government export tax revenue, corporate profit tax revenue, or producer income is above the average, percentage fluctuations in savings will be greater than those of income. Since government savings and investment out of profit tax revenue tend to fluctuate more than profits and profits fluctuate more than returns to other factors, particularly labour when changes in demand are met by changes in inventory, we may expect government savings to exhibit significantly greater instability than returns to factors other than equity capital. Government savings and investment from export tax revenue may similarly fluctuate more than returns to factors if export earnings fluctuate more. A progressive export tax may destabilize revenue in the face of fluctuating export earnings and consequently government savings, even if the government's marginal propensity to save is no higher than the average. In a planned growth situation dependent on a calculated flow of private and public sector investment, a climate of economic uncertainty would create greater factor rigidity, distortion in the distribution of resources and disruption of planned investment. Investment planning even in centrally planned countries is, however, an unstable process. If the optimum path of investment is unstable, inverse movements in foreign exchange earnings would complicate the process, but sympathetic fluctuations would not.

c. EXPORT EARNINGS

Fluctuations in income from single exported primary commodities may affect the level of foreign exchange earnings and, thus, the ability to import. On the other hand, if resources are highly mobile they may flow between alternative export industries, maintaining export earnings in the face of fluctuations in receipts from specific exports. If such an ideal situation does not exist, periods of scarce foreign exchange will raise the price of imported consumer goods if scarcity is met with depreciation or devaluation of the domestic currency or artificial restrictions on imports such as quotas or surcharges. Such action could temporarily create a more favourable climate for import substitution industry while turning the terms of trade against the primary producing sector, further lowering real incomes and the market for consumer goods in that sector. A decline in export earnings from primary products accompanied by an increase in consumer goods prices will raise profits and reduce the wage to industry if industry's wage is determined by average or marginal income in the primary producing sector. That is, fluctuations in primary commodity export earnings may destabilize industrial sector profits by causing opposing movements in prices and wages. Reduction in wages will be limited by a greater demand for labour because of higher prices and increased domestic production of import substitutes. If, in the production of a crop for export, periods of low gross income coincide with large harvests for most crops, costs of those employing labour will be higher without import substitution industries bidding up wage rates. The consequent reduction in net income to owners of primary producing units will occur in a period when prices of purchased imports are high.

If the primary commodity export is a staple food crop produced in part by food deficit farmers, the effect on their well-being of fluctuations in price will depend on whether periods of low export earnings coincide with low or high incomes. If, for instance, periods of high staple food prices correspond with low export earnings and a low yield on the food deficit farmer's land and periods of low prices with high export earnings and yield, his outlays for food and essential imported consumer goods will be destabilized. However, his off-farm wage rate may increase in the periods of high food prices and decrease in those of low prices if fluctuations in aggregate foreign exchange earnings alternately stimulate and depress industrial production.

Where foreign exchange earnings are normally devoted to necessities such as fuels, capital equipment, raw materials, medical supplies and staple foods, a decline in earnings may severely impair current production and well-being. Fluctuations may be absorbed largely by variations in capital goods and raw material imports when imports of other more essential items like staple foods and medical supplies cannot be further reduced.

Fluctuations in foreign exchange earnings will increase consumption of imported consumer goods if in periods of favourable export earnings habits of high consumption of imports are formed, and during a decline an attempt is made by the consumer to maintain these levels despite greater scarcity of foreign exchange. Alternatively, the government might find it expedient to gear imports of consumer goods to foreign exchange available in a period of low export earnings, such that fluctuations in export earnings would reduce consumption of imports.

For a country experiencing a fairly constant demand and fluctuating export supply, export earnings instability could be expected to be a decreasing function of the proximity of export demand to unitary price elasticity. This, in turn, will depend on the country's share of the world market and on aggregate demand elasticity. (The demand facing a single country will fluctuate despite a constant world demand if output of other suppliers fluctuates. Thus, a single exporting country with stable supply may be in a demand shift market when the aggregate demand function is constant.) The general level of economic activity, foreign exchange reserves and the export producer's income may be insulated against market instability by distributed lags to changes in consumption and investment patterns as these respond to changes in export earnings. Built-in stabilizers such as progressive income and export taxes and a high marginal propensity to import will further insulate the domestic economic environment.

d. The Consumer

Unpredictable variations in commodity prices will complicate investment planning for fabricators for they will add uncertainty to the ranking of expected relative returns from alternative investment opportunities. An increase in an input price could result in a loss to the manufacturer if product price is fixed by contractual commitments or the manufacturer faces a very elastic demand. Such factors will increase in importance to the manufacturer as the commodity input's share of total production costs increases. Risk aversion on the part of the manufacturer, as with the primary producer, will tend to influence the manufacturer's choice of outputs and inputs. Given a choice between two economically and technically substitutable inputs, the manufacturer will choose the one of least price risk. The high price risk input may be sufficiently more risky than the low price risk alternative as to induce the use of the latter even if its average price is higher. Where there is no less risky substitute, price risk of a major material input may discourage a manufacturer from using his resources to produce the end product using that input. He will prefer another activity offering similar average returns to his resources, but of less input price risk. This deflection of investment to other uses will be limited by the rise in price of the end product as it becomes scarce relative to demand. As the resources and income of a manufacturer increase, preoccupation with risk tends to be displaced by an overriding interest in average returns. That is, less value is placed on the risk premium.

Instability in a commodity price will cause fluctuations in foreign exchange expenditures of an importing country with a stable demand if demand for the commodity is not of unit price elasticity. The unfavourable effect of these fluctuations will be dependent upon the proportion of the commodity in the total value of imports and consumption. In food deficit countries, a low yield period for food surplus and deficit farmers may necessitate large imports to correct for a deficiency in domestic supply. Foreign exchange available for imports of other consumer items might be reduced giving rise to higher prices for importables to both categories of food producers as well as non-food producers. Whether the net real incomes of food and non-food producers change will depend on the price of imported food, the effect of reduced foreign exchange on the cost of other imports, and the effect of increased prices for consumer imports and lower harvests on wage rates.

e. SOME EMPIRICAL FINDINGS

In studies by Coppock, MacBean, Massell, and Michaely, instability in total export earnings was found to be positively correlated with the degree of commodity concentration of exports and the proportion of export receipts derived from primary products, and negatively correlated with the concentration of exports by geographic area of destination and per capita income in exporting countries. Coppock (1962) found virtually no correlation between export earnings instability and the rate of growth in real gross national product of 30 countries tested. The geographical concentration of demand for primary exports from developing countries to the developed countries has had a stabilizing effect on export earnings relative to the prewar period because of the relatively smooth progress of the developed countries in the post-war period. The level of per capita income reflects export earnings stability because it is a rough measure of the level of economic sophistication of a country and the mobility of its resources. These in turn are important determinants of the types of goods produced and their export supply elasticity. The more advanced a country economically, the more likely it is to export capital and skill intensive items for which demand may be fairly stable. Moreover, with greater flexibility in the allocation of resources, a country is better able to shift resources among products in response to or in anticipation of changes in demand conditions and thereby reduce the impact of a sudden change in demand. The instability of total export receipts depends not only on the instability of individual export items, but also on the degree to which opposing fluctuations in the receipts of different export items tend to neutralize one another. Export earnings from goods that are affected by similar market forces will tend to move together while those from products that are affected by dissimilar market forces will fluctuate independently. Thus, a country's total export receipts will tend to be more stable the more dissimilar its exports, the more evenly its resources are spread over the different exports and the greater the number of its export items. The more developed a country, the more diversified its economy is likely to be, and the greater the number of different goods in its exports.

Countries whose exports consist largely of goods with unstable demand and/or supply functions, whether primary commodities or manufactures, will tend to experience instability in earnings. The particular goods exported, rather than the category into which they fall, primary or manufactured, will tend to be of greatest importance. MacBean (1966) and Massell (1964) found that the proportion of the value of exports derived from primary products is positively related to instability in earnings although this relationship is weak. In Coppock's earlier study, manufactures were found to experience greater price instability than primary commodities. Food, agricultural raw materials and manufactured consumer goods were found to be relatively stable while base metals, minerals, capital goods and fuels, in order of decreasing instability, were more unstable. Such analysis of aggregated data, while indicative of tendencies, obscures the experience of individual products. There are countries which experience all the classical maladies of dependence on primary commodity exports because they rely on exports of those primary commodities which experience instability. Those exporting countries which do not experience hardship at the macroeconomic level may do so at the individual producer level for reasons already covered. Individual producer income could well be destabilized even as national fluctuations in export earnings for different commodities neutralize one another. Average producer income from an export might be stable while income of an important minority of producers of that export remains unstable.

Michaely (1962) found that the ratio of exports to the national product is slightly higher on average in the developed countries. It has often been argued, however, that fluctuations in the terms of trade of any given magnitude should exert a relatively larger impact on the income of developing countries because their ratio of export earnings to national income is higher. Michaely also observed that there is only a weak relationship between the ratio of export earnings to national income and fluctuations in a country's terms of trade. Serious fluctuations in the terms of trade do not tend to occur where export earnings are of pronounced importance to a country. Fluctuations in foreign exchange reserves are similar for developed and developing countries, suggesting that greater fluctuations in the terms of trade of developing countries have not induced wider fluctuations in their foreign exchange reserves. Other factors, such as autonomous or compensatory capital movements, may be more influential in determining movements in foreign exchange reserves than changes in the terms of trade. Since, on average, the developing countries have larger reserve-import ratios than the developed countries, the former may be in a better position to absorb fluctuations in foreign exchange reserves. With large reserves relative to imports, the volume of imports may be more effectively insulated from fluctuations in foreign exchange earnings. Aggregation in his tests for developing countries raises the possibility that Michaely's findings may not be representative of individual countries. Single countries might have a high average reserve-import ratio and also extreme foreign exchange difficulties because the terms of trade tend to remain depressed for prolonged periods before reversal. Despite a high average reserve-import ratio, reserves may be depleted while the terms of trade remain depressed. Favourable reserve-import ratios could also reflect artificial controls on trade in the developing exporting country that are costly in terms of administration and distortion in the use of resources. Investment in normally low return foreign exchange to mitigate effects of earnings fluctuations can, as well, divert resources from much needed high return domestic investment.

Contrary to conventional opinion, MacBean maintains that variations in export supply rather than demand has been the leading source of price instability. Yield variability and political disturbances in exporting countries are the most common causes.

3. THE SECULAR DECLINE IN THE TERMS OF TRADE

The threat of a long run deterioration in the terms of trade of developing countries may be of greater importance than short run instability in price or income. Problems of definition and detection frequently give rise to doubts as to whether or not a secular decline in fact exists. By deliberate selection of an unrepresentative base period in the construction of a terms of trade time series and bias in the period of the series itself, one can often produce evidence to support alternative inclinations. The prices used in the series will also influence conclusions. Thus, if prices ruling on markets in importing countries are used, a relative decline in primary product prices may be indicated because of reductions in transport costs or tariffs over time, everything else being equal. Conversely, if prices of exports and imports in primary product exporting countries are used, and transport costs increase, a decline in the terms of trade of the exporter will be indicated. A commodity terms of trade index must by its very nature be highly aggregated, masking the existence of commodities with rapidly rising prices, and results will be influenced by the weights given to different commodities in the index. The impression of declining terms of trade for the primary producer may be exaggerated if no account is taken of increased costs of manufactures due to quality improvements. Because an automobile imported thirty years ago is only remotely comparable to one imported today, a long-term time series of automobile prices assumes little meaning for it will not represent a single product. Most primary commodity exports, however, have qualities today similar to those in the past.

A secular decline in price may be expected for those agricultural commodities whose production is likely to expand faster than demand at given prices. As previously mentioned, output expansion can depend in large part on the development of marketing facilities and of farmers' awareness that a market exists. Increased planting of a crop is likely to be accompanied by productivity increases since research, extension work and improved variable inputs offer a prospect of high returns at little cost. Resulting price declines will have a limited effect on production because of these initially easy productivity increasing measures, low opportunity costs for existing farm resources, and possible irreversibility of investment even when alternative opportunities become attractive. Irreversibility may occur because of sunk fixed costs, such as a stand of tea bushes, which cannot be recovered, or of what seems to be the perseverance of man's optimism over any tendency to despair. If prices have been favourable in the past when investment was undertaken and are not excessively depressed in the present, producers will attach considerable weight to the likelihood that they will recover in the future.

One common reason for expected secular declines in prices of some primary products is the development of synthetic substitutes. In the post-war period, however, synthetics have largely served as supplements to a deficient supply of the natural product, as evidenced by the low level of average stocks for many natural products compared to pre-war years. In some cases synthetics are complementary inputs to the natural product. A decline in certain synthetic rubber prices, for instance, may significantly increase demand for natural rubber which is a complementary input in some of the major end products using synthetic rubber. Synthetics may not be perfect technical substitutes if they have been created for specific uses where the natural product is unsuitable or if an exact chemical duplication of the natural product has not been found. Technical substitutes may not be economical substitutes for the natural product if their cost is high. If, for instance, the cost of petroleum, from which synthetic rubber is derived, and labour wages in the synthetic rubber industry continue to rise faster than natural rubber input costs, particularly those of labour, in the major natural rubber producing countries, synthetic rubber will not in time represent as formidable an economic substitute for natural rubber as at present. However, synthetics, as manufactured products, generally enjoy the competitive advantages of price stability, scientifically determined quality standards and predictable and assured supply at short notice since production is usually situated in the country of further processing and final use. Production and use of synthetics as substitutes during periods of high natural product prices tends to be irreversible because the costs of synthetic production fall with the scale of output and experience in production. As production is generally capital intensive, investment will not be liquidated unless the low variable cost component is not being covered and prices are not expected to become remunerative in the foreseeable future. The vertical integration of synthetic product production with end-product production could reduce demand for the natural product because substitution of the natural product for the synthetic would entail reducing production of part of the integrated enterprise. Such captive markets exist for synthetic rubber in the petro-chemical and tyre industries and for synthetic fibres in the textile industry.

Deterioration in the commodity terms of trade over time may be of nominal interest if productivity in the production of primary commodity exports is increasing rapidly. If unit costs are declining faster than price, or relative prices, for a commodity export, resources could continue to be most usefully employed in its production and, consequently, production and profits may expand in the face of declining prices. (This is not to deny that greater gains in export earnings could be made by restricting production where demand is inelastic or that producers' surplus could be increased by limiting output to the point at which marginal revenue is equated with marginal cost for the industry.) The benefits from improvements in productivity, however, may be seen as exported to rich consuming countries through lower prices. Real income is transferred abroad, for instance, whenever labour productivity in export industries is higher than the marginal industry where the wage rate is determined. Products imported from the developed countries do not decline in price with reduction in unit costs because labour's strong bargaining position in labour scarce economies insures that the benefits of increased productivity are channelled to labour, rather than to the consumer through lower prices. Such a distribution of benefits will limit demand and export earnings where demand is elastic. Likewise, reduction of primary product export prices with improvement in productivity, may cause an increase in export earnings in the long run if demand is elastic.

A secular decline in a country's terms of trade implies a gradual change in the economic environment of the primary producer and thus sufficient time for resources to move into other activities without dislocation. The importance of a decline to the national economy will depend on the contribution of the export sector to the total value of economic activity, the prospects in the long run for alternative employment of resources, and the degree to which alternative uses offer comparable returns to old uses. Methods of coping with a secular decline are discussed in the following chapter.

4. BARRIERS TO TRADE

Motives underlying the erection of barriers to trade, such as tariffs, preferential arrangements and quotas, differ according to whether or not the affected product is competitive with similar products produced in the importing country. Where domestic producers compete with the imported product, they are likely to exert pressure on their governments to engage in restrictive trade practices and national support policies. Considerable barriers do exist, particularly in importing developing countries, not only against imports similar to goods made locally but against imports of products not produced domestically, as a means of conserving foreign exchange, raising revenue and augmenting import substitution polices of development. Commodity exports produced in both exporting and importing countries are subject to trade restrictions designed to protect the domestic producer in the importing country to the detriment of the developing country exporter. This phenomenon is found, for instance, in importing developed countries producing fats and oils, cotton, tobacco, beet sugar and wheat and in developing countries interested in fostering local synthetic production or self-sufficiency in staple foods. The widespread desire for food self-sufficiency in food deficit countries in the face of greater productivity elsewhere with improved plant varieties and methods of cultivation is having an increasingly unfavourable effect on the access to markets by developing countries dependent on food exports. Protection of beet sugar and oil seeds in nearly all major developed temperate zone countries and food grains in developing countries has reduced demand for cheaper imports. In response to the negative implications of curtailing trade, increasing international effort has been turned toward reducing restrictive practices.

a. TARIFFS, QUOTAS AND SUBSIDIES

Tariffs and quotas on tropical zone products with no close temperate zone substitute tend to be low for major consuming countries and, in a number of important cases, non-existent. Removal of those that do exist may have a very marginal effect since demand in developed countries is often derived and consumption near saturation. However, the expansion of potential markets in other developing countries with rapidly rising incomes and un-cultivated tastes for these tropical zone products is severely limited by the typically high import duties and low quotas dictated by balance-of-payments and revenue considerations. Although the effect of a tariff under normal supply and demand functions will be to lower income for the producer in the exporting country, actual price change will be shared between the consumer and producer. In the extreme case of a perfectly inelastic demand, a tariff will be absorbed entirely by the consumer while producer's income will remain unchanged. (See Chapter 3, Section 7b.)

In some instances price support in developed countries has led to overproduction and subsidized export of products in which the exporting country does not have a comparative advantage. Such 'dumping' of surpluses accumulated under domestic support programmes depresses international prices and lowers export earnings of developing countries. The developing country is thus disadvantaged from two angles in a pincer action. The restrictive trade practices of the developed country necessitated by a domestic support programme is one while the dumping of the consequent overproduction is the other. The gain to importing developing countries from lower prices through dumping must be weighed against the losses suffered by developing exporters. Lower world prices will cause a redistribution of income from the producer to the domestic consumer in developing export countries, which may or may not be desirable on socio-economic grounds. Low international prices for wheat through dumping will directly affect export earnings only in some Middle Eastern countries and Argentina among the developing countries. Indirectly however they may reduce demand for substitute foods, like rice, exported by other developing countries. Concessionary sales of wheat and soybean oils to developing countries from the developed may similarly limit demand or retard development of markets for substitute products exported by developing countries. Such concessionary sales, however, lend muscle to domestic support policies in developed countries by providing a moral or economic return to the burdensome surpluses that develop under price support without adequate production control. Where world prices are near the cost of production in developed countries with price support programmes, as has been argued in the case of cotton and soybeans, markets relieved of restrictions may find the geographic distribution of production unchanged. Moreover, the typical subsidy and production quota device in developed countries has, in the case of tobacco, allowed developing tobacco exporting countries to increase their share of the world market.

b. DIFFERENTIAL TAXATION

While some tropical zone primary products escape high duties in developed countries because they are not a source of competition with a local product, fabrication in developing exporting countries may represent a threat to fabricators or labour in the fabricating industry in the developed importing country. Where the latter group of fabricators or labour associated with the industry is organized, pressure will most likely be exerted upon their governments to apply differential import duties that discriminate against fabrication in the developing export country. Particularly where such discrimination occurs in developing import countries, it may also be an expression of the government's aspirations for full employment.

Discrimination in tariffs is effected by a larger tariff on value added in fabrication than on the value of the raw material. For instance, if the value of the raw material is $100 and that of the fabricated product $150, and the respective tariffs are 10 percent and 20 percent (or $10 and $30), the tariff on value added is 40 per cent ($20) compared to 10 per cent for the raw material. Since a fabricated export realizes earnings not only on the value of the raw material but also on the value added during fabrication, such discrimination reduces export earnings in developing countries. More elaborate products have lower price elasticities of demand because they are not as subject to economies and substitution as the raw materials of which they are made. If, through such change in the form of the exported product, demand elasticity moves toward unity from a more elastic position for the raw material, export earnings would be stabilized in a supply shift market. There is a tendency, moreover, for speculation to decrease as a product becomes less standardized, since non-standardized products are less interchangeable on spot and future markets than standardized materials. Movements in the price of the raw material for speculative and other reasons will affect export earnings less, when the raw material is included in a processed product, as its proportion of total costs in the fabricated product diminishes.

c. PREFERENTIAL ARRANGEMENTS

Preferential arrangements represent a further form of discrimination which may reduce export earnings of some exporters and, like tariffs and quotas on tropical zone products which have temperate zone substitutes in importing countries, distort the world-wide distribution of resources. While tariffs and quotas normally discriminate against all importers, preferential arrangements discriminate against groups of importers who are not party to the arrangements. Favoured exporters are given relatively low tariffs and/or high import quotas by the importing country. Such preference is frequently granted by a metropolitan country to former colonies in exchange for reciprocal preferences for the metropolitan country's exports. The net gain to the developing country may be small if reciprocal preferences induce consumers to buy goods which are not the cheapest available on world markets. Removal of preferential arrangements would tend to shift the pattern of world production to the most efficient producers, possibly increasing world income. However, changes in the total volume of trade may be marginal if unit cost savings are small or demand inelastic. Gains might also be small if the replacement of preferences by uniform tariffs or equity in the distribution of quotas involves an averaging of tariffs or a redistribution among all exporters of a fixed aggregate quota, rather than a reduction of average tariffs or an increase in aggregate quotas. In this event, the effect on total demand could nevertheless be expected to be nominal for tropical zone products with no temperate zone counterpart if demand is derived and saturated. Where preferences coincidentally correct disparities in actual or social costs or for disequilibria in exchange rates, their removal would probably bring no net gains.

d. INTERNAL TAXES

Taxes in consumer importing countries represent a barrier to trade if they discriminate against certain primary commodities. General sales or turnover taxes applicable to all commodities alike, or to all consumer goods which are not considered to be household necessities like food, clothing and medicine, will affect consumer net income, but not the distribution of income between alternative consumer items to any great extent. Efforts on behalf of developing export countries to have such general internal taxes removed from certain products may meet with limited success since their removal would tend to introduce more specific forms of discrimination. Where the internal tax is applied to an end product using a material input produced in both tropical and temperate zone countries, removal would not cause a switch in manufacturing to the tropical zone inputs. If the raw material itself is taxed, a reduction in the tax would stimulate aggregate demand without inducing a substitution of the imported input for the domestically produced input since internal taxes do not discriminate against imports (otherwise they would fall within the category of tariffs). Internal taxes tend to be low in major developed countries. Their elimination is likely to create only a marginal effect on demand for the end product, particularly if the tax is on the raw or semi-processed material and demand is derived or if it is on the end product and demand is inelastic. Where internal taxes apply to specific end products such as cigarettes and confectionery, which use raw material inputs from developing countries, they are likely to be heavy because the inelasticity of demand for the product allows high taxes at little cost to the producer or because the products are to be discouraged as a possible source of social harm. The former justification would suggest that the taxes have small effect on producers' incomes.

The chief villains among countries applying high internal taxes tend to be the fellow developing countries of the tropical exporters. Like tariffs, sales and turnover taxes are a major source of government revenue in developing countries because they represent an administratively convenient form of tax collection where illiteracy, lack of household and business accounting, and widespread evasion make other more direct forms of taxation, such as property and income taxes, unattractive. That is, sales taxes and tariffs allow greater revenue, given the amount of government resources devoted to their collection.

5. THE OBJECTIVES OF CONTROL DEVICES

Possible goals of national and international control devices have been implied in the discussion of primary commodity market problems in the preceding paragraphs. Although twenty-four 'objectives' can be identified in post-war conventional international draft or ratified commodity agreements, the number can be pruned somewhat by minimizing the characteristic overlap in the definition of individual objectives. Control is normally designed to increase and/or stabilize producers' incomes, export earnings, government tax revenue and world absolute or relative prices. Stability is desired in order to minimize personal hardship, distortion in resource use and costs to society associated with frequent factor movements. Increasing the levels of the earnings and revenue variables is seen as a means of correcting for secular declines in price, incomes or terms of trade or simply as a means of transferring wealth from rich importing countries to poorer exporting countries.

Those who adhere to the 'concessionary-trade-not-aid' objective believe that the possible disadvantages to developing importing countries from concessions to commodity exporters such as higher than equi-librium prices are more than compensated for by the advantages to developing export countries. Price support results in discouragement of demand growth in the other developing countries where potential demand increases are greatest for a number of tropical zone primary exports because of rapidly growing incomes and new felt wants. This must be included as a debit in weighing the net long run effects of price raising objectives. Short run gains due to an aggregate inelastic de-mand would have to be balanced against losses in the long run under undoubtedly elastic demand in all markets (bearing in mind that export earnings now are worth more than in the future). High preference for current income often accounts for income increasing efforts taking the form of price increases rather than decreases. A related motive for con-cessionary trade is the transfer of control over the financial means as well as the plans to achieve development to countries which are the object of aid programmes. Debt-servicing and predictability, perhaps more than total foreign exchange receipts, are frequently the con-cern of those who support a concessionary trade objective. Concessions could be granted in the form of a high price range, a price 'range' with-out a ceiling, consumer finance of surplus disposal or the operation of a buffer stock, and consumer co-operation in increasing the strength of a buffer stock so that unpopular adjuncts such as export quotas are not needed.

A number of other subsidiary objectives support the primary ones of higher and more stable prices and incomes. So-called objectives which express a desire for new markets, new uses, reduction in trade barriers and increased sales promotion, in fact, indicate means to in-crease aggregate demand which, as an objective, is already included in those relating to the increase of the variables cited above. Where pro-duction and demand potential are separated by institutional barriers, high market costs or ignorance, one objective of market control in the broadest sense may be to make potential trading parties aware of exchange possibilities and draw them into a market relationship. Such an objective sometimes includes a specific desire to improve market efficiency, eliminate unfair trade practices, transmit information re-garding price ratios and technical input-output relationships of produc-tion, or the like. In effect these goals coincide with the general objective of increased producer income as would subsidiary objectives aimed at quality control through regulation sizes and packages, safety and health standards, and standardized grades and labels. Similarly, the frequently stated objective of diversification of commodity exports and resource use in developing countries refers to a means to accomplish balance-of-payments, income and revenue stability objectives. Diversification may also be used to increase incomes. Concern for the prevention of dislocation of resources due to excessive market fluctuations or a chronic imbalance of supply and demand is often stated separately although this is a subsidiary objective to income stabilization. If incomes are stabilized avoidance of dislocation would necessarily follow.

One use to which national control devices may be put is the artificial manipulation of resources between alternative uses for purely strategic or political reasons. Redistribution of wealth to those historically disadvantaged or for whom a strong economic stimulus is necessary is difficult in a barter economy. A further objective of market control then would be to monetize market activities since, short of collectivization or confiscation, redistribution efforts will be most efficiently accomplished in a commercialized environment.

A clear statement of objectives is useful in providing a reference point against which performance of a device can be measured. A judgement on the effectiveness of a control device should be based on the efficiency with which it accomplishes its objectives after an allowance has been made for the inevitable undesirable effects of the device. (The benefit from successful accomplishment of a stated goal may be diminished by the undesired side effects which are created.) Those who negotiate commodity control agreements frequently find deciding upon control measures difficult because they either have an ill-defined idea of what their objectives are or are unable to agree on what they should be. Compromise or lack of understanding may result in the inclusion of conflicting objectives or objectives for which no functional means of accomplishing them is provided. Price stability may, for instance, destabilize and reduce producer income and profits. The increase of producer income through an average price higher than the long run equilibrium price is likely to work contrary to the goal of increased demand, particularly in underdeveloped markets, yet in articles of agreement the objectives of price increase and expansion of demand may be found together, suggesting a certain amount of confusion. In effect participants are defining their objectives as both the contraction of demand and the expansion of demand. Although an agreement may aspire on the one hand toward controlling price fluctuations around an unimpeded trend, the inflexibility of export quota allocations, emphasis on surplus disposal of stocks or provisions that make a change in the price range unlikely after the agreement is signed, would suggest that negotiators are interested in controlling the trend itself. Conventional price stabilization devices may accompany the goal of maintaining the balance-of-payments of high output risk exporting countries. These are not, however, particularly good devices for meeting this objective for individual exporting countries since such strict emphasis on the control of price disregards income, particularly the export earnings of producing countries whose supply moves contrary to most other producers or with world price. Further ambiguity in goals is seen in the revision of objectives rather than of control methods when an existing control device is not working.

Ambiguity is heightened when one objective is given a strong device to back it up while another stated objective receives none. As window dressing, for instance, the development of new uses of the commodity may be included as a goal without the administrative and research funds to make it feasible. Other stated goals, for which there is frequently no tangible backing given, are 'production control' and 'elimination of trade restrictions'. It is not uncommon to find some objectives supported by weak provisions, suggesting a lack of conviction in their possible net favourable effects. Because objectives are not fully complementary, policymakers must make value judgements about their relative importance and, preferably, assign specific weights to them—a subject that will be taken up in the last chapter.

6. SUMMARY

The vagaries of the market place affect the stability of the primary commodity producer's income through relative changes in the prices of those things the producer buys, including credit and factor inputs, and those that he sells. His income may be further destabilized by unplanned changes in output due to unexpected changes in production coefficients or the availability of inputs. Such risks will cause dislocation or underemployment of resources and distortions in the allocation of resources away from a strict consideration of average returns. While severe risks are admittedly undesirable, particularly at low income levels, not all producers will be affected alike by similar market phenomena, nor will they all place the same value on given risks.

Where a crop is both produced and consumed domestically, the effect of market volatility on the producer must be weighed against its opposite effect on the consumer. This is especially important for food as a major source of income and expenditure in developing countries. Those market forces which influence the food surplus farmer's net income, for instance, tend to have an opposite effect on the incomes of the food deficit farmer and the non-food producer. Inverse fluctuations in the real incomes of food producers and consumers suggest that consequent changes in the level of savings on both sides of the market will tend to cancel one another. However, for products that are exported, fluctuations in income will produce fluctuations in savings, and thus resources available for investment, that may not be rectified by compensating international capital movements. Wide fluctuations in producer and government savings because of changes in receipts and marginal propensities to save that are higher than average propensities, could create a climate of economic uncertainty, disrupt planned investment, increase factor rigidity and distort the distribution of resources. However, income fluctuations may increase savings and thus investment where consumption patterns are based on permanent or average income expectations.

Foreign exchange availabilities often fluctuate with export earnings from a primary commodity which, with compensatory exchange rate alignments and import controls, will in turn influence import prices. Compensatory exchange rate alignments will further depress the terms of trade of the primary producing sector during periods of low export earnings and prices, and conversely. High import prices and low wage rates during periods of depressed export earnings will encourage import substitution industries while the opposing decline in economic activity due to low export earnings will discourage them.

Empirical tests indicate that commodity instability may not be an important problem for developing countries on average and in relation to the experience of developed countries. Nevertheless, individual countries and individual producers in all countries may experience hardships attributable to market instability. Analysis that aggregates the experience of nations or individual producers may not reveal the urgency of specific problems. Tendencies lose significance in the priority ranking of areas needing attention, for instance, if there is a wide variation in relative abilities to bear risks. The problem is not so much ascertaining which class of countries, developing or developed, has greater fluctuations, but how much hardship, particularly at the individual level, these fluctuations cause.

Actual secular declines in terms of trade will be demonstrated by a representative base period and time period of comparison, weights indicating the relative importance of separate commodities over time, account of quality changes over time, and prices undistorted by changes in transport costs or tariffs. Any secular decline shown to exist will not necessarily imply that returns to resources are declining. If productivity is increasing faster than relative prices are declining, resources may continue to be most usefully employed in that commodity's production. Increased productivity, reflected in lower prices, may increase export earnings in the face of an elastic demand. The existence of a synthetic substitute does not necessarily mean substitution in manufacturing; synthetics may supplement a deficient supply of the natural product and reduce price instability. Secular declines in the prices of the synthetic and the natural product may be a sign of increases in productivity of both rather than substitution of one for the other.

The removal of barriers to trade could be expected to have small effect on total demand where demand is derived and saturated, as it is in developed importing countries for a number of tropical zone products. Restrictions tend to be higher and possible gains from reduction greater for products common to both tropical zone exporting and temperate zone importing countries. However, high levels of domestic price support linked with production quotas may obscure marginal costs that would be competitive with tropical zone imports in an unrestricted market. Although developing countries with rapidly growing incomes and tastes offer the best prospect for demand expansion, high import duties and low quotas dictated by balance-of-payments and revenue considerations severely restrict the growth of over-all demand for primary exports from their fellow developing countries. Tropical exports considered to be luxuries, such as coffee and cocoa, face particularly high barriers in a number of these countries. Full employment policies in developed and developing countries and import substitution policies in the latter foster discriminatory tariffs which reduce the amount of processing in exporting countries and, in turn, lower export earnings and increase their susceptibility to the vicissitudes of markets in raw materials.

The primary control device objectives of stable and/or high producer price, export earnings, government revenue and absolute or relative world prices are frequently accompanied by a host of secondary objectives, such as diversification and creation of new markets, which can be seen as means to accomplish the more general objectives. Ambiguity and possible confusion in the negotiation of agreements is frequently reflected in the inconsistency of objectives and the stated commitment to objectives which are given weak or no tangible backing.

Readings

Baldwin, R.E., *Non-Tariff Distortions in International Trade*, Washington, D.C., 1970.

Belassa, B.A., *Trade Prospects for Developing Countries*, Irwin, Illinois, 1964.

Berman, D.M., & Heineman, R.A., 'Lobbying by Foreign Governments on the Sugar Amendments of 1962', *Law and Contemporary Problems*, Vol. 28, No. 2, 1963, pp. 416–27.

Boyle, S.E., 'Government Promotion of Monopoly Power: An Examination of the Scale of the Synthetic Rubber Industry', *Journal of Industrial Economics* Vol. 9, No. 2, April 1961, pp. 151–69.

Caine, S., 'Instability of Primary Product Prices: A Protest and A Proposal', *Economic Journal*, Vol. 44, September 1954, pp. 610–14.

Coppock, J.D., *International Economic Instability*, New York, 1962.

D'Amico, S., & Evans, J.W., 'The International Effects of National Grain Policies', *Commodity Policy Series No. 8*, FAO, Rome, September 1955.

FAO, 'The Stabilization of World Trade in Coarse Grains, a Consideration of the Underlying Economic Issues', *Commodity Policy Series No. 14*, FAO, Rome, 1963, esp. pp. 52–8.

————, 'Synthetics & Their Effects on Agricultural Trade', *Commodity Bulletin Series No. 38*, Rome, 1964.

Johnson, H.C., 'Sugar Protectionism and the Export Earnings of Less Developed Countries: Variations on a Theme by Snape', *Economica*, Vol. 33, February 1966, pp. 34–42.

Johnson, L.L., 'The Theory of Hedging and Speculation in Commodity Futures', *Review of Economic Studies*, Vol. 27, (3), No. 74, June 1960, pp. 139–51.

Honan, W.D., 'Wheat Policies and Programs: U.S.A.', *Quarterly Review of Agricultural Economics*, Vol. 19, No. 2, April 1966, pp. 73–82.

Kaldor, N., 'Stabilizing the Terms of Trade of Underdeveloped Countries', *Economic Bulletin for Latin America*, Vol. 8, No. 1, March 1963.

Lipton, M., 'The Theory of the Optimizing Peasant', *Journal of Development Studies*, Vol. 4, No. 3, April 1968.

MacBean, A.I., *Export Instability and Economic Development*, London, 1966.

Maizels, A., *Exports and Economic Growth of Developing Countries*, Cambridge University Press, 1968.

Massell, B.F., 'Export Concentration and Fluctuations in Export Earnings: A Cross-Section Analysis', *American Economic Review*, Vol. 54, No. 2 March 1964, pp. 47–63.

Michaely, M., *Concentration in International Trade*, Amsterdam, 1962.

Pincus, J., *Trade, Aid & Development*, New York, 1967.

Porter, R.C., 'On Placing the Blame for Primary Product Instability', *International Economic Review*, Vol. 11, No. 1, February 1970, pp. 175–8.

Reynolds, C.W., 'Domestic Consequences of Export Instability', *American Economic Review, Papers & Proceedings*, Vol. 53, No. 2, 1963, pp. 93–102.

Ruttan, V.W., & Hayami, Y., *Agricultural Development: an International Perspective*, Johns Hopkins Press, 1971, especially Chapter 11.

Snape, R.H., 'Some Effects of Protection in the World Sugar Industry', *Economica*, Vol. 30, 1963, pp. 63–73.

Swann, P.L., 'Natural Rubber Trade: The Implications of Synthetic Rubber Innovations', *Applied Economics*, Vol. 3, 1971, pp. 57–66.

Tolley, G.S., & Gwyer, G.D., 'International Trade in Agricultural Products in Relation to Economic Development', in Johnson, B.F., & Southworth, H.M., Eds., *Agricultural Development and Economic Growth*, Cornell University Press, 1967, pp. 403–47.

Warley, T.K., 'Problems of World Trade in Agricultural Products', *Agricultural Producers and Their Markets*, Basil Blackwell, Oxford, 1967, pp. 50–74.

Wheeler, L.A., 'Government Intervention in World Trade in Wheat', *Journal of World Trade Law*, Vol. 1, No. 4, July–August 1967 pp. 379–98.

Viner, J., 'Stability and Progress: The Poorer Countries' Problems', in Hague, D.C., Ed., *Stability & Progress in the World Economy*, London, 1958, pp. 41–65.

III
Commodity Control and National Devices

1. INTRODUCTION

THE objectives of commodity control suggested by the market problems covered in the last chapter have brought forth a plethora of quantitative, fiscal, informational and other measures. The present chapter defines the general categories of control devices and relates some of the national devices to their effectiveness in accomplishing alternative goals. Attention is given to criteria for fixing the producer price and the effects of price control on producers in different risk categories and on domestic consumers. Since the analysis of some popular national devices, particularly buffer funds and buffer stocks, is similar to that for international buffer stock and export quota devices, these are covered concurrently in the following chapter. Counter-cyclical fiscal policies, tenancy reform, subsidy of improved inputs, crop insurance, diversification, import quotas, tariffs, and the popular export tax device, all means of increasing or stabilizing incomes, are strictly national measures in historical application and, thus, are given consideration here.

2. GENERAL TYPES OF CONTROL DEVICES

Market instability is influenced by a number of factors, some of which are within the scope of short run control devices while others will be influenced only by longer run efforts. The size of the export sector, geographic concentration of demand and per capita income are perhaps the least subject to the direct influence of control, although these are frequently important sources of instability and hardship. Domestic consumption of exported goods, commodity concentration

of exports and geographic concentration of supply can be more directly influenced while price, quantum and the balance-of-payments are
artificially manipulated in the short run with *relative* ease. Control tends
to become slower in its effect as it attempts to reach fundamental causes
of instability or low incomes. What are commonly referred to as control devices are frequently palliatives which treat the symptom rather
than the underlying cause but enjoy the advantage of a quick effect.
Of those considered, the devices easiest to handle and negotiate nation-
ally and internationally are those which attempt to directly control
the quantities marketed through the use of stocks, funds and production control. General fiscal and other types of devices tend to be slower
in response and less specific.

Among those controls which might serve as remedies, as distinct
from palliatives, would be monetary and fiscal devices that stabilize the
levels of economic activity in importing countries and thereby reduce
market instability caused by shifts in demand. Such remedies could
also be used in producing countries where fluctuation in local demand
is a source of instability. On the supply side of the market, diversification at the national level or possibly counter-cyclical fiscal policies
would offer remedies for fluctuations in macroeconomic variables, but
would not solve the problems of individual producers. Yield stabilization of a crop through control of the water regime, for instance, or
by plant protection measures would offer a remedy for individual producers in a supply shift market. Spreading of risks through diversification at the individual producer level would offer a possible remedy
to individual producers in demand shift markets. Diversification at the
national level through industrialization or self-sufficiency in the production of domestically consumed food crops will insulate the national
economy from exogenous forces and the consequent internalization of
instability may facilitate control. The characteristic weakness of monetary and fiscal instruments in the institutional environment of some
developing countries could be expected to disappear with industrialization, for the institutions which allow effective control through such
instruments are the infrastructure of modernization.

Remedies which aim at a structural transformation of the economy
offer a favourable long term prognosis and look to the interests of the
country as a whole. Those remedies which are associated with yield
stabilization and producer level diversification are also a long term effort because of the considerable resources required for them to reach
fruition. For instance, the magnitude of resources for control of the
water regime or plant protection will over time depend largely on the

rate of expansion of the income base. In balancing the urgency of the short run against the greater effectiveness of these long run efforts, a number of palliatives are opted for which produce rapid results at the individual and national levels. Because of their specific and direct nature, these may frequently be used for fine adjustments. Price controls, for example, can be used to raise producers' incomes during a single season or to influence a cropping pattern. In contrast, more general efforts such as extension education and subsidy of improved inputs could be expected to have a significant effect on incomes and production patterns only in the longer run. They will influence these variables slowly but in a cumulative, dynamic manner as they affect producers' incomes through an actual change in techniques. Although, admittedly, this offers a better remedy than the price increase palliative, the urgency of a solution to welfare problems associated with low incomes or food shortages may necessitate the use of price support. Price support will increase incomes under normal assumptions and may increase output through more intensive use of existing resources and employment of new resources. This non-cumulative once-and-for-all increase in output, however, should be complemented by longer term efforts to raise productivity through the encouragement of innovation.

3. PRODUCERS' PRICE CRITERIA

Aside from direct on the spot controls, coercion, appeals to national pride and moral suasion, prices remain the only known way to influence the production activities of numerous primary producers. In historical application, the manipulation of price of a primary product has been an expression of objectives, however ambiguous and ill-defined. These objectives should ideally be given precise formulations which protect them from the arbitrary changes (or lack of change) which inevitably occur if goals are diffuse and no regulating influence forces consistency in setting price from period to period. Once the goals of price control have been established, their incorporation in a mathematical formulation will lend security to the producer and reduce the effort and friction generated in *ad hoc* changes.

a. EFFICIENT GROWTH AND DISTRIBUTIVE EQUITY

The general goal of increased producers' or consumers' welfare would argue for the establishment of prices which stabilize income. With the price of inputs and consumption items held constant, producers in supply shift markets would, for instance, be given controlled prices which fluctuate inversely with output so as to insure a stable income. The controlled price for an agricultural commodity could be set either before harvest, in which case there would be an element of error relating to the reliability of forecasting techniques used, or after harvest when the level of output is known. The latter controlled price would have to be administered in the form of a rebate that would stabilize income. Such control implies close contact with individual producers and, therefore, its application is limited to crops which are not produced by numerous, widely dispersed smallholders. In a demand shift market the welfare aim can be met with a stable producer price. If the prices of inputs and consumption items fluctuate, these fluctuations would have to be given expression in any mathematical formulation designed to stabilize real net incomes. Stabilization of the price of primary commodities to the consumer will help stabilize his terms of trade and, thus, his real income.

Another and possibly conflicting objective is efficient growth or the allocation of resources according to highest average returns and the distribution of income to those who have a high marginal propensity to save and an ability to invest at high returns. Patterns of investment distorted by risk aversion activities may be overcome either by stabilizing returns or by placing investment funds in the hands of those who will not discount average returns when short-term returns fluctuate. Stable prices would enable holders of resources (including individuals embodying human resources in the form of skills) to decide more effectively between alternative uses. If producers, in allocating resources, look to income risk rather than price risk, the means of meeting efficient growth and welfare objectives (in both cases, stable income) are likely to coincide providing income stabilization is not accompanied by reduced profits or income for reasons covered in Section 5 of this chapter and Chapter 4, Section 2b, p. 121. Attempts to satisfy the efficiency objective may entail the channeling of resources to those who use them with highest returns whereas opposing welfare considerations dictate that resources be distributed to those to whom they provide the greatest utility. Those who can use resources at highest returns are not necessarily the same individuals as those who should be recipients of income transfers on the basis of distributive equity. On an international level and under certain types of control, the developed consuming countries will make net gains at the expense of the developing exporting countries. The transfer of wealth here is from those who need it most to those who may arguably use it more efficiently. Neither efficient growth nor distributive justice goals will be met if the developing exporter is in fact the more efficient user of resources. This may be the case if, for instance, his investments can be saturated with abundant labour of low opportunity cost. On the national level a similar conflict of aspirations will be encountered between different classes of producers and producers and their governments. The argument that the producer uses resources more productively than his own government or consumers in a developing country may be countered by his possible lower rate of saving. But if he is poor, additional wealth may allow him to dissave less, releasing resources of lenders for other uses. On an international scale this would mean that developing countries would be in a position to borrow less from the developed countries.

b. Export Earnings, Profit and Work Effort Maximization

The maximization of export earnings is a more specific form of the welfare criterion, for its application involves efforts to maximize the transfer of wealth from importing countries to the exporting country. Export earnings can be maximized with a producer price that elicits the export supply necessary for a world price, P, at the point of unitary demand elasticity for the exporting country. In Figure 3.1a (p. 67) this is illustrated with linear demand and supply functions D and S. If the supply function, S, intersects the demand function, D, below the point of unitary demand elasticity, as shown, the export earnings maximizing producer price, P^*, will be below the world price. As supply becomes more inelastic, the optimum fixed producer price will move further below the world price. (Linear functions will give the mistaken impression that if supply is very inelastic the optimum producer price may be below unit costs of production or even negative.) Intersection of the supply and demand functions at the point of unitary demand elasticity would argue for an optimum producer price equal to the world price. Where the maximization of export earnings is of overriding concern in price policy, producer price will fluctuate with the market price but probably not coincide with that price. Subject to the constraint that the producer does not receive a price higher than the world price, the export earning maximizing price will be the world price when demand is elastic at uncontrolled world market prices, and less than the world price when demand is inelastic.

Linear demand functions imply the debatable assumption that demand is price elastic at high prices and inelastic at low prices. World demand elasticity may be higher in periods of high prices since competition from synthetic substitutes may be greater and lower in periods of low prices because a point of consumer saturation has been met. Demand may be less elastic at high prices because of unwillingness to risk substitution during a boom. Where demand is derived, moderate changes in prices can be absorbed by profits with no retail price adjustments so that demand remains inelastic through this range. Extreme movements in prices, however, might induce more economical use, noticeable changes in retail price and switching, causing demand to become elastic at high and low prices. Thus when world price is low, export earnings in a supply shift market could be maximized by offering producers a lower price that moves world price into the inelastic section of the demand function. Export earnings will be increased if the arc elasticity between the uncontrolled and controlled price is inelastic. At high prices in a supply shift market the producer would be offered the world price. Assuming constant world demand elasticity, the elasticity of demand facing the single country would tend to be higher in periods of stockpiling (low price periods) and lower in periods of selling (high price periods) because of changes in its share of the world market. An approach which offers a compromise between these conflicting persuasions is one in which the demand function retains the same elasticity throughout the range of normal price variations. If such a logarithmic linear demand function is inelastic, export earnings will be maximized by the lowest possible producer price, and if it is elastic they will be maximized with the highest possible producer price.

The maximization of monopoly profits to the exporting country is an objective which, in its application, may roughly coincide with that of export earnings maximization. An exporting country in a position of market power will maximize national profits by fixing the producer price in any period at the point where aggregate marginal costs equal marginal revenue. Under conditions of competitive national production, the supply function, S, in Figure 3.1b will correspond to the aggregate marginal cost function, MC, and, under normal conditions of positively sloped supply and negatively sloped demand, intersect the marginal revenue function, MR, below world price. Thus, producer price will be below and fluctuate with world price, as is the case when export earnings are maximized with an inelastic demand. This will hold with linear or normal curvilinear functions and an elastic or inelastic demand. The optimum producer price under this criterion will decrease with increases in supply inelasticity. Although it may be difficult to know what the profit maximizing price is in any period, this line of analysis suggests that it can be approached by a producer price below the world price. Implied in this and the export earnings maximization criteria, when used for short run price fixing, is the substitu-

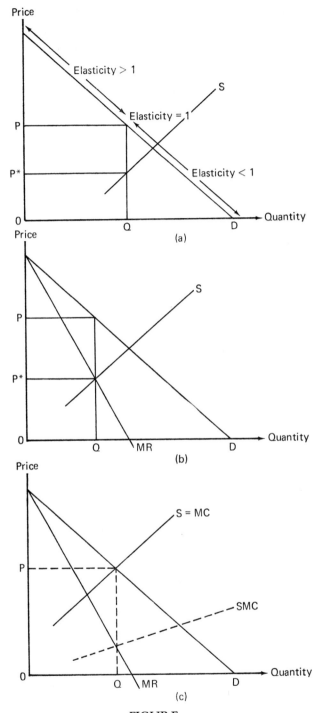

FIGURE 3.1

THE OPTIMUM PRODUCER PRICE FOR EXPORT EARNINGS, PROFIT
AND WORK EFFORT MAXIMIZATION

tion of a traditional mercantile psychology for the long term production and sales goals of modern capitalism; maximum gain on the immediate transaction is preferred over long term market expansion.

Maximization of profits and export earnings can be obtained with reduced output, implying a release of factors of production which may remain under-employed or unemployed. For countries in which unemployment is chronic and a source of social and political tension, price policy might instead be formulated around maximizing work effort. If aggregate work effort is reflected in the level of output of the commodity under consideration, it is maximized by the highest possible producer price. If the producer price is not to be supported above the world price, work effort is maximized by giving the producer the world price (net of market margins). Support of the producer price above world levels may not maximize work effort in general if the subsidy is financed domestically out of taxes or government borrowings since such financing will reduce work effort elsewhere and the availability of savings for other uses. A domestic currency overvalued at fixed exchange rates may, however, justify an export subsidy if the equilibrium rate would make the primary commodity competitive on world markets. A strict application of the work effort criterion without subsidy would leave the producer's price, and possibly his income, fluctuating with world price. Sufficiently wide and frequent fluctuations might discourage work effort and, thus, operate contrary to the objective. A balance could be struck by the stabilization of producer price around the trend of prices as indicated, say, by a moving average of world prices.

Where money wages do not reflect low opportunity costs because they are based on the average income of a prevalent extended family system or on other institutional transfers, wages will not decline in order to accommodate unemployed labour. The social marginal cost function, which reflects the opportunity cost of labour, may lie below the money marginal cost function of Figure 3.1b and intersect the marginal revenue function at a higher level of output. If price policy is directed toward the maximization of social profit and work effort, both objectives might be accomplished with a high producer price. Figure 3.1c shows, for example, that profit to society is maximized with output Q when the social marginal cost function is SMC. Q is elicited with a producer price equal to the world price, P, in an uncontrolled market. P is also the work effort maximizing price.

Historically agricultural price policy has been negative and often formulated without reference to any of the above goals. Exported commodities have been taxed heavily without a thorough consideration of market parameters and the effect on export earnings, work effort or profits to society. Domestically produced and consumed primary products have been given artificially depressed prices so as to provide cheap food and raw materials to an industrial sector and to facilitate the transfer of wealth from primary producers to the industrial sector or the government for industrial or general development. Normally some of the 'tax' is returned to producers in the form of market facilities, education, subsidies and research. In defense of a policy of low fixed producer prices it has been argued that the low producer prices of the West African marketing boards have allowed world price to fluctuate without affecting the producer and without necessitating the use of buffer funds. Producers have been little affected by periods of severely depressed world prices since world prices, even in depressed periods, remain above the low fixed producer price. There is no danger of exhausting a buffer fund or other device designed to stabilize producer price above world prices in periods of low world prices.

Where the marginal income of labour in the primary sector is kept above the marginal value product by institutional transfers, the industrial wage level, determined in the primary sector, will be artificially high. World price for the primary export will be above social costs based on low opportunity costs for labour. Since this works to the disadvantage of industry, lower producer prices or high import taxes will reduce real incomes of primary producers to their rightful level, directly through the tax or indirectly through higher prices for domestically manufactured import substitutes, giving to industry the incentives she would enjoy under a competitive labour market. On the other hand, low primary product prices represent a tax on marginal output and, thus, discourage marginal effort. Moreover, in the West African case they discriminate against those who produce for export and make no distinction between income levels among producers of an export. A more equitable system, which would have the advantage of creating a positive income effect without a negative substitution effect, would be a land tax or property tax which is based on potential output and which increases progressively as the land or property belonging to a single family increases. By basing the tax on potential output, owners would be encouraged to use their resources fully, while its progressive structure would insure distributive justice. However, the possible additional costs of collecting such taxes, compared to export taxes, have discouraged their use in economies where administrative talent and integrity are scarce.

The popularity of monolithic policies of development through industrialization, with the consequent artificial turning of the terms of trade against the primary producing sector through low prices and in favour of the industrial sector through protective tariffs, may be attributed in part to the attraction of the most vocal, educated and powerful elements of society to the urban centres where industry is normally located. This concentration of elites results from the economies of locating in centres of communication and of a close physical proximity of central government and business head offices to the professionals who serve them. Those in positions to influence decisions, such as politicians, planners and other high level civil servants, have daily contact with an urban industrial elite from whom they absorb ideas and on whom they depend socially. This phenomenon serves to dilute the representation of the primary producer even where there is universal adult franchise and a majority of the population in the primary sector. Experience has shown, however, that development is dependent upon the contribution each sector can make to the other. At early stages in development when most of the population is in the agricultural sector, growth in the industrial sector will be dependent upon growth in the flow of savings, labour, food and raw materials from that sector. Since agriculture is primarily a competitive sector, the benefits of technological progress in agriculture are passed on to the industrial sector in the form of lower prices for agricultural commodities. Moreover, expansion of markets for industrial consumer goods and agricultural inputs will depend upon the growth of income in the large agricultural sector.

c. INPUT COST, INCOME PARITY, INTER-PRODUCT PARITY, AND RULING PRICE CRITERIA

A criterion which relates producer price to input costs may be more easily expressed in a formula than some of those already cited for it is less dependent in application on knowledge of market parameters and more on the relationship of easily observed variables. This may be considered as a criterion when, in the interest of welfare and growth, it is undesirable to let the producer's price fall below paid out or total unit costs. It can be used to assure him of a favourable minimum ratio of return to cost in order to induce him to undertake costly and risky innovations. Innovations may be risky in their uncertain yield effects. Misapplication because of inadequate or incorrect information and, in the case of agricultural inputs, unsuitability depending on local soils, climate, water supplies or farm labour requirements, add considerable risk to purchased inputs. A particular hybrid seed might offer a higher yield in good periods than the traditional variety but a lower yield in a period of drought because it has not been selected for its drought-resistant properties. Although it may offer a higher average yield, yield variability is increased. The hybrid may have been developed for use under conditions of reliable rainfall or irrigation but the farmer may be unaware of this or unable to afford the necessary tube well or other irrigation expense. Modernization involves a switch from self-sufficiency in generating inputs to dependence on purchased inputs and, thus, increases in net money income risks and the risk of debt cycles if purchased inputs are financed by loans. Individual innovations often give a prospect of high return only in combination with complementary innovations. Complementary groupings of improved inputs, such as a tube well, commercial fertilizer, hybrid seeds and plant protection materials, increase the risk of a mistake, because of the relatively large amount of new knowledge which must accompany them, and the penalty for a mistake because of the large cash outlay for their purchase.

Although costs of production will be relatively easy to calculate for any given producer, a difficulty arises under the application of this criterion when producers experience different unit costs because of variations in production coefficients due to conditions beyond their control, or differences in the efficiency with which resources are used. Estates, for instance, may have radically different costs from smallholds for which a given crop is a side-line. One possible solution is to take the average cost of a representative sample of producers. But this may hurt the efficient producer working under adverse conditions (poor soil, unreliable water, or debilitating disease) and those concerned about protecting the interests of the high cost inefficient producer may oppose it on welfare grounds. A price based on average costs would reward the low cost inefficient producer and the low cost efficient producer alike. Calculating a single farm's costs for a given crop is also likely to present problems, notably in assessing the division of overhead between different products, the treatment of unpaid labour of the farmer and his family, and the imputed rate of return and depreciation schedule for capital equipment. If the product being considered for control is an essential commodity, such as a staple food, concern for possible inequities and errors in measurement may be overshadowed by the need for a minimum output that can be assured only with a high price. A high minimum price rewards the efficient producer with the means to expand his production while the inefficient producer might be enabled to become an efficient producer only if he is given additional income. Care must be taken, however, not to support prices above costs when inputs are in inelastic supply. Efforts to increase output under such circumstances will be met by cost inflation and further increases in a producer price based on costs.

One frequent upshot of the conceptual difficulties, errors in measurement, and inequities in a general application of the input cost criterion is that attention is focused on a particular type of producing unit to the exclusion of others. The type of unit chosen for sampling might be one which conforms to policy objectives regarding farm size and techniques. If an element of arbitrariness is unavoidable in either extensive or intensive sampling, producers' price could be based on a weighted index of a limited number of input prices as recorded in major markets with perhaps no increase in the inequality of effects. When using this approach one should bear in mind that marketed inputs for which prices can be obtained will generally be improved inputs. A producer price based on a package of improved inputs which have not been widely adopted may be lower than the uncontrolled market price since improved inputs bring down unit costs of production. The cost of wage labour should be included in the index for those employing labour have probably expanded production to the point of needing non-family help through superior efficiency and thus, are to be encouraged. A producer price designed to leave the producer a stipulated net income after account is taken of input costs and risks might assume the form:

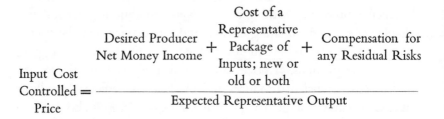

$$\text{Input Cost Controlled Price} = \frac{\begin{array}{c}\text{Desired Producer}\\\text{Net Money Income}\end{array} + \begin{array}{c}\text{Cost of a}\\\text{Representative}\\\text{Package of}\\\text{Inputs; new or}\\\text{old or both}\end{array} + \begin{array}{c}\text{Compensation for}\\\text{any Residual Risks}\end{array}}{\text{Expected Representative Output}}$$

In international commodity control, the input cost criterion was roughly applied in the 1963 Coffee Agreement. Negotiators, unwilling to submit to a price range based on an unreliable forecast of prices, specified that prices were not to decline below the average level of 1962 prices. These prices were felt to be 'fair' to producers. Although determination of this minimum level was not worked out beforehand, nor the role different coffees should play in determining the average 1962 prices, such an arrangement does put off price decisions which have been stumbling blocks for a number of prospective agreements and increases the scheme's potential flexibility.

Income parity, a more comprehensive system, relates the producer's price to the relative prices of his inputs, consumption items and output, such that either his real net income or the purchasing power of a unit of output is guaranteed at a minimum level during periods in which the device operates. Where the income parity criterion is expressed through a complete stabilization of the purchasing power of the producer's net unit output, it reduces income uncertainty to a consideration of yield uncertainty alone. In this case it does not smooth income fluctuations arising from variations in yield (or the pattern of production) and may therefore be usefully supplemented with a crop insurance scheme. A limited application of the parity criterion would use only changes in actual receipts and expenses in adjusting the controlled price whereas a comprehensive application would also include imputed receipts and expenses taking into account interest and depreciation on equipment. As with the cost criterion, the likely value of any remaining risk premium due to a measurable margin of error in calculations or to differences between the environments in which individual producers operate may be included in the controlled price. A price based on income parity that takes overall yield variations into consideration is expressed in the following relationship:

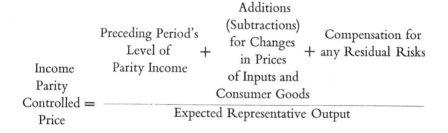

In historical application the parity principle has primarily been designed to redistribute income in favour of producers and is usually expressed through control of output prices. The recent emphasis on income parity, in contrast to the negative price policies of the past, comes with the increasing awareness that the relatively low real income of the agricultural community is not compatible with the incentive required for a steady increase in production. Nor does it assure a large and expanding market for the products of industry. The cost principle discussed earlier conventionally is aimed at stimulating output by insuring a margin between costs and price and has operated either through output or input prices or both. Income parity would be the preferred of the two approaches if the object of control is either a redistribution of real income or output expansion, if real incomes are significantly affected by rising consumer goods prices, and if producers do not suffer from money illusion. Any advantage to the primary producers whose price is being supported under either criteria should be weighed against the effect of a supported price on the competitiveness of exports of raw materials and their end products, on industrial wages through the influence on food prices and primary producer income, and on the level of savings through the effects on the distribution of income.

Under policies of diversification or food self-sufficiency, the production pattern can be influenced by control of price relatives. An application of the inter-product parity criterion has the advantage of influencing the allocation of resources at all price levels. Floor-ceiling price limit devices directly affect relative prices only at the price limits, although support at the limits may influence the production pattern between the limits. While the criterion is normally applied to groups of primary commodities, a rough application is seen in international efforts to influence relative prices of primary commodities and manufactures.

The ruling price criterion reflects the preferences of consumers as well as the strength of supply and is useful when both consumer and producer interests are to be represented. All the draft or ratified international agreements have, in effect, used this criterion. By allowing the price range to be changed either in council or when an agreement is up for periodic renegotiation, the negotiators by contrivance or necessity allow the range to be influenced by trend movements. Trend control under conventional international devices is limited in the long term by the exhaustion of control resources. The ruling price criterion may be applied through a price range mean based on a moving average. Forecasting and its uncertain reliability is avoided by fixing the mean of the price range to a moving average of prices (the ruling price) over previous periods. In the course of time, however, the controlled prices would gradually replace the uncontrolled ones in the moving average and, consequently, perpetuate the influence of the base period. The influence of reliable forecasts may be introduced if it is clear that the moving average will be out of line with a changed trend. To preclude the introduction of political bias, forecasts used in any mathematical formulation for determining the controlled price should be those of an independent agency. If the period of the moving average is sufficiently long, producer price will change only gradually and therefore serve to avoid dislocation of resources during a period of secular price deterioration. The producer will receive a price higher than the world price, allowing him a period of grace during which to consider alternative employment for his resources. Such support must be temporary and *be known to be temporary* if the producer is to be induced to actively search for alternative uses.

The moving average price or price range mean should ideally be based on a clearly defined formula that the producer knows is not tied to the discretion of politicians and civil administrators. Bauer and Paish (1952) have suggested a formula which is fairly representative of its type and also includes some novel features. The variations on this theme are, of course, numerous and can be expected where the application of the criterion differs from one socio-economic environment to another. Their fixed producer price in any period will equal:

Expected Market Price (The Proportion of the Expected Market Price Given to Producer) $+ \dfrac{1}{\text{Expected Quantity}}$ (Export Earnings over a Moving Series of Past Periods — Producers Receipts over the same Period) $\times \dfrac{1}{\text{The Number of Periods in the Moving Series}}$

The larger the proportion of the expected price given to producers, the greater will be the weight given to the current period, and the more the controlled producer price will fluctuate with the free market price. This proportion will be high, for instance, if the supply elasticity is high, since a high supply elasticity implies that producers can reallocate resources rapidly and, consequently, need less price stabilization. Since only a proportion of the expected price is paid to the producer in each period, it is likely, with reliable forecasts of the expected price, that the agency operating the device will accumulate funds. The amount accumulated is given by the second bracketed expression in the equation. Division of this expression by the number of periods in the series indicates how much is available for distribution in the current period. Further division by the expected quantity in the current period reduces this amount to a figure showing the funds available for each expected unit of output. Upon the completion and publication of the forecast of expected output this latter amount will be known by the producer to be available to him. As the number of periods in the moving series increases and the proportion of expected price given to the producer decreases, producer price will increasingly reflect earnings and price in past periods. The fund and payments out of the fund will diminish in size if export earnings decline in the long run but will protect the producer against single periods of deviation from the trend. A drawback of this formula is that it relies heavily upon guesswork about expected prices and output. Errors in forecasting may not allow the favourable effect anticipated for smoothing income can depend not only on getting the direction of the change right but also its magnitude. Moreover, the formula does not deal with the individual producer whose yield is not related to the average experience. The formula is perhaps most useful in ensuring that the control agency through conservatism in fixing producer prices does not accumulate a surplus on a continuing basis.

No one of the criteria discussed here need be used alone. A multiple factor formula may be used to combine, say, market trends as indicated by a moving average price, with the price of inputs, consumption items and outputs to arrive at a fixed producer price. The different elements in the formula may be given weights which indicate their relative importance in satisfying price policy objectives. The multiple factor and preceding criteria may most usefully be expressed in formulae for, if it is known by the producer how his price will respond to changes in a number of economic indicators, he may, by observing the changes, be able to plan output more intelligently. Where, because of conceptual problems and errors in measurement under formulae schemes, *ad hoc* methods of price support are used, the security obtained under price determination by formulae can be maintained by assuring the producer that his price will not fall by more than a specified percentage (4–5 per cent is common) in a single year.

4. PRICE CONTROL AND THE INDIVIDUAL PRODUCER

The effect of price stabilization in a supply shift market on the stability of producer income will depend in part on the elasticity of demand. This point is illustrated in Figures 3.2a and b. Figure 3.2a shows a supply shift market with elastic demand, D, where ceiling and floor prices, P_c and P_f, respectively, are within uncontrolled market prices P_1 and P_2 in two periods. In the first period control reduces a low uncontrolled market income from $OP_1.OQ_1$ to $OP_c.OQ_1^*$ and in the second period a high uncontrolled market income is increased from $OP_2.OQ_2$ to $OP_f.OQ_2^*$. In Figure 3.2b, showing control in a market with an inelastic demand, control is seen to decrease income in the high income period from $OP_1.OQ_1$ to $OP_c.OQ_1^*$ and increase it in the second period of low income from $OP_2.OQ_2$ to $OP_f.OQ_2^*$, stabilizing income over

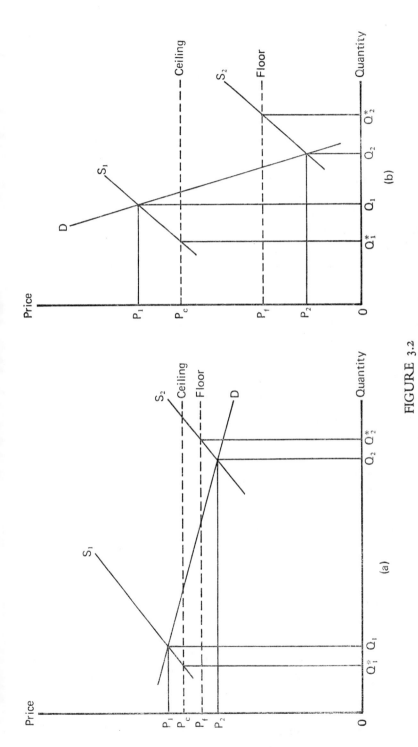

FIGURE 3.2

EFFECTS OF PRICE CONTROL WITH PRICE ELASTIC AND INELASTIC DEMAND AND A SUPPLY SHIFT MARKET

the two periods. Control may, however, destabilize gross income in a demand inelastic market if demand is only slightly inelastic. If the difference in uncontrolled market incomes is small because demand is only slightly inelastic, the loss in the period of high income and price and the gain in that of low income and price under control could be enough to cause a reverse instability of greater magnitude. Similarly, if supply is very elastic (again in the supply shift market of the figure) and is therefore greatly reduced in a period of ceiling price support (in the extreme it may be reduced to zero) and greatly increased in one of floor support, control may destabilize producer income regardless of the demand elasticity. The likelihood of gross income being destabilized under these conditions will increase with the narrowness of the price range spread.

Stable prices that stabilize gross income of the low or no output risk producer because his output and price are stabilized may destabilize relative prices and net real income. If, following Lipton's (1970) example, the volumes of different agricultural crops in a market or isolated part of a larger market tend to move together because they are subject to the same destabilizing factors, price movements for all crops will be in the same direction in any period. If producers are specialized in the production of specific food crops, stabilization of one crop price will destabilize relative prices of food the farmer produces and buys and real incomes. Since the price controlled producer's demand for other farm products is reduced by control in periods of high prices and increased in those of low prices, income derived from their purchases would be destabilized if this demand is elastic (for without similar control, income from the other products will already be high in low price periods and low in high price periods). Periods of high output and income for the price stabilized high output risk producer will be periods of high output and low prices for food products produced by other farmers from whom he buys, and conversely. The higher income in good crop periods of farmers under price control will increase demand for the crops of other farmers and prevent their prices falling as low as otherwise. The net effect over periods of high and low prices will be increased stability in incomes of non-price-stabilized crop producers producing for an inelastic demand and destabilized incomes of those producing for an elastic demand. That is, price stabilization of one or a few crops will have spillover effects on the stability of other crop prices and incomes.

In a low crop high price period for all farmers, the lower demand for harvest labour will decrease wage rates and increase the net unit income of all who are employers of labour providing the decrease in wages is not offset by increased unit costs as fixed costs are spread over a smaller output. With ceiling price control and a price responsive supply, the demand for labour will be further reduced. Unit variable costs of production and relative and absolute prices will be lower than without control. The reverse will occur during periods of good harvests and floor support. Price stabilization will, of course, benefit the non-food producer, the consumer of agricultural raw materials and the food deficit farmer by reducing the price risk attached to that which he buys. Benefits may, however, be offset by wage destabilization. Price stabilization reduces the food deficit farmer's off-farm wage in a period of generally poor harvests since ceiling price support reduces production below the uncontrolled market level. This occurs in a period in which he needs off-farm employment most since his own food harvest is low and price of purchased food high. The limit placed on price increases will in part or completely offset the loss in wages. In a period of low prices and good harvest, the increase in the wage rate by floor price support is needed least since his own food crop is likely to be good.

If the high output risk producer is preoccupied with income risk, to the exclusion of price risk, we may expect him to steer his resources away from the production of the price stabilized commodity. The producer of low output risk will be attracted to the price stabilized commodity by the benefits of a coincidence of stable prices and stable yield. He will be provided with the additional incentive of rising prices as the high output risk producer retracts resources. This switch of production from high to low output risk producers will have favourable effects on the supply side of the market for the product but may be expected to destabilize the production of other crops. As high output risk producers switch to the production of other crops, a greater proportion of those crops will be produced by output volatile producing units, increasing aggregate output fluctuations and destabilizing markets for those crops. Low output risk producers, who move out of production for uncontrolled markets, leave behind a larger proportion of high output risk producers, causing increased instability in these markets as well.

By conferring most benefits on the low output risk producer, price stabilization could benefit those groups which need it least. Low output risk producers could be expected to be among the wealthier producers since output stabilization entails either considerable expenditure for plant protection and water control or producing units which have natural advantages that exclude them from marginal prosperity. Wet double cropping padi cultivators, for instance, not only experience less yield fluctuation than dry padi cultivators, but generally are better off because their land is more conducive to high yields. Moreover, if moneylenders are risk avertors, they will lend more or at a lower rate of interest to the producer whose uncertainty is reduced. Price stabilization that involves a price range symmetrically distributed between the un-controlled equilibrium prices (e.g. in Figure 3.2a $P_f - P_1 = P_2 - P_c$) will, however, increase producers' incomes. The gain in price under floor price support will be at a larger volume of output than the loss at the ceiling price. When this benefit accrues to the high output risk poor farmer it may encourage him to remain in the production of the price-stabilized-income-destabilized primary product. He may, in fact, pro-duce more of the product to cover himself in low income periods and thus increase average output. In this case, greater income instability may be accompanied by a higher average income. But if the high out-put risk producers of a controlled crop continue to produce at least as much as before and the low output risk producers switch to production of the controlled crop, price will *ceteris paribus* decline providing the controlled price is related to equilibrium prices over time.

In sum, price stabilization designed to stabilize price around the trend, will disadvantage the poor high output risk producer and benefit the rich low output risk producer. The net effect on aggregate pro-duction of a product and welfare will be dependent upon the proportion of output produced under different risk and income conditions. If most is produced under conditions of high output risk, there may be more switching out of the product than into it by low output risk producers. If the product is an export the net welfare effect to the exporting country may be negative since the increased instability of producers' incomes is not offset by benefits to domestic consumers. Where the product is consumed in the country of production, gains to consumers through more stable prices must be weighed against possible higher prices as high output risk producers switch to alternative products.

5. THE EFFECT OF PRICE CONTROL ON PRODUCER SURPLUS

Oi (1961) has shown that under certain conditions producers gain from price fluctuations and hence lose from price stabilization. In Fi-gure 3.3a, showing a short run demand shift market with linear, parallel shifting functions, producers are confronted with two prices, P_1 and P_2, which are equally likely to prevail at any moment in time. Under con-

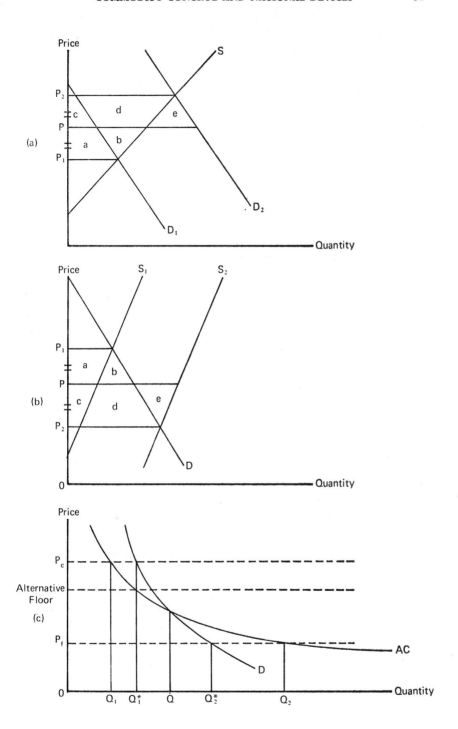

FIGURE 3.3

THE EFFECT OF PRICE CONTROL ON PROFITS

ditions of perfect competition the aggregate supply function, S, will equal the sum of individual marginal cost functions. Where resources are mobile or price changes are anticipated, S will be less than perfectly inelastic. The competitive industry maximizes short run profits in each period by producing up to the point at which marginal cost equals price. With supply positively sloped, equal increases in price, P_1P and PP_2, will create increasingly larger profits. Stabilization of producer price at P, the mean of the uncontrolled market prices, increases producer surplus by $a + b$ in periods when P_1 would otherwise have ruled on the uncontrolled market and decreases it by $c + d$, when P_2 would have ruled. The expected value of producer surplus is $\frac{1}{2}(a + b - c - d)$. This is less than on the uncontrolled market since $a + b < c + d$, but this unfavourable effect is offset in part by reduction in the problems of management (or mismanagement) associated with output variation. Reduced profitability can, of course, be avoided with a fixed price somewhat higher than the mean. Producer surplus is stabilized since the gain occurs in a period of low surplus and the loss in one of high surplus. (When applied to social surpluses such analysis is indicative only of tendencies if social and money marginal costs differ. Should the two differ substantially, the above and subsequent analysis of surpluses would be further complicated.)

In a supply shift market with a negatively sloped demand the reverse outcome holds, as Waugh (1944) has demonstrated. In Figure 3.3b stabilization of price can be seen to increase the expected surplus of producers by $\frac{1}{2}(c + d + e - a)$. The promise made in the preface to avoid unduly fastidious analysis notwithstanding, it is worthy to note Zucker's (1965) qualification that, if Oi's supply function is given constant elasticity between prices P_1 and P_2 and producer gross income with and without control is equal, profitability will not be affected by control while gross income will be stabilized. By dropping Oi's implicit assumption of an adjustment of output to change in price and substituting a rigidly preplanned output, Tisdell (1970) has shown that profits increase with stabilization of price; this finding is particularly relevant where output once planned is unalterable in the span of time in which variations in price take place. Most primary commodities could be expected to fall between the Oi and Tisdell assumptions. The possible losses in profits with control will be reduced if the fixing of price limits cause prices between the limits to move more rapidly in a particular direction. What is euphemistically labelled 'market psychology' may cause price to gravitate toward a fixed point if one is provided, with the result that fluctuations within the price range are destabilized with control. In this event price stabilization in the demand shift market above would reduce profits on wide fluctuations and increase them on narrower ones.

Porter (1950) has argued that in the short run agricultural commodities may be assumed to have declining average costs (or money outlays) because fluctuations in production due to natural causes do not give rise to proportionate variations in costs. If the demand function, D, cuts the average cost function, AC, as shown in Figure 3.3c, producers will make losses at outputs above Q, and profits at outputs below this point of intersection. With floor and ceiling producer price control at P_f and P_c, respectively, production above Q_2 will give profits and below Q_1 losses. Profits will decline with control for production between Q_1 and Q_1^* and losses will decrease for production between Q_2^* and Q_2 compared to the uncontrolled market. Thus, moving from high to low prices in a supply shift market, producers experience a double sequence of alternating losses and profits. If short run equilibrium prices tend to move about the ceiling price, P_c, stabilization may cause hardship for producers who cannot afford periods of losses because of indebtedness, low incomes, or reliance on profits to provide cash for the next crop's purchased inputs. Should the normal level of production be at output below Q, with floor price control at the 'alternative floor', profits will be destabilized because losses will be made in periods of low output and in periods of bumper harvests profits will be increased above their uncontrolled market level.

6. THE EFFECT OF PRICE CONTROL ON EXPORT EARNINGS

A widely debated argument of Nurkse's (1958) maintained that a producer price control below world prices for an exported primary product will reduce export earnings since low producer prices restrict output and exports. Although this was proferred as a rule of thumb, it relates in fact to a specific set of conditions, as later rebuttals made clear. In periods of high world prices, low fixed producer prices will reduce export earnings only if the demand facing the country imposing a low fixed producer price is elastic and supply is responsive to price. In the short run supply may be sufficiently inelastic to allow a small reduction in export earnings to be compensated by the reduced producer income risk that accompanies control. Where supply is unresponsive to price, no loss will be made regardless of the world price elasticity of demand, while gains will be experienced with an inelastic demand and price responsive supply. Moreover, what occurs during periods of ceiling price support must be weighed against effects during periods of floor price support, if the device is one which fixes the producer price between extremes in world prices. In a period of low prices, elastic demand, and floor support, export earnings will be increased over the uncontrolled market if supply is responsive to price. Under devices which control both producer and world prices, such as international buffer stocks and export quotas, periods of ceiling price support will be ones of reduced supply and lower price and, thus, reduced producer income. A national buffer stock for an export will maintain a ceiling price by selling from stock, increasing export earnings in a market of elastic demand despite reduced producer earnings. If the buffer stock is held internationally, however, export earnings will be the same as producer earnings. Possible gains in export earnings under a national buffer stock in periods of ceiling price support will be countered by losses at the floor when stocks are withheld from the market.

7. NATIONAL DEVICES

Some control objectives are most effectively met with national devices while others are, by necessity, sought through national devices because international agreement is difficult to reach. Stabilization of products produced and marketed domestically is, of course, a national problem. National devices may be used to control the influence of volatile international markets on the national economy or to control the international market itself. Counter-cyclical fiscal policies, progressive export taxes, buffer funds, and crop insurance programmes are devices which fall into the former category while national buffer stocks and export restriction schemes fall in the latter. Buffer stocks and export restriction are common international as well as national devices.

a. THE SLIDING-SCALE EXPORT TAX AND EXPORT SUBSIDY

The sliding-scale or progressive export tax is a popular form of producer price control because it fits easily into existing administrative machinery designed to raise government revenue through a uniform *ad valorem* tax on exports. The relatively small cost of collection at the few points where primary products cross the producing country's border accounts in part for the use of export taxes as a revenue raising measure. The export sector may, moreover, be the most prosperous sector at early stages in development and a logical source of development funds. Where it is not the most prosperous, the tax may be seen as a way of generating savings from a low income and low saving sector. In doing so, however, it may reduce private savings more than it increases public savings or it may shift savings from possible high-return private use to a lower return public use. Whether income is best left in the hands of the producer rather than transferred to the government begs questions regarding the relationship of immediate and postponable consumption, interpersonal comparisons of utility, and the concept of the welfare state in the context of development which are beyond the scope of this text. Export taxes have been justified on the basis of a need for diversification or increased productivity that can only be promoted by public agencies. Revenue in this case would be used to broaden the resource base, in the face of unstable commodity markets or secular deterioration in commodity prices, or to counter secular declines through productivity-increasing research in the production of the disadvantaged commodity.

Unlike a buffer fund, where earnings of producers are averaged out over time with, by definition, no net gains to the fund, the export tax constitutes a net change in earnings of the export sector. The graduated tax structure under a sliding-scale tax allows the siphoning off of excess purchasing power arising from high export prices, reducing the primary and secondary effects of increased export earnings on the economy. Inflation is restrained if the amount removed by the tax is not spent by the government while export earnings remain high. It may not act in an anti-inflationary manner, however, if high prices are accompanied by low incomes and low prices by high incomes in a supply shift market characterized by an elastic demand. In a demand shift market the tax may destabilize government revenue, for revenue will be high in periods of high prices and low in those of low prices. If the government is committed to planned expenditure over several years, it may have to make up the loss in revenue in low price years with an underbalanced budget and risk ensuing inflationary pressures.

Whether a progressive tax is, in fact, an anti-inflationary device will depend on whether public expenditure is based on average revenue, some amount above or below the average, or is allowed to fluctuate with or inversely with receipts. The more direct and progressive the tax on the export industry the more tax revenue fluctuations will exceed export earnings fluctuations in a demand shift market and the greater will be the influence of government expenditure policy in determining the effect of export earnings fluctuations on the domestic economy. The influence of the expenditure policy on the economy will increase with the contribution of the export industry to the total level of economic activity and with the proportion of total government revenue derived from it. The government can avoid transmitting export earnings fluctuations to the system by allowing expenditure to vary inversely with export earnings or running a surplus in periods of high and a deficit in periods of low export earnings and revenue.

The conventional partial equilibrium analysis of the export tax device is demonstrated in Figure 3.4a where S is domestic supply, D domestic demand and P_2 the world price. P_2 constitutes the average revenue function facing a small country for a given exchange rate. (All prices—producer prices, world prices and domestic market prices—are expressed on a common, strictly comparable basis, i.e. allowance is made for differences in the costs of marketing functions). Under a nominal tax rate of P_1P_2, domestic production is reduced by Q'_2Q_2, domestic consumption increased by $Q_1Q'_1$, and consumer and producer price reduced to P_1. (From this it is seen that an export tax is essentially an antiprotection device.) Consumers' surplus increases by $a + b$, government revenue by d and producers' surplus is reduced by $a + b + c + d + e$. The unfavourable effect on export earnings could be avoided by use of a consumption tax of P_1P_2 instead of an export tax. In effect this would reduce the demand function to D'', allow the government to collect some revenue and increase exports. Similarly, a unit production subsidy of P_1P_2 would increase exports by moving the supply function down to S'' but it would also have a negative tax revenue effect. An export tax with a consumption tax of the same amount would leave consumption unchanged at Q_1, raise revenue $a + b + c + d$, and increase exports by Q_1Q_1'. Finally an effect identical to that which export tax P_1P_2 exerts on export earnings could be obtained by a production tax and consumption subsidy of similar magnitude. The production tax would, in effect, move the production function up to S' and the consumption subsidy would move the demand function up to D'. Revenue $a + b + c$ would be neutralized by the consumption subsidy of like magnitude, leaving revenue d, as under an export tax.

If export demand is not perfectly elastic, the tax will to some degree fall on foreign consumers. The share each side of the market bears will depend on the relative elasticities of supply and demand. With reference to Figure 3.4b, where D_1 and D_2 represent price responsive foreign demand (no domestic demand exists in the exporting country), it is seen that the effect of the tax is to shift the demand facing producers downward by the amount of the tax, from D_1 to D_1^*. World supply is reduced and price increased. Thus, while the producer suffers a loss in

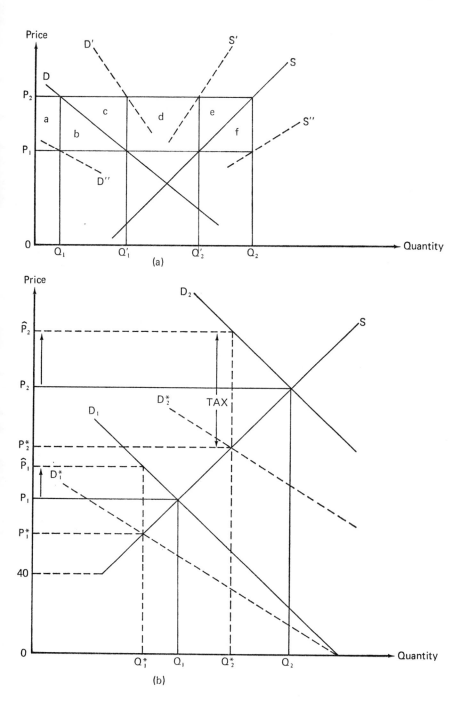

FIGURE 3.4

THE EFFECT OF EXPORT TAXES AND SUBSIDIES IN PARTIAL EQUILIBRIUM

income under the normal conditions of a positively sloped supply function and negatively sloped demand, foreign consumers pay some of the tax through higher prices. The greater the inelasticity of demand and the more elastic is supply, the greater will be the consumer's share. Producers will suffer no income loss if demand is perfectly inelastic and supply responsive to price. On the other hand, the entire tax will fall on producers if supply is perfectly inelastic and demand is responsive to price. Where supply is price responsive, increases in export earnings, despite reduction in producer income, will occur if the demand confronting the exporting country is inelastic. In the event of a perverse supply function, due perhaps to speculative stock accumulation in the exporting country, the incidence of an export tax falls entirely on the consumer so long as the elasticity of supply is greater than that of demand.

Under normal circumstances, with producers receiving lower than world prices, domestic users of a taxed raw material export will experience lower costs of production than without the tax because of lower material input costs and wage rates if the wage rate is determined by incomes in the primary producing sector. If the tax reduces foreign exchange earnings, prices of imports will rise, further turning the terms of trade against the primary producer and in favour of import substitution industries. Reduced output will be indicative of a movement of resources out of the export industry and a movement of the country away from production according to its greatest comparative advantage if the domestic currency is not overvalued at fixed exchange rates. The effect on returns to resources will be compounded if displaced factors cannot find alternative employment. Conversely, where severe unemployment problems exist they may be relieved by reduction of export taxes. If the tax is placed on the raw material export but not the end product, it will encourage further processing before export, increase employment and possibly increase export earnings since they will include the value added in processing. In the long run, reduced domestic output and higher world prices under an export tax will encourage other producing countries to expand production. Consequent price declines may leave a single country applying the tax with reduced output, reduced share of the world market and a pre-tax world price.

The effect of export taxes on the level and stability of prices and income may be illustrated in a two period analysis. Figure 3.4b shows a demand shift market with a fixed percentage export tax. Demand in the first period, D_1, is parallel to that of the second period, D_2. Where the tax is of a fixed percentage, the effect in the first period will be identical but on a smaller scale to that in the second period of high prices; the lines in the figure relating to the first period are a miniature of those relating to the second period in which demand D_2 rules. Although over the two periods absolute fluctuations in world price and export earnings will increase and in producer income will decrease, percentage fluctuations will be unaffected when the percentage is measured as the difference in price in relation to the mean of two observations.

Appendix 3, Table A3.4, shows results under varying market parameters when the demand and supply functions are given a logarithmic-linear expression. Comparison of Table A3.1 with A3.2 and A3.4 indicates that the tenor of results with an *ad valorem* export tax over the uncontrolled market is the same as with linear functions. Percentage fluctuations in world price, export earnings, and producer income are seen not to change with the tax. Under normal supply and demand assumptions profits decrease, while export earnings increase with inelastic demand functions and decrease with elastic ones.

Figure 3.4b may be used to illustrate the effects of a progressive tax, relative to a fixed percentage tax, if we make the simplifying assumption that no tax exists in the period of low price and one does exist in the period of high price. Percentage fluctuations in producer prices will decrease compared to the uncontrolled market because the producer receives a lower price in the second period of high price and no change in price in the first period. On the other hand, world prices will be destabilized since world price increases in the second period with the tax. Producer income will be stabilized because a lower price and volume of output in the second period moves income in that period closer to the low income of the first period. Export earnings, however, may be destabilized if, in the second period of high export income with the uncontrolled market, output contracts in the face of an inelastic demand. Government tax revenue is destabilized regardless of how little tax is collected in the second period, since under our assumptions no tax is collected in the first period. If the tax reduces the producer price in the period of high price below the export earnings maximizing price P^* of Figure 3.1a above (p. 67), each of three policy variables would assume a less desirable level: export receipts and domestic producer income plus tax revenue would be lower than without control and world price would be higher. That is, P^* places a possible lower limit on the range over which the taxing authority might reasonably elect to alter producer price.

Progressive or fixed percentage export taxes will reduce producer and consumer surpluses in both supply and demand shift markets since in any period in which a tax exists there will be an increase in price to the consumer and a decrease in price to the producer. With reference to Figure 4.2b in Chapter 4, Section 2b (p. 124), for instance, in the period in which P_1 would have prevailed on an uncontrolled market, tax PP_1' will decrease producer and consumer surpluses by $c + d$ and $a + b$, respectively. The exporting country realizes a net gain (loss) of $a - d$ and the exporting country and consumers jointly suffer a loss of $b + d$, the amount by which producer and consumer losses exceed tax revenue. Surpluses of both producers and consumers are destabilized in the supply shift market of Figure 4.2b since the loss occurs in a period of low surplus.

One limitation of the line of analysis taken here and in the preceding paragraphs is that the demand function for a given period is assumed to be independent of what happened in preceding periods, and in particular is not affected by the world price destabilization of the progressive export tax. Control may, however, alter the demand and supply functions and the conclusions reached. In the case of a normal good, the income effect of price stabilization will reduce and destabilization increase the elasticity of the demand function. Where producer real income moves with price, devices which stabilize real income will increase the supply responsiveness to price by allowing the substitution effects on the side of production to predominate. Decreased market price stability would tend to cause speculation to be price destabilizing if, as is often argued, the greater the range of price fluctuations caused by non-speculative factors the more likely speculation will be price destabilizing. The degree of control in the first period of the analysis is important for the second period; price in a previous period often appears as significant as current price for explaining a particular position of the market. This frequently occurs because of a possible delay between the conclusion of a contract and the actual delivery of the goods or because purchases and sales decisions are taken on the basis of an 'expected price' related to the evolution of prices during the recent past. Even if the appropriate changes in the functions were included in the above analysis, it would be misleading to evaluate the device entirely within this simple supply and demand context. Market activities are inherently institutional and, consequently, influence the way in which basic supply and demand forces come into being and interact. Control devices not only determine the results of market activities cited above, but change the way in which those results are obtained; they involve dynamic, possibly irreversible, effects such that even a short term two period device may produce conditions which linger long after its termination.

A corollary to the export tax is the export subsidy, used to support prices paid to domestic producers at levels above export prices. The relatively large size of the primary producing sector in developing countries, however, precludes wide use of this form of income transfer which is more typical of developed countries. If P_1 in Figure 3.4a is the world price (in contrast to the export tax case above in which P_2 was the world price), a nominal unit export subsidy of P_1P_2 would have the reverse effect to the export tax, except on government revenue. What would result is a negative consumption effect of $Q_1Q'_1$, a positive production effect of $Q'_2Q'_2$, a redistribution from consumers to producers of $a + b$ and a negative revenue effect of $b + c + d + e + f$, assuming, of course, that a tariff exists to make import price at least equal to P_2. The unfavourable effect on consumer price could be avoided by a production subsidy of the same amount, causing the supply function to shift down to S''. Likewise, an export subsidy combined with a consumption subsidy of the same amount would leave consumption unchanged. Both alternatives would reduce the level of exports compared to the effects of an export subsidy alone. Too ambitious a food self-sufficiency programme may inadvertently produce a trade reversal entailing an implicit export subsidy. In effect, a prohibitive tariff is supplemented by domestic price support above the equilibrium of domestic supply and demand, at least in good harvest periods. During those periods producers are paid the high support price while the surplus above domestic consumption is sold at the lower world price. Variable subsidies may be used to stabilize producer price and output, both of which will be completely stabilized, for instance, in an export demand shift market where the unit subsidy varies inversely by the same amount as world price. Dropping the small country assumption of Figure 3.4a, assuming a fairly rigid domestic demand, and allowing a price responsive export demand, production, exports and world price are less for export subsidy P_1P_2/OP_2 than when export demand is perfectly elastic. The value of exports will increase over the uncontrolled market if demand is elastic and decrease if it is inelastic.

b. IMPORT QUOTAS AND TARIFFS

Import quotas and tariffs are national devices frequently used to control foreign exchange expenditure, to redistribute income to primary commodity producers and to encourage self-sufficiency in essential foods for economic and strategic reasons. Figure 3.5 illustrates the effects of each on a country which has a stationary domestic supply, S, and de-

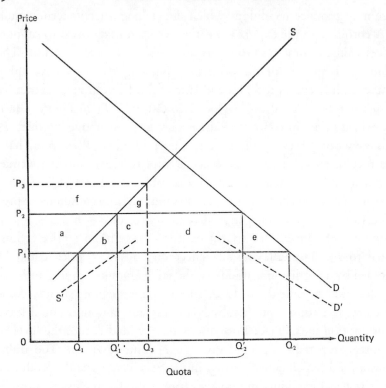

FIGURE 3.5

IMPORT QUOTAS & TARIFFS IN PARTIAL EQUILIBRIUM

mand, D, for a commodity over two periods and which at world prices P_1 and P_3 produces less of it than is needed to satisfy domestic demand. Without control, Q_1 is produced locally in the first period and $Q_1 Q_2$ imported. Internal price may be raised to a stipulated floor price, P_2, with quota $Q'_1 Q'_2$ or tariff $P_1 P_2$, assuming that the tariff is imposed on a perfectly elastic international supply and that there is no domestic price rigidity such as might exist if the quota or tariff were considered temporary and importers allowed price increases to be absorbed by profits in order to maintain goodwill. Since the import quota is equal to the volume of imports which would occur from the imposition of tariff $P_1 P_2$, the effect of each device on domestic consumption, price, production and redistribution of income is the same. Consumption in either case is reduced by $Q'_2 Q'_2$, production increased by $Q_1 Q'_1$, price increased to P_2 and there occurs, as well, an income redistribution between consumers $(-a-b-c-d-e)$, producers $(+a)$ and others $(+c+d)$. If the level of imports affects world price, internal price will rise and production increase with a given *ad valorem* tariff but by less than with a perfectly elastic import supply. Likewise, consumption and redistribution effects will be less and there will be a smaller decline in the volume of imports.

During the first period, that of low producer income, control increases income from $OQ_1.OP_1$ to $OQ'.OP_2$, bringing it closer to the second period of higher income, $OQ_3.OP_3$, and no control. Since the second period is without control, the net income change is positive. (If domestic supply or demand shifts from one period to the next, however, these effects would not necessarily hold.) On the one hand we have a transfer to producers of a, and on the other an equal loss to consumers, a loss, b, attributable to the inefficient use of resources fostered by protection (assuming resources used to produce $Q_1Q'_1$ have an opportunity value of OP_1) and a loss, e, in consumers' surplus caused by reduced consumption of the controlled commodity by Q'_2Q_2 (assuming the expenditure diverted to other items produces a happiness equivalent to the marginal satisfaction of consuming the commodity before control, OP_1). The loss in consumers' surplus shown by area $c + d$ is transferred to the government, importers or foreign exporters. The consumer surplus loss, $a+b+c+d+e$, could be avoided by a grant of $a+b$ to producers. If this were financed by a progressive income tax, the burden would fall largely on the wealthy. The reduction in world market demand by $Q_1Q'_1 + Q'_2Q_2$ may induce a decline in the price of imports $Q'_1Q'_2$ that offsets the net surplus loss $b+e$. Utilizing a unit domestic production subsidy and a unit consumption tax of P_1P_2/OP_2, and thus moving the supply curve to S' and the demand curve to D' could achieve an effect like that of import quota $Q'_1Q'_2$ during the period of quota support. The subsidy would cost $a + b$ and be exceeded by tax revenue $a + b + c + d$.

Control effects similar to those under tariffs can be achieved with consumption taxes, with results identical to those cited in the preceding paragraph. If it appears necessary to avoid the protection and redistribution to producers found under a tariff, a domestic sales tax of the same magnitude as the tariff could be used to shift domestic demand downward to D'. This would raise revenue $a + b + c + d$, more than the tariff, but would not be as effective in reducing imports. Production and consumption subsidies could be used separately or in mixed schemes with the same effect as under quotas. With world price at P_2 an import subsidy (negative tariff) of the same specific amount, P_1P_2, would have the converse effect to a tariff (or quota).

Whether or not the quota $Q'_1Q'_2$ has a revenue effect identical to the specific tariff P_1P_2 will depend on how the quota profits, $c + d$, are distributed between importers, their government and foreign exporters. Where the importing country faces a perfectly competitive international market, this amount will accrue to either importers or their government. On the other hand, if foreign exporters enjoy a strong bargaining position vis-à-vis importers, they may be able to increase their price above P_1 without losing sales. Where this condition exists a tariff will improve the country's terms of trade while the quota may make it worse. The tariff will bring a larger reduction in the foreign exchange value of imports than would occur under the quota. In the small country case of perfectly elastic import supply, if the government auctions licences to competitive importers, importers should be willing to pay $c + d$ for the licences as this represents prospective receipts in excess of those needed to induce imports $Q'_1 Q'_2$. It represents the scarcity value of the quota licences. If there is a monopoly importer or an importers' cartel, however, the auction returns will not be as large as $c+d$ and some quota profits will go to importers. By distributing the quota beforehand, auctioned licences avoid the awkwardness and imprecision of determining that point in time, in the flow of the commodity into the country, at which the quota has been filled. Without such a system for distributing the quota among importers before the period of restriction, each importer might be inclined to import as much as possible at the onset of the restriction in order to insure a large share of total imports, with the possible effect of causing scarcity at the end of it.

Since import licences are a source of livelihood for importers that receive them, government officials may come under pressure to accept bribes and distribute them according to favour. Licensing will be popular among those who for political reasons wish to increase the representation of indigenous peoples in external trade. In this case, licences will be given to those who could not survive in trade without them. Where licences are not auctioned, they may not go to importers and their quota profits may go to neither importers, consumers nor the government if they are given to politicians and officials as bribes or as favours to relatives, military officers, political supporters, or to the ruling party itself. Auctioning of licences, on the other hand, might serve to increase an already high degree of concentration of imports in the hands of a small number of merchants. The popular alternative method of distributing licences according to the proportion of an importer's historical share of the market could also reduce competition if it excluded new entrants who have no historical share.

Political groups may prefer a combination of quotas and licences over tariffs as a means of control because these allow tighter government supervision of the environment in which the importer operates. Consequently this creates influential and possibly remunerative positions which their holders would not otherwise enjoy. A scheme which benefits those in power is likely to set up forces for its perpetuation or extension. One frequently inevitable extension is the replacement of private importers and intermediaries by state trading, with the consequent disregard of marginal efficiencies because of an absence of competition and the existence of salaries which are not directly related to performance. Where salaries of civil servants are tied to cost of living indices based on high controlled prices, governments could be tempted to perpetuate even ineffective price control.

Very severe quotas may bring in no licence revenue and eliminate imports altogether if reduced imports increase importers' average costs above price. Since prices increase with quotas, the effect on profits will depend on their relative effect on average costs and price. Where importers' cost curves differ only some of them are likely to terminate imports. Reduced imports might, in fact, reduce average costs and increase the auction price of licences if importers are operating beyond the point of lowest average cost on their cost curves. Nontransferable quotas distributed to importers according to historic share in the market require all importers to reduce the magnitude of their operations. Under a tariff, however, marginal importers could be expected to drop out while other importers maintained their level of imports. If the level of imports is maintained so that average costs do not increase, the level of profits of those remaining will be greater under a tariff than under a quota. Importers of staple food may encourage licensing combined with retail price control since the government in establishing a fixed margin between the import price plus licence fee and the fixed domestic retail price is likely to increase profits on imports. To err in the opposite direction could discourage imports and create political unrest with the consequent price increase. With such price control importers will make greater and relatively riskless profits while licensing serves to protect them from competition from new entrants.

Intermediaries who buy from importers may be expected to encourage a system of licensing and price control that fixes the price at which importers can sell. When the domestic price is above the fixed price intermediaries will receive windfall gains. In such a situation importers would be tempted to evade price control, sell conditionally and show preference toward particular intermediaries, possibly of their own ethnic or kinship group. This would provide grounds for political ten-

sion between those who do not benefit from the scheme and importers
if the latter are of a different ethnic group than the population at large.
In short, the combination of the scheme and human nature would work
to discredit the useful functions performed by the importers. The more
effective the price control over importers, the greater will be the riskless profits of intermediaries at the next stage in marketing. If these intermediaries are unable to survive without such gains, they will oppose
the removal of control. They would also oppose taxes designed to reduce the differential between the supply and domestic prices.

A quota may be preferable to a tariff where both produce an identical
effect if, as is so often the case, the flexibility of a tariff is impaired by
international agreements on its use and magnitude. The outcome of a
quota can also be more predictable if international supply is not fairly
elastic. When suppliers absorb some or all of the tariff, the efficacy of
the tariff in raising price to domestic producers will be limited. The tariff
will be preferred, however, if the improvement of the importing country's terms of trade in a market with a less than perfectly elastic supply
is of overriding consideration, since importers under quotas may find
it expedient to relinquish quota profits to foreign exporters. In an inflationary situation quotas will exacerbate inflationary pressure by restricting supply. Tariffs will restrict supply but also reduce the general
level of spending, compared to quotas that are distributed among
importers without charge, if revenue collected is not used to increase
government spending. Neither import quotas nor tariffs, as restrictive
measures, can be used to defend a ceiling price as this calls for a reserve
of stocks or funds. Where tariff revenue or revenue from licences under
a quota scheme are used to subsidize low priced imports during periods
of high world prices, the device becomes a buffer fund, a subject discussed in the following chapter, Section 2 (p. 118). Employing tariff and
quota devices concurrently can be useful since the quota will assure a
maximum level of imports while the tariff permits the government to
transfer some of the quota profits to itself. This is so even if the quota is
stronger than the tariff, thus in effect, rendering the tariff redundant.

When a source of subsidy funds cannot be found elsewhere, a mixed
tariff and subsidy self-financing scheme provides an alternative. With
reference to Figure 3.5, tariff P_1P_2 may be used to subsidize producer
price by P_2P_3, with tariff revenue d in this case equalling subsidy
$f + g$. Alternatively, control authorities could impose a ratio of domestic purchases to imports of $OQ_3/Q_3Q'_2$ on importers such that their
gain of d is just offset by loss $f + g$ on compulsory domestic purchases
at price P_3. In order to maintain either price P_2, the consumer price,

or P_3, the producer price, in the face of a downward shift in S, as well as to uphold the equality of the gains and losses to importers (represented by d and $f+g$ before a shift), one would increase the ratio. Under a downward shift in either S or D, if P_2 is to remain constant the producer price would have to decrease while if P_3 is to be held constant the consumer price would have to increase. If world price P_1 fell, inducing an expansion of imports, the equality of tax and subsidy for a given ratio could only be achieved with an increase in producer price above P_3, decrease in consumer price below P_2, and increased production and imports. To control price at P_3, the ratio and P_2 would have to decrease. If instead P_2 was fixed, the ratio would be increased so as to hold total supply at Q'_2. A variant of this general type of mixed scheme, found for instance in the Malaysian rice price support device, fixes producer and consumer price at P_2 by requiring importers to purchase government stock at P_3 in a stipulated ratio to imports. Schemes may be devised that directly convert tariff revenues into export subsidies. For instance, when primary commodity exporters are awarded bonuses in the form of import licences for foreign exchange earned, the net effect, when these licences are sold, is to tax imports and subsidize exports. The partial devaluation aspect makes them akin to some multiple exchange rate schemes discussed in Chapter 4, Section 3 (p. 129).

c. GENERAL COUNTER-CYCLICAL FISCAL MEASURES

General counter-cyclical fiscal measures can be used in producing and consuming countries to reduce the effects of unstable market variables on the level of economic activity in producing countries. On the demand side of the market, control of the business cycle would stabilize shifts in demand due to shifts in macroeconomic variables and, thus be of particular value as a stabilization device in demand shift markets. Such general fiscal measures would be most effective on demand shifts caused by fluctuations in the general levels of disposable income and less effective in markets destabilized on the demand side by political disturbances affecting specific industries, labour strikes, national defence expenditure, strategic stockpiling, or changes in trade policies.

On the supply side, counter-cyclical fiscal measures could be used to stabilize the general level of economic activity over periods of fluctuating export earnings. Producers of the unstable export would be affected only indirectly through changes in the general level of taxes, wage rates and opportunities for alternative employment. The government budget would be manipulated to provide a surplus during a period of high export earnings and a deficit in one of low earnings through variations in taxes on all sectors. This procedure is extolled for its ability to stabilize national income without directly controlling the producer price of specific destabilized commodities where fluctuations in producer prices, or relative prices, are seen as necessary incentives to funnel resources into their most efficient uses. Neglect of the income instability of the commodity producer may itself, however, decrease efficiency in the allocation of resources as producers distort investment patterns through risk aversion activities. If price fluctuations are excessive, in the sense that they serve no functional purpose in reallocating resources, they could cause situations of alternating employment and unemployment or full employment and underemployment of individuals. Such factor immobility may exist as the result of land tenure, custom, specificity of resources and other causes mentioned in the first chapter. An elastic export supply might not, as already noted, indicate the rapid readjustment of resources. It may be more a reflection of a negative elasticity of inventory accumulation or of the elasticity of imports for re-export.

By shifting the burden of adjustment from investment to consumption through changes in the level of income taxes, all sectors will be directly affected. Whether a general tax policy is preferred to the progressive export tax depends on its relative equity, ease of collection and the tendency to have export earnings fluctuations generalized to the rest of the economy. If the exchange rate is appreciated with export earnings, the benefits of increased earnings would, given a positive income effect for domestically produced goods, be generalized simultaneously through improved terms of trade and real income for all. Where domestic non-export goods are inferior, variable import quotas could be used to convert inferior goods to normal ones in times of high earnings and exchange appreciation. In the absence of exchange appreciation, the slower generalization of increases in export earnings to non-export sectors would argue for a delayed general tax which would also last longer than the rise in export earnings. (A stabilization effect similar to counter-cyclical general taxes will arise if customs duties or other consumption taxes are systematically higher on semi-luxury or luxury goods where consumption is likely to increase in times of high export earnings.) Counter-cyclical general taxes may not be needed if it is seen that the domestic non-export sector is less stimulated by the income effects of favourable international terms of trade than by the substitution effects of an unfavourable one. General counter-cyclical taxes may be preferred to export taxes if the frequently observed unresponsiveness of export volume to world price is, in fact, due less to immobility than to a generalization of the export boom which leaves relative prices of exports and domestically produced consumption items confronting producers unchanged. Where the choice is either a progressive export tax or a counter-cyclical fiscal policy, use of the latter may allow greater remittances abroad during periods of high earnings if the export sector is externally financed, while avoiding the inequities of the former. Finally, the counter-cyclical device often suffers from slowness of response. Unless the counter-cyclical measures are automatic and can be anticipated, there will be a lag between a change in export earnings and the change in taxes together with the possible further lag between the change in taxes and their collection.

d. CONTROL OF MONOPOLY-MONOPSONY IN MARKETING

Selection of prices to be controlled always presents some difficulty in price stabilization. There may be considerable difference between the level and stability of prices received by producers and those on international or main domestic markets. At all levels constant and unpredictable changes in a multiplicity of grades and types of a commodity makes the choice of a single controlled price designed to limit market power difficult. Moreover, the same commodity can change hands at different prices according to the volume of the consignment involved (with 'odd-lots' generally receiving lower prices). Where international transactions are subject to bilateral agreements and short and long-term contracts, the nominal unit price of each deal may give little indication of the prices at which further trading could take place. In practice, international and often national stabilization schemes have concentrated on the control of nominal prices in the larger markets because of the extreme intricacies involved in determining and keeping track of the price the producer actually receives.

Price control at several levels in the market hierarchy implies controlled price differentials between markets that reflect market margins. It is, however, difficult if not impracticable to try to determine uniform costs of moving goods from different localities to where they are consumed, for cost depends on distance, the conditions of the roads, time involved, special handling problems, the amount of processing and so forth. These will differ for individual products and for the same product in different areas. Thus, in establishing uniform prices at each market level, the inefficient middleman may be rewarded and the efficient one penalized. It is difficult to imagine how uniform margins could be enforced at the producer and higher levels without considerable administrative expense or inequities in the distribution of their effects on traders. The practice in some countries of requiring traders to possess certificates signed by producers attesting to the price the producer received does not assure that the producer knows what he is signing or that he signed it himself. If subsequently questioned by officials, the producer may falsely admit signing a certificate for fear of reprisals. A scheme which offers the same price in all markets at a given level, will induce a production shift away from relatively high cost producing areas to relatively low cost ones regardless of their proximity to the ultimate consumer or point of export. Unless the government engages in arbitrage, the artificial maintenance of uniform prices between markets will give rise to black market operations and discourage private arbitrage. Private arbitrage frequently needs wide margins to cover risks where communications and transport are slow and grades not standardized.

Problems associated with control of monopoly-monopsony power through price regulation may be circumvented by increasing the producer's bargaining power through public provision of market advice and information and increased competition among market intermediaries. The government can facilitate entry into the market by granting more licences or by not restricting licences to those who can afford a yearly fee. It may actively seek to detect and punish collusion among intermediaries or enter the market itself as a competitor with private enterprise in providing outlets for primary products, and inputs in the form of consumer goods, credit and production materials. If history provides an indication of the long run efficiency of prospective government marketing agencies, replacement of private traders with government monopolies may be unwise. Private agents provide useful functions that cannot easily be replaced by a bureaucracy. Buying and selling by private traders is often conducted in a more relaxed and friendly atmosphere with more attention given to accurate grading and less time spent waiting in queues. In replacing the private trader, government statutory monopolies may eliminate the efficient, competitive trader along with the monopolist or monopsonist.

The unfavourable aspects of government intervention have been particularly noticeable in the creation of credit facilities which attempt to control the price of the credit input. Typically government loans require much red tape, long delays which reduce timeliness, and payment schedules which are rigid and unsuited to the recipient's income stream. Public agencies may unwittingly offer interest rates which do not reflect the high risks and diseconomies of small scale credit. Instead of increasing competition in the credit market they reduce it by eliminating the local moneylender. Private moneylenders in even the most competitive situations may need 20 to 40 per cent per annum to cover the administrative costs and risks of small loans, particularly where collateral is not offered. In rural areas local moneylenders have an advantage over bureaucracies in personal knowledge of clients. The personal nature of such credit links implies reduced risk and more flexible terms of payment. The latter is an important service which may in part account for high credit costs.

There are few known cases in which governments have performed marketing functions in open competition with private intermediaries at a lower cost. Often finding themselves bankrupt, statutory agencies cover up inefficiencies with subsidies out of public revenue or grant themselves monopsonistic privileges. The most common monopsonistic privilege is the statutory elimination of private competition. As in private monopoly or monopsony, the government finds it can make profits with little effort and has few incentives to increase efficiency. Public managers of monopsonies may have no problem showing profits despite inefficiencies and may be judged, in any event, on the basis of political allegiance, social contacts and general presentation. In time public agencies tend to forget in whose interest they have been established and may, in fact, find their vested interests competing with those of the producers whom they represent. Statutory elimination of private traders has been justified on the grounds that it is the only way to combat cheating in the market place: fixing scales, defrauding accounts and incorrect grading. In light of probable inefficiencies (and historical malpractices) of government monopolies and the ease with which alternative solutions can be found, this would not seem a convincing excuse. One possible alternative would be government supervised market places in which scales, accounts and grading procedures were periodically checked by officials. Officers could also adjudicate disputes arising between buyers and sellers over alleged irregularities.

e. CONTROL OF SPECULATION

If it is found that speculators make net gains over time that do not reflect their useful market functions or that their activities are detrimental to the smooth operation of the market, these can be limited by government provision of reliable projections of the market situation. The consequent foresight would eliminate over and under-storage at the local and national levels and permit future scarcity or abundance to be reflected in current prices. If future abundance or scarcity is registered in harvest prices of crops, producers would assume some of the losses and gains of speculators. Producers of seasonal crops will normally find their price low immediately after harvest as farmers eager for cash or fearful of theft or deterioration put their crop on the market with as little delay as possible. As the product becomes scarcer with time, price will rise giving the impression of gains to stockholders. In competitive markets price increases will normally be related to the often high costs of warehousing, financing, risk, insurance, handling and bulk building and breaking during this period. Speculative gains and losses may be extended to producers if credit to finance stockholding is provided to them by the government. To transfer these skilled functions into the naive hands of the farmer, however, could be a disservice to him if it decreases specialization of function and volume marketed. Storage losses at the local level from pests and mould, amounting to as much as 15 per cent, and in traditional methods of processing, frequently reaching a similar percentage, reduces total volume marketed. These actual losses in crop may exceed in value possible cash savings from storage and processing using low opportunity cost traditional methods.

An alternative to increased market information and producer storage would be contra-market price control by a government buffer stock, import quota or buffer fund which by stabilizing prices limits windfall gains and losses to those who store commodities. A controlled market price or price range designed to encourage storage by private traders should increase with unit storage costs over time. If the controlled price does not increase with costs, there will be no incentive for private storage and the burden of storage will unnecessarily fall on the government. Private traders, often with marketing skills accumulated through long experience, will become redundant, storage will revert to possibly less experienced public agencies, and these agencies will suffer losses since the controlled price does not cover costs of storage.

f. CROP INSURANCE

Various forms of voluntary or compulsory insurance may be used to stabilize producer income and avoid a number of problems involved in other forms of stabilization. The most common application is found in agriculture but insurance may be used as well for non-agricultural primary commodities. It can be related to unexpected changes in output or price and may be comprehensive, covering all farm output, or specific to certain farm products. Specificity may also apply to certain destabilizing factors such as flooding, pests or disease. Where insurance is not compulsory, however, many producers may not participate, preferring to leave themselves open to risk. This could be expected where producers are poor and the insurance premium is paid in cash rather than by a withholding of income through official price control agencies. Where the insurance is provided by governments or government backed cooperative agencies, there may be a tendency to under-rate risks so as to minimize premiums with the result that in unfavourable periods there are not sufficient funds to meet claims. If the government succumbs to pressure to subsidize payments in these periods the programme will unwittingly assume characteristics of a deficiency payments scheme. In their analytical aspects insurance programs are similar to buffer funds discussed in the following chapter since funds are accumulated in good periods to tide producers over bad ones.

g. DEFICIENCY PAYMENTS

Deficiency payments offer a fiscal measure which, unlike the counter-cyclical device, is designed to directly protect the producer against severe hardship. The transfer of wealth to those in the primary producing sector during periods of low income would in its effect on producer income be similar to some forms of output insurance. Like the counter-cyclical fiscal policy and output insurance schemes, it does not interfere directly with price and, therefore, fosters the efficient allocation of resources as well as the welfare of producers. Its operation does not raise the price to the domestic consumer, except indirectly through lower income if the subsidy is financed through increased taxes. The demand for domestic products may be little affected if the subsidy is financed out of increased taxes on those in higher income brackets who have a high marginal propensity to consume imports. The foreign consumer of an export would have less inclination to search for substitutes than under devices, such as the buffer fund or progressive export tax, that raise or destabilize consumer prices. Unlike the devices discussed in the next chapter, deficiency payments avoid the risks associated with stock accumulations. They involve a net transfer of wealth to producers which may be considered inequitable and, where producers are numerous, the close administrative supervision required may not be feasible.

a 8. LONG RUN COMPLEMENTS TO SHORT RUN FISCAL AND QUANTITATIVE DEVICES

. DIVERSIFICATION

Diversification of production into areas which do not experience similar market forces offers a *remedy* to exporting countries producing a limited range of exports for volatile markets or markets characterized by secular price decline. Incentives for diversification away from those products in which a country has its greatest comparative advantage, in the conventional sense, will depend on the importance of the risk attached to their production. Concentration of resources on export production, rather than diversification into a less efficient import substitution industry, can provide a strong stimulus to growth if the export industry induces the development of domestic backward and forward linkages with other industries related to the export sector. That sector may additionally serve as an important source of savings, imported ideas and experience, and expanded market for import substitution industry. Backward linkages are formed when demand from the export sector makes domestic production of inputs used by the sector viable, while forward ones would come about through the establishment of enterprises to process the raw materials or perform any of the market functions. In the ideal situation, the economy would grow rapidly around and be led by the export sector. This sequence, however, is frequently not found among developing countries reliant on an export industry, possibly because returns to the export sector revert to foreign factors, insufficient attempts are made to transmit imported technology to indigenous factors, or domestic labour in the export sector acquires foreign consumption patterns with attendant high propensities to consume imports. Under these circumstances, the high technology and income export sector enclaves do little to stimulate overall growth, although they do offer a source of tax revenue and a source of foreign exchange to import capital goods as the absorptive capacity for capital goods is increased. One of the few instances where diversification goals have been given concrete encouragement in an international commodity control agreement is in the 1968 International Coffee Agreement. It provides for a diversification fund to be raised by a cess on unit exports of member countries with yearly exports exceeding 100,000 bags.

An argument for diversification away from exports, which in effect means away from primary commodity exports, is that the benefits of technological progress in terms of decreased prices tend to be exported in the manner previously described. That this argument ignores the capture of productivity increases through the widely used export tax limits its persuasiveness. In developed countries exporting to developing countries labour wages may rise with productivity but export taxes tend to be low or non-existent. The widespread use of export taxes as a revenue raising device in developing countries suggests that, although the benefits of increased productivity may not accrue directly to labour, they are captured to some extent by the government. The benefits of technological change could also be captured by the diversification to production for the domestic market. This implies a shift of resources to food production and import substitution industries. Such structural readjustment can be facilitated by the export tax if tax revenue is used to encourage industrial development. If the import substitution industry is competitive on world markets, diversification into industry may, as well, allow a country to maintain export earnings. Stabilization of industrial activity would replace that of primary production. Overall national stabilization would increasingly become an internal problem and more amenable than exported primary commodities to control by national stabilization devices.

b. IMPROVED INPUT SUBSIDY

Expansion of trade through national and international control devices may lead merely to a higher level of stagnation unless increased incentives to production are accompanied by basic changes in the producer's economic environment. Attempts to raise income levels by price support or stabilization might meet with a limited production response, and that which does occur may be a once-and-for-all event. More positive approaches, including those sought through extension education, subsidy of improved inputs, provision of incentive-increasing consumer goods, land reform, and credit facilities which tie credit to the use of new inputs, induce producers to increase income through an increase in their productivity. In encouraging innovation, these approaches will have an ongoing, cumulative effect. They enjoy the advantage over price control of greater certainty of increased output and reduction in prices to domestic consumers as unit costs decline. Under favourable conditions, the foreign consumer can be made to pay part of the cost through the imposition of an export tax, the revenue from which is used to finance improved inputs. Such subsidy is a form of price and income control on the input side of the producing unit, but may lack the capacity of output price control to effect marginal adjustments in production patterns unless it is possible to insure that a given subsidized input is used only to produce a given output. Thus, subsidies on specific improved seeds might influence production patterns while those on fertilizers may not.

Productivity-increasing *remedies* may bypass the limitations of a number of popular devices. Tariffs designed to raise domestic prices of primary products are, for instance, not effective if the products are in very inelastic import supply; price support financed out of general revenue can be used only for minor products if political friction is to be avoided; and unilateral restrictions of exports can be effective in raising incomes only where the exporting country faces an inelastic demand. Raised or stabilized prices, as mentioned in Chapter 1, may meet a limited production response because of limited income expectations. This is not to minimize the fact that income expectations are increasing over time. But at any point in time additional income may not be seen as worth the effort to obtain it, particularly if the return on normal output has been increased by a supported or stabilized price. Price support or stabilization in such cases will not have substitution effects on the side of production that outweigh income effects. The increased reward for marginal effort through reduced risk or increased price would not exceed the countervailing decrease in the marginal utility of income at higher income levels. Those whose consumption patterns are less rigid may be discouraged from making additional efforts because of unfavourable past experience in efforts to increase output, social taboos against getting too far ahead of their neighbours, or characteristic traditional attitudes of hopelessness and resignation. Unlike price stabilization or support, improved input subsidy will raise both income and output and often without additional effort on the part of the producer (e.g. subsidies on improved seeds). In the case of extension education (also a subsidized input) the producer will be directly encouraged to increase output.

The extent to which subsidized new inputs are used by the farmer depends on their price, availability at the right time, form and place, physical productivity, risks and the ability of the producer to channel the benefits to himself. Many improved inputs, such as inorganic fertilizer, use resources of high opportunity cost in the form of local industrial capacity, expensive marketing facilities or foreign exchange. Encouragement of their use should occur only where they offer a competitive return to society. Subsidies should not mask low returns, but rather cover the discount primary producers place on their cost for real or imagined risks attached to their use. As these risks are overcome in time through increased experience in the local application of the inputs and with the demonstration of their effectiveness, the subsidy should be reduced and eventually eliminated, leaving producers better off through increased productivity alone. Where returns to new inputs with their complements are not sufficiently high to meet opportunity costs, effort should rather be placed on the more time consuming process of research into their greater productivity and local adaptation. A necessary interim measure may be price support or subsidy.

c. TENANCY REFORM

Investment in the land and the adoption of improved techniques in agriculture, even if subsidized, are often retarded by insecurity of land tenure. If a farmer can be dispossessed of the land he farms at the whim of the landlord or relatives who maintain residual rights in his land, he will be disinclined to make improvements to the land, particularly long run improvements in the form of wells, irrigation ditches, leveling, tree crops, fences or buildings. He may also be discouraged from improving his own house. Traditional land tenure arrangements may thus work contrary to price support and stabilization policies and thwart their effectiveness. The redistribution of land to cultivators involves a transfer of wealth from landlord to tenant in physical land and rent returns to land. The farmer's ability to provide collateral for production-increasing credit or to provide his own financing is increased together with incentives to improve the land. If rent was formerly tied to output, he may be expected to increase effort on the land, even if investment in the land does not increase, because the reward for marginal effort is increased. On the other hand, if rent was fixed and unrelated to marginal output, redistribution will bring a negative income effect on the side of production without a substitution effect. The negative income effect could, nevertheless, be compensated for by increased ability and the incentive to invest in the land which comes with ownership. Land reform may stimulate import substitution industry through increased demand for improved farm inputs and by broadening the market for consumer goods. Where much of the surplus of the land is channeled into the hands of a small class of landlords, both markets for luxuries consumed by them and other goods consumed by the landless class may be too small for economies of scale in domestic industry. Habits of conspicuous consumption and, thus, low levels of saving, among the landlord class will be fostered if opportunities to invest savings are limited because low disposable incomes of the tenant class restricts market size. With a more equitable distribution of the means of production, aggregate savings may increase because of incentives of farmers to invest in their land and increased opportunities for remunerative industrial investment. Land redistribution will, like price stabilization and support, have a once-and-for-all effect on output and incomes unless coupled with efforts to improve productivity. It will not increase aggregate income where activities enjoying economies of scale in large producing units, before fragmentation, such as obtaining credit, processing, marketing and the use of skilled manpower, are not provided on the same scale after fragmentation.

Increases in producers' incomes from price support, input subsidy or redistribution of land with compensation to landlords can be financed out of general revenue. At early stages of development with most of the population and income in the primary producing sector, the accompanying tax increases will fall largely on those who directly benefit by their use. The tax itself, as well as the way in which the tax revenue is spent, could have a production increasing effect, if the tax is, for example, a fixed progressive land tax based on potential output. Such a tax would be equitable, encourage the use of idle land and, moreover, have a positive income effect and no substitution effect. The producer will continue to receive the same reward for marginal effort as before the tax, but his reduced income will induce him to work harder to make good the loss. Taxes on income, consumer goods or exports will be accompanied by negative substitution effects while taxes on specific sectors, products or persons discriminate and distort resource use. Direct and general taxes are to be preferred, and of these the land tax may be the most suitable given the constraints imposed on collection of income taxes in developing countries. Whatever the tax, the government must leave enough income in the hands of producers to provide incentives to increase production and, preferably, to finance improved inputs. If not enough is left behind for investment purposes, producers may be drawn into debt syndromes or the government may be impelled to provide larger subsidies out of tax revenue.

Primary commodity sector surplus can be siphoned off for investment in industry, without heavy taxes, through the development of institutions that allow or encourage private savings: commercial and postal savings banks and organized stock markets. Investment in industry by holders of primary production surplus may not materialize because of the lack of markets in which to turn surplus into cash and inter-sectoral financial markets to convert cash surplus into claims against the industrial sector. Lack of investment in industry and much investment in primary commodity production may also be due to unmet economies of scale in industry which can be satisfied only by expanded markets in the large primary sector through increased productivity and income there. Consequent higher returns to investment in industry will attract the savings of primary producers.

9. SUMMARY

Primary commodity control tends to be slower in its effects as it attempts to reach the fundamental causes of low incomes or instability. Among the more temporary symptom-alleviating measures or palliatives, international control devices are difficult to negotiate and, therefore, used less frequently than national devices. Of the national devices which may be considered palliatives, the progressive export tax and tariff are two of the easiest to administer because they will frequently fit into existing fiscal machinery designed to raise revenue in countries where other forms of self-financing are more expensive. Remedies, such as counter-cyclical fiscal and monetary policies can be applied to the underlying causes of commodity production and trade problems. Counter-cyclical measures are useful where world markets are destabilized by fluctuations in incomes in consuming countries. Goals of increased producer income can be met in the long run by remedies in the form of extension education, subsidy of improved inputs, land reform, improved market facilities, and research.

The price paid to the producer may be artificially manipulated in attempts to reach the goals of control outlined at the end of Chapter 2. The manner of this manipulation will depend on the objectives sought. If the objective is growth in incomes through the efficient allocation of resources, price stabilization at the predicted trend would be called for when resources are allocated according to unit price. If, on the other hand, high yield risk producers look to income and its uncertainty, growth can be promoted by controlling price fluctuations to neutralize the effect on income of changes in yield. The twin goals, price and income stabilization, can be met with price stabilization in a demand shift market. Growth considerations might conflict with those of welfare if stable prices destabilize incomes or cause wealth to be transferred from the poor to those who are not so poor. Growth considerations may include the transfer of wealth to those who save most and/or invest at greatest returns. A conflict of goals and means arises when the poor producer does not fall in this category.

Other price criteria which include welfare and growth elements are those of export earnings, profit and work effort maximization. The goal of export earnings maximization suggests a low producer price when the exporting country or group of countries is confronted with an inelastic demand, and a producer price equal to the world price when demand is elastic. National profit maximization under normal market functions with demand less than perfectly elastic will occur with production restriction or producer prices below world equilibrium prices. Both the maximization of export earnings and profits may be brought about by a producer price below world price in a market characterized by an inelastic demand. In an environment of under-employment or unemployment, however, the pursuit of these goals through low producer prices may reduce total resource use and, there-fore, operate contrary to welfare aims. Where wages do not reflect low opportunity costs or social marginal costs, profits and work effort may concurrently be maximized by producer prices close to world prices. A period-by-period application of the export earning, profit and work effort criteria would leave producer prices fluctuating with world prices. This in itself may conflict with growth and welfare goals and thus call for a smoothing of the controlled producer prices.

Welfare and growth goals can be expressed through a price crite-rion which assures the producer a minimum unit price related to the costs of inputs (input cost criterion) or a unit price which maintains its purchasing power (income parity criterion) or that stabilizes price around a trend (ruling price criterion). If the producer's output is stable, the ruling price criterion would meet both goals, whereas an income parity criterion would allow producer price to deviate from the trend with possible consequent distortion in resource use. Problems in the practical application of the input cost criterion might also lead to distortion if the controlled price supports high cost production. Once goals have been decided upon and given weights, their corresponding price criteria preferably should be expressed in a mathematical formula in order to give the producer an assurance that his price will not be tampered with by opposing political or economic interests and to avoid the effort and friction in frequent *ad hoc* changes (or reviews resulting in no change).

Price stabilization can bring a number of unanticipated effects, as well as those that are sought. At the individual producer level, for example, the price stabilization of one commodity may destabilize relative prices and incomes of consumers and other producers, even if the stable price stabilizes the gross income of the producers of the controlled commodity. The higher income of farmers under price control in good crop periods will increase demand for crops of other farmers and prevent their prices falling as low as otherwise, and conversely in periods of low harvests. Wage rates will be destabilized if supply is responsive to price and price stabilization reduces demand for labour in low crop periods and increases it in high crop periods. The price stabilized commodity will attract producers of low output risk and cause high output risk producers to seek other uses for their resources. Thus, output of the price stabilized commodity will increase in stability while that of other commodities to which high output risk producers switch will be destabilized. Welfare considerations are unlikely to be served if the high output risk producer is poor and low output risk producer not so poor. Low output risk in agriculture is normally associated with a naturally well endowed farm environment or the means to invest in water control and plant protection.

Price stabilization may reduce profits (producers' surplus) on equal fluctuations either side of the price limits where profits are a monotonically increasing function of price and the market is one of demand shift. On the other hand, profits might increase in a supply shift market. If the establishment of price limits increases instability between the limits because of an inclination of the market to gravitate to fixed points, profits on fluctuations between the limits may be increased in a demand shift market. Where average costs decline with output, such that they are below high market prices and above low market prices, price stabilization may destabilize profits and cause losses at high prices.

Sliding-scale or progressive export taxes designed to increase producer price stability will destabilize world price and cause a net loss in surpluses to the exporting country and consumers considered together. In a demand shift demand inelastic market producer income will be stabilized at the cost of greater export earning instability. As an anti-inflationary device, the progressive export tax may be unsuccessful in a demand shift market if government spending follows revenue in high price periods. Where demand is elastic and a supply shift market operates, the tax (and possibly producer cost) will be highest in low gross income periods and lowest in periods of high gross income. If the tax serves to reduce net export earnings and the demand for imports is unaffected by lower producer incomes, the price of imports may rise from the consequent imposition of import restrictions further turning the terms of trade against the primary producing sector. Export subsidies will generally have effects opposite to those of export taxes. Some of the possible unfavourable effects of export taxes and subsidies may be circumvented by combining them with production and consumption taxes and subsidies.

Import quotas or tariffs can be applied to maintain a minimum price to producers of a domestically produced and consumed importable. In those instances where a quota in a market with a perfectly elastic import supply has the same effect on domestic price as a tariff, both will reduce consumption and imports and increase domestic production by identical amounts. The revenue effect of the two will be equal if quota licences are auctioned under conditions of perfect competition among importers and foreign exporters and if average costs of importers remain unchanged. The judicious use of sales taxes or production subsidies can avert some of the undesirable effects of either device.

General counter-cyclical fiscal measures are often effective in stabilizing demand in consuming countries where demand fluctuations result from changes in the level of disposable income. They will have more limited effect if demand fluctuations derive from labour disputes or changes in national defence expenditure or trade policies. On the supply side of the market these measures can be used to insulate the general level of economic activity against the market vagaries of single exports without directly influencing the price of the exports. Without further specific intervention, dislocation or underemployment of resources resulting from market instability for the single export would go unchecked. Deficiency payments offer a fiscal measure which, unlike the counter-cyclical device, is designed to directly protect the producer against severe hardship.

The undesired activities of market intermediaries and speculators can be overcome in part by increased market information, advice and reliable forecasts. Direct control of market margins is undesirable since they are not likely to be uniform for all market intermediaries. Any attempt to enforce a uniform margin will have unequal effects on traders. Where unfair trade practices are found to warrant the expense of intervention, governments might increase competition by facilitating market entry or by entering the market themselves *on a commercial basis*. Government statutory monopolies may not be preferred because of efficiency disincentives accompanying market power and the fact that trade may be transferred to relatively inexperienced civil servants who exhibit little motivation for pursuing marginal efficiencies. The discouraging known history of the efficiency of statutory monopolies would suggest that efforts to establish them are an indication that governments cannot compete on equal terms with private traders.

In the long run, goals of stable and increased producer income and export earnings can be met by more fundamental national efforts. Diversification can be used on a national level or individual producer level in order to spread the risks of reliance on single products. At the national level this may take the form of a greater variety of primary product exports and a more even distribution of resources among these exports, or it may occur through a calculated structural transformation of the economy away from primary production and toward import substitution industry. In the latter event, problems of industrial instability gradually replace those of primary commodity instability, and control is facilitated by the internalization of destabilizing forces. Efforts to increase or stabilize producer income through conventional formal control devices could merely lead to a higher level of stagnation unless they are accompanied by efforts to improve the producer's productivity. Extension education, subsidy of improved inputs, provision of incentive-increasing consumer goods, land reform, and credit facilities which tie credit to the use of new inputs offer a more positive and dynamic approach for they stimulate producers to increase their income through an actual change in techniques. Success with these demonstrates to the producer that change is beneficial and that he is capable of making successful innovations himself. Subsidies on inputs may be needed to cover the real or imagined risks attached to the use of new inputs until the risks are overcome. Even with subsidies, improvements to the land will be retarded if the producer does not have security of tenure. Land reform would seem to be a necessary prerequisite to efforts to improve productivity and to offer an effective long run complement to more formal control measures.

Readings

Abbott, J.C., 'The Development of Marketing Institutions', in Johnson, B.F., & Southworth, H.M., Eds., *Agricultural Development and Economic Growth*, op. cit., pp. 364–98.

————, & Creupelandt, H.C., 'Agricultural Marketing Boards', *Journal of Farm Economics*, Vol. 49, No. 3, August 1967, pp. 705–22.

Ady, P.H., 'Cocoa Marketing in French West Africa', *West Africa*, Nos. 2245–2247, June 1960.

————, 'Fluctuation in Income of Primary Producers: A Comment', *Economic Journal*, Vol. 63, September 1953, pp. 594–607.

Bauer, P.T., 'Price Control in Underdeveloped Countries', *Journal of Development Studies*, Vol. 2, October 1965, pp. 19–37. Also in Bauer & Yamey, *Markets, Market Control and Marketing Reform*, London, 1968, pp. 251–69.

————, *West African Trade*, London, 1963, esp. Chaps. 20–24.

————, & Paish, F.W., 'Comment, the Quest for a Stabilization Policy in Primary Producing Countries', *Kyklos*, Vol.11, 1958, pp. 169–79.

————, & Paish, F.W., 'The Reduction of Fluctuations in Income of Primary Producers', *Economic Journal*, Vol. 62, December 1952, pp. 750–80.

————, & Paish, F.W., 'The Reduction of Fluctuations in the Incomes of Primary Producers, Further Consideration', *Economic Journal*, Vol. 64, December 1953, pp. 704–29.

————, & Yamey, B.S., 'The Economics of Marketing Reform', *Journal of Political Economy*, Vol. 62, June 1954, pp. 210–35.

————, & Yamey, B.S., *Markets, Market Control and Marketing Reform*, London, 1968.

Brown, C.P., 'The Malawi Farmers Marketing Board', *Eastern Africa Economic Review*, Vol. 2, No. 1, June 1970, pp. 37–52.

————, 'Marketing of Food Crops in Blantyre, Malawi', *African Social Research*, Vol. 12, December 1971, pp. 111–28.

————, 'Rice Price Stabilization and Support in Malaysia', *Developing Economics*, Vol. 11, No. 2, 1973 and in Lim, D., ed., *Readings on the Malaysian Economy*, Oxford University Press, forthcoming.

Candler, W., & McArher, A., 'Efficient Equalization Funds for Farm Prices', *American Journal of Agricultural Economics*, Vol. 50, No. 1, February 1968, pp. 91–110.

Chen, H.Y., & Chuang, W.F., 'Report on a Case Study on the Impact of Agricultural Price Policies at the Farm Level in Taiwan', in *Getting Agriculture Moving*, Ed. Borton, R.E., Vol. II, New York, 1966, pp. 738–57.

Cordon, W.M., *The Theory of Protection*, Oxford University Press, 1971, esp. pp. 5–27 and pp. 199–238.

FAO, *Commodity Stabilization Funds in the French Franc Area*, Rome, 1962.

————, *An Enquiry into the Problems of Agricultural Price Stabilization and Support Policies*, Rome, 1960.

————, *Food and Agricultural Price Policies in Asia and the Far East*, Bangkok, 1958, pp. 81–5.

Friedman, M., 'The Reduction of Fluctuations in The Incomes of Primary Producers: A Critical Comment', *Economic Journal*, Vol. 64, December 1954, pp. 698–703.

Goode, R., Lent, G.E., & Ojha, P.D., 'The Role of Export Taxes in Developing Countries', *IMF Staff Papers*, Vol. 13, No. 3, November 1966, pp. 453–501.

Hazelwood, A., 'Stabilization and Development, A Proposal', *Kyklos* Vol. 12, 1959, pp. 307,–15.

Helleiner, G.K., 'The Fiscal Role of the Marketing Boards in Nigerian Economic Development', *Economic Journal*, Vol. 74, September 1964, pp. 582–610.

————, 'Marketing Boards and Domestic Stabilization in Nigeria', *Review of Economics and Statistics*, Vol. 48, February 1966, pp. 69–78.

Hill, P., 'Fluctuations in Incomes of Primary Producers', *Economic Journal*, Vol. 63, June 1953, pp. 468–71.

Howell, L.D., 'Benefits and Costs of Price Support', *Quarterly Journal of Economics*, Vol. 30, February 1954, pp. 115–30, and comment by Koo, A.Y.C., *Journal of Farm Economics*, Vol. 37, November 1955, pp. 731–4.

Krishna, R., 'Agricultural Price Policy and Economic Development', in Johnson & Southworth, op. cit. pp. 530–35.

Lewis, S.R., Jr., 'Agricultural Taxation in a Developing Country', in Johnson & Southworth, op. cit. pp. 468–70.

Lipton, M., 'Farm Price Stabilisation in Underdeveloped Agricultures: Some Effects on Income Stability and Income Distribution', in Streeten, P., Ed., *Unfashionable Economics*, London, 1970.

Massel, B.F., 'Price Stabilization and Welfare', *Quarterly Journal of Economics*, Vol. 83, No. 2, May 1969, pp. 284–98.

Miracle, M., 'An Economic Appraisal of Kenya's Maize Control' and rejoinder by Haller, A.A., *Eastern Africa Economic Review*, Vol. 6, December 1959, pp. 117–32.

Mishan, E.J., 'What Is Producers' Surplus?', *American Economic Review*, Vol. 58, No. 5, December 1968, pp. 1269–82.

Morley, J.A.E., 'Marketing Boards', in *Agricultural Producers and their Markets*, Oxford, 1967, pp. 341–51.

Mubyarto, —, 'Rice Price, Marketing and Food Policy in Indonesia', *Malayan Economic Review*, Vol. 13, No. 2, October 1968, pp. 103–14.

Niculescu, B., 'Fluctuations in Incomes of Primary Producers: Further Comment', *Economic Journal*, Vol. 64, December 1954, pp. 730–43.

Nurkse, R., 'Epilogue', *Kyklos*, Vol. 12, 1958, pp. 244–65.

——————, 'Trade Fluctuations and Buffer Policies of Low-Income Countries', *Kyklos*, Vol. 11, 1958, pp. 141–154. Also in Eicher, C., & Witt, L., Eds. *Agriculture in Economic Development*, 1964, Ch. 19.

Ogunsheye, A., 'Marketing Boards & the Stabilization of Producer Prices and Incomes in Nigeria', *Nigerian Journal of Economic and Social Studies*, Vol. 7, No. 2, July 1965, pp. 131–44.

Oi, W., 'The Desirability of Price Instability under Perfect Competition', *Econometrica*, Vol. 29, January 1961, pp. 58–64.

——————, 'Rejoinder', *Econometrica*, Vol. 31, January 1963, p. 248.

Porter, R.S., 'Buffer Stocks and Economic Stability', *Oxford Economic Papers*, Vol. 2, January 1950, pp. 95–118.

Preston, L.E., 'Market Control in Developing Economies', *Journal of Development Studies*, Vol. 4, No. 4, July 1968, pp. 481–96.

Roy, H., *Tea Price Stabilization: the Indian Case*, World Press, 1965

Sengupta, J.K., 'Cobweb Cycles and Optimal Price Stabilization. through Buffer Funds', *Indian Economic Journal*, Vol. 13, No. 3, January 1966, pp. 351–64.

Shan, V.C., 'Agricultural Price Policy in a Developing Economy', *Indian Journal of Agricultural Economics*, Vol. 22, No. 3, July–September 1967, pp. 16–27.

Smith, J.H., 'The Eastern Regional Marketing Board, Nigeria', *Journal of Agricultural Economics*, Vol. 14, May 1961, pp. 368–74.

Swerling, B.C., 'Income Protection for Farmers: A Possible Approach', *Journal of Political Economy*, Vol. 67, April 1959, pp. 173–86.

Tisdell, C., 'Price Instability & Average Profit', *Oxford Economic Papers*, Vol. 22, 1970, pp. 1–12.

——————, 'Some Circumstances in which Price Stabilization by the Wool Commission Reduces Incomes', *Australian Journal of Agricultural Economics*, Vol. 16, No. 2, August 1972, pp. 94–101.

——————, *The Theory of Price Uncertainty, Production & Profit*, Princeton University Press, 1968.

————, 'Uncertainty, Instability, Expected Profit', *Econometrica*, Vol. 31, January 1963, pp. 243–47.

Walker, D., 'Marketing Boards', *Problems in Economic Development*, Ed., Robinson, E.A.G., MacMillan 1965, pp. 574–96.

————, & Ehrlich, C., 'Stabilization and Development Policy in Uganda,' *Kyklos*, Vol. 12, 1959, pp. 341–53.

Wallace, T.D., 'Measures of Social Costs of Agricultural Programs', *Journal of Farm Economics*, Vol. 44, 1962, pp. 580–94, & symposium passim, pp. 564–97.

Waugh, F.V., 'Consumer Aspects of Price Instability', *Econometrica*, Vol. 34, April 1966, pp. 504–8.

————, 'Does the Consumer Benefit from Price Instability?' *Quarterly Journal of Economics*, Vol. 58, August 1944, pp. 602–14.

Wells, J.C., 'Price Stabilization of Nigeria's Export Crops', *Nigerian Journal of Economic and Social Studies*, Vol. 4, 1962. pp. 40–48.

Zucker, A., 'On the Desirability of Price Instability: An Extension of the Discussion', *Econometrica*, Vol. 33, April 1965, pp. 437–41.

IV
Buffer Funds, Buffer Stocks and Export Quotas

1. INTRODUCTION

FORMAL international control which conforms to the egalitarian spirit of the Havana Accords has, in the post-war period, been confined to the buffer stock, export quota, multilateral contract and compensatory finance devices. The analytical similarities between buffer stocks and export quotas on the one hand and multilateral contracts and compensatory finance on the other argue for treating these devices in pairs. The first pair is considered in the following pages while the second is discussed in the next chapter. There is, as well, a comparability of international buffer stocks and export quotas to national buffer funds and multiple exchange rate control. And if applied unilaterally, national buffer stocks are largely identical in their effects to international export quotas, for the former device operates directly or indirectly through export control. The present chapter progresses from devices which are primarily national devices to those used in international co-operation.

2. BUFFER FUNDS

National buffer funds stabilize the producer price by withholding part of earnings in periods of high market prices and, conversely, supporting the producer price out of the accumulated 'stabilization fund' in periods of low market prices. Unlike the export tax device, there is no net transfer of income on a continuing basis; the 'tax' in periods of high prices is matched by a 'subsidy' in periods of low prices. Where a net transfer of income occurs the scheme would not be an unadulterated buffer fund but would include elements of tax or subsidy schemes for which corresponding changes would have to be made in any analysis. Buffer fund reserves built up in periods of high prices are, by definition, depleted over time in periods of low prices. Even where the fund is designed to break-even over the long run, very large losses in the short run may not be economically desirable and very large profits not politically expedient. There is a range, as under export taxes, over which the short run average profits of the fund are an instrumental variable of government policy. The export earnings maximizing price of Figure 3.1a of the last chapter (p. 67) may be seen as a lower limit to the fixed price if it is intended simultaneously to increase export earnings, increase the sum of fund profits plus producer income and restrain world price increases. If the controlled price is above the average world price, producer incomes might increase at the expense of fund losses. Countries that choose a producer price above average world price, because of producer pressure, may pay for this in terms of reduced foreign exchange earnings and of government budget deficits. Countries which hope to maximize foreign exchange earnings in the face of short run inelastic demand or to use the 'fund' as a revenue raising device will tend to choose producer prices below average world prices, and possibly pay a price in terms of long run substitution on the demand side of the market and producer dissatisfaction. For these reasons the break-even fund proffered in the following discussion is likely to be popular.

The effect of a buffer fund on the producer's income will differ from that of an insurance programme or deficiency payments scheme if, as is usually the case, it is concerned strictly with price stabilization. Under the *caisses de stabilisation des prix* of 'French' West Africa, however, an attempt is made to stabilize producer income directly through the buffer fund device. Partial payment for crops is made at harvest, with the remainder being remitted later according to considerations of volume as well as price. Such control, however, is limited to those situations over which direct farm or mine level control is feasible. Buffer funds of the *caisses de stabilisation* and the alternative type described below are essentially the same as those operated expressly in the form of variable export taxes and export subsidies. A system of forced loans issued in boom periods and repaid in slumps would have equal revenue effects though weaker allocative effects than the export tax-cum-subsidy device. Multiple exchange rates, to be discussed later, offer a further alternative form of buffer fund device.

a. THE ROUTINE

The effects of producer price control through national buffer funds in a demand shift market are illustrated in Figure 4.1a. The demand shift case would appear to be of particular importance as post-war experience indicates that most metals and a number of agricultural raw materials operate in such a market. With perfect foresight of the uncontrolled market equilibrium prices P_1 and P_2, the buffer fund agency establishes price limits symmetrically between these such that $P_1 P_1^* = P_2^* P_2$. Since linear functions are used and D_1 is parallel to D_2, $Q_1 Q_1^*$ will equal $Q_2^* Q_2$. During the period of floor price support at P_1^*, output will exceed the uncontrolled market level causing world price to decline to $\hat{P}_1$, while in that of ceiling price support at P_2^* output will decline and world price increase to $\hat{P}_2$. Since $P_1 P_2 < \hat{P}_1 \hat{P}_2$ and $\hat{P}_1 P_1 = \hat{P}_2 P_2$, one effect of the buffer fund is to increase market price fluctuations. Funds $P_2^* \hat{P}_2$. OQ_2^* are accumulated in the period of ceiling price support and $\hat{P}_1 P_1^*$. OQ_1^* disbursed in that of floor price support. While waiting to be used for floor price support, these funds can be invested in foreign exchange, thus not only reducing the degree of inflation due to increased export earnings but also diminishing the level of domestic investment that would have prevailed without control. If investment tends to be based on income in boom periods, the average level of investment may decline with control. If the fund is invested domestically, this could have a counter-cyclical effect if the gestation period is such that new investment plans reach fruition as a downturn approaches. Where local financial markets are not well developed, however, a domestic investment policy would entail the additional risk that sufficient funds could not be liquidated at short notice to meet the device's needs.

The device as illustrated might not be considered a true buffer fund if its life ends with the second period since more is accumulated than disbursed and, thus, a tax element is involved in its functioning over the two periods. The net revenue gain to the agency is represented by areas A and C. A higher floor or ceiling price or a single fixed price at the mean of the two uncontrolled market prices would enable the fund to break even over the two periods. In Figure 4.1b the buffer fund breaks even over the two periods since gains in funds $OQ^*.P^*\hat{P}_2$ equal disbursements $OQ^*.\hat{P}_1 P^*$. On the assumption that producer price P^* lies at the mean of OP_1 and OP_2 and that D_1 and D_2 are parallel, it follows that P^* is also the mean of OP_1 and OP_2 and that $\hat{P}_1 P_1 = P_2 \hat{P}_2$. Thus $Q_1 Q^* = Q^* Q_2$. Gains in export earnings $O\hat{P}_1.Q_1 Q^*$ and $P_2 \hat{P}_2.OQ_1$ are cancelled, respectively, by losses $O\hat{P}_1.Q^* Q_2$ and $\hat{P}_1 P_1.OQ_1$. A net loss in export earnings will occur since area A representing a gain is matched by B, ($Q_1 Q^* = Q^* Q_2$ and $\hat{P}_1 P_1 = P_2 \hat{P}_2$) leaving the net loss indicated by cross-

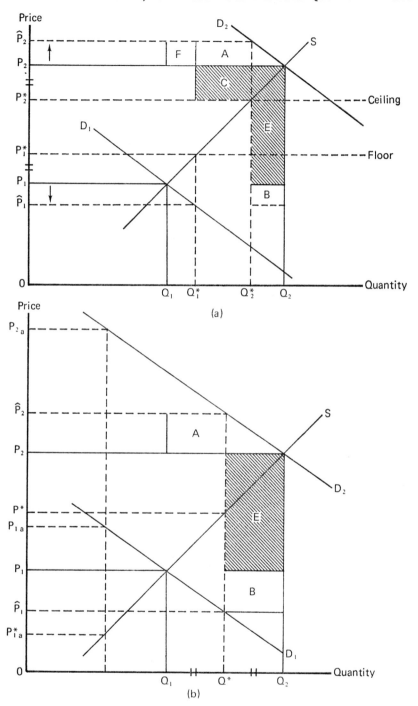

FIGURE 4.1

THE ROUTINE AND POSSIBLE EFFECTS OF A BUFFER FUND IN

A DEMAND SHIFT MARKET

hatching. This loss and the producer income loss discussed below will be reduced as the controlled prices approach the uncontrolled market prices. A single fixed price at the mean of the uncontrolled market prices would increase market price fluctuations over a price range with that mean (i.e. $\hat{P}_1\hat{P}_2$ of Figure 4.1a < $\hat{P}_1\hat{P}_2$ of Figure 4.1b and their means are equal) and perhaps work against an efficient allocation of resources while a higher floor or ceiling price would reduce average market price and export earnings for an exported commodity if demand was inelastic.

If the buffer fund operates for an exported commodity, export earnings will be destabilized in a demand shift demand inelastic market. The small export earnings in the first period will be further reduced with the increase in exported volume from Q_1 to Q_1^* in Figure 4.1a and the large earnings in the second period will be further increased with a reduction in exported volume of $Q_2^*Q_2$. Where demand functions D_1 and D_2 are linear and parallel as shown, the gain in export earnings during a period of ceiling price support may be greater than the loss in the period of floor price support depending on the elasticity at which the supply function S cuts the demand functions. If demand is elastic in a demand shift market, export earnings will be stabilized. Under our assumptions regarding the positioning of the price range, export earnings will always be destabilized in a supply shift market regardless of the elasticity of demand, because in periods of high earnings on the uncontrolled market they are increased and in those of low earnings they are decreased.

Buffer fund schemes are most readily adapted to commodities which are entirely or in part exported, since the difference in producer and consumer price can be maintained by a monopsony exporting agency with relative ease. Where producing and consuming units are numerous buffer fund control of a domestically produced and consumed commodity would entail expensive surveillance and adjudication facilities to insure that the price differential was not eroded by black market activities. Moreover, if the world price for the commodity is to remain uncontrolled, additional measures would be necessary to insulate the domestic from the world market.

b. POSSIBLE EFFECTS ON THE LEVEL OF GROSS INCOME AND SURPLUSES

In the demand shift market illustrated in Figure 4.1b producer income is stabilized since volume and price increase in the low income period and are reduced in the high income period. Gruble (1964), Snape and Yamey (1963) have shown that in a demand shift market this favourable aspect may be offset by a net loss in producer income if the producer price is fixed at the mean of the two uncontrolled market equilibrium prices, which is the case if the buffer fund is to break even over the two periods. Producer income losses $OP_1.Q^*Q_2$ and $P^*P_2.OQ^*$ are neutralized by gains $OP_1.Q_1Q^*$ and $P_1P^*.OQ^*$, respectively, leaving a net income loss of E. Their observation will also hold for the market and controlled prices of Figure 4.1a. The gain to the producer at the floor price, $P_1P_2^*.OQ_1^*$, is countered by the loss $P_2^*P_2.OQ_1^*$ at the ceiling, leaving a net loss of C. Similarly the gain of $OP_1.Q_1Q_1^*$ at the floor is offset by loss $OP_1.Q_2^*Q_2$ at the ceiling, leaving a net loss to the producer of E. The producer's total net loss is $C+E$. Likewise, reference to the figure shows that the exporting country makes net losses (gains) of $A+F-E-B$. The producer will always lose under our assumptions and the country as a whole will lose an equivalent amount if the fund has a single fixed price and a break-even policy. A break-even buffer fund which establishes a single fixed price at the mean of the uncontrolled market prices, as shown in Figure 4.1b, will completely stabilize producer income, collect no 'tax' and cause producer and export earnings losses of E.

In the supply shift market of Figure 4.2a, with producer price fixed at the mean of the uncontrolled prices, P^*, losses of a, b, d, and f in the first period are cancelled by gains c, e, d, and g, respectively, in the second period (each pair of rectangles share the same height and width) leaving a net gain in producers' income indicated by cross-hatching. In evaluating this gain one should consider the greater income instability when demand is elastic (control increases income in the period of large income and decreases it in that of small income) and bear in mind that income stability increases when demand is more than slightly inelastic. (See Chapter 3, Section 4, p. 76). If the level of investment is based on average to highest income, investment will increase when demand is elastic since both the average and highest income are increased with control. The converse is true of control in the demand shift market above, whether demand is elastic or inelastic.

A comparison of Tables 1 and 2 with 7 and 8 in Appendix 3 shows the effects of a buffer fund under logarithmic-linear functions of varying elasticities in demand and supply shift markets. A summary of effects with linear functions is given in Tables 4.1 and 4.2 of this chapter. The effects indicated will decline and in some cases reverse as the controlled prices approach the uncontrolled market prices.

Under the assumptions underlying Figure 4.2a, buffer funds will increase both producer and consumer surpluses in a supply shift market.

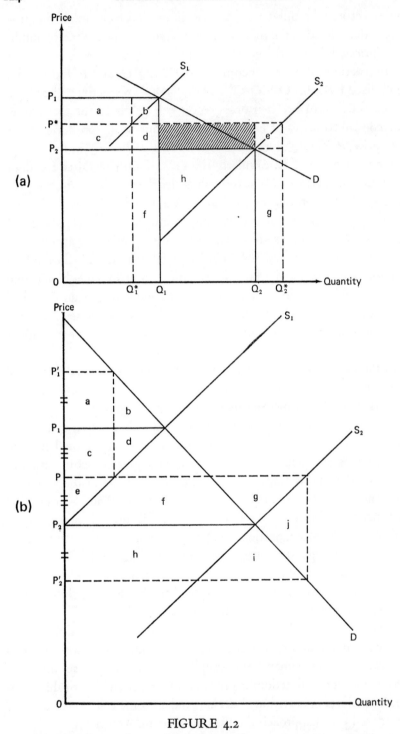

FIGURE 4.2

THE POSSIBLE EFFECT OF A BUFFER FUND IN A SUPPLY SHIFT MARKET
ON PRODUCER INCOME AND PRODUCER AND CONSUMER SURPLUSES

TABLE 4.1

THE EFFECTS OF CONTROL DEVICES IN RELATION TO THE UNCONTROLLED MARKET IN A DEMAND SHIFT MARKET

WITH LINEAR FUNCTIONS AND PARALLEL SHIFTS

Demand Elasticity	World Price		Producer Income Level		Producer Income Stability		Export Earnings Level		Export Earnings Stability		Surplus Level		Net Change	Surplus Stability	
	Elastic	Inelastic	Elastic	Inelastic	Elastic	Inelastic	Elastic	Inelastic	Elastic	Inelastic	Producer	Consumer		Producer	Consumer
Progressive Export Tax[a]	Destabilized	Destabilized	Less	Less	Stabilized	Stabilized	Less	More	Stabilized	Destabilized	Less	Less	Less[e]	Stabilized	Stabilized
National Buffer Fund[a]	Destabilized	Destabilized	Less	Less	Stabilized	Stabilized	Less	Less	Stabilized	Destabilized	Less	Less	Less	Stabilized	Stabilized
National Buffer Stock or Export Quota with Stocks[a]	Stabilized	Stabilized	Less	Less	Stabilized	Stabilized	Less	Less	Destabilized	Stabilized	Less	More	More	Stabilized	Destabilized
Export Quotas with Production Control[a]	Stabilized	Stabilized	Less	More	Destabilized	Stabilized	Less	More	Destabilized	Stabilized	-	Less	-	-	Destabilized
International Buffer Stocks[a]	Stabilized	Stabilized	Less	Less	Stabilized	Stabilized	Less	Less	Stabilized	Stabilized	Less	More	More	Stabilized	Destabilized
Multilateral Contract[a,b]	Stabilized[c]	Stabilized[c]	Same	Same	Same	Same	Same	Same	Stabilized	Stabilized	Same	Same	Same	Same	Same
Compensatory Finance with Loan Compensation for Full Shortfall	Same	Same	Same[d]	Same[d]	Same[d]	Same[d]	Same	Same	Stabilized	Stabilized	Same	Same	Same	Same	Same

Key: a. The price range mean coincides with the mean of uncontrolled prices and the range is narrow.
b. A multilateral contract under which the producer and consumer prices remain unchanged.
c. Weighted average price will be stabilized but residual market price is not likely to be affected in the short run.
d. No change if, as is usual, the compensatory transfer is not passed on to the producer.
e. The joint loss in producer and consumer surplus exceeds the revenue gain.

TABLE 4.2

THE EFFECTS OF CONTROL DEVICES IN RELATION TO THE UNCONTROLLED MARKET IN A SUPPLY SHIFT MARKET WITH LINEAR FUNCTIONS AND PARALLEL SHIFTS

Demand Elasticity	World Price		Producer Income Level		Producer Income Stability		Export Earnings Level		Export Earnings Stability		Surplus Level		Net Change	Surplus Stability	
	Elastic	Inelastic	Elastic	Inelastic	Elastic	Inelastic	Elastic	Inelastic	Elastic	Inelastic	Producer	Consumer		Producer	Consumer
Progressive Export Tax	Destabilized	Destabilized	Less	Less	Destabilized	Stabilized[f]	Less	More	Destabilized	Destabilized	Less	Less	Less	Destabilized[k]	Destabilized
National Buffer Fund[a]	Destabilized	Destabilized	More	More	Destabilized	Stabilized[g]	Less	Less	Destabilized	Destabilized	More	More	More[i]	Destabilized[k]	Destabilized
National Buffer Stock or Export Quotas with Stocks[a]	Stabilized	Stabilized	More[j]	More[j]	Destabilized	Stabilized[g]	More	More	Stabilized	Stabilized	More	Less	More	Destabilized[k]	Stabilized
Export Quotas with Production Control[a]	Stabilized	Stabilized	Less	More	Stabilized	Stabilized	Less	More	Stabilized	Stabilized	–	Less	–	–	Stabilized
International Buffer Stocks[a]	Stabilized	Stabilized	More[j]	More[j]	Destabilized	Stabilized[g]	More	More	Destabilized	Stabilized[k]	More	Less	More	Destabilized[k]	Stabilized
Multilateral Contract[a,b]	Stabilized[c]	Stabilized[c]	Same	Same	Same	Same	Same	Same	Destabilized	Stabilized[h]	Same	Same	Same	Same	Same
Compensatory Finance with Loan Compensation for Full Shortfall	Same	Same	Same[d]	Same[d]	Same[d]	Same[d]	Same	Same	Stabilized	Stabilized	Same	Same	Same	Same	Same

Key: a, b, c and d see Key Table 4.1.
f With a slightly progressive tax income may be destabilized.
g If the price range is sufficiently narrow, supply sufficiently elastic, and/or demand only slightly inelastic, producer income may be destabilized.
h If the price range is sufficiently narrow and/or the contract a sufficiently large proportion of total exports, a reverse instability may result.
i The loss to the fund may exceed the joint gain in surpluses.
j If the price range is not very wide and/or supply not very elastic.
k Assuming the supply curve intersects the vertical axis at a positive price.

With reference to Figure 4.2b, when producer price is stabilized at P, the mean of the uncontrolled market prices P_1 and P_2, $P_2'P_2 = P_1P_1'$ for reasons previously stated. Loss in producer surplus (profits) $c + d$ during periods when price P_1 would otherwise have prevailed is exceeded by gains $e + f + g$ in periods of low uncontrolled market price. Similarly, loss in consumer surplus $a + b$ is smaller than the gains $h + i$. The loss to the fund in a supply shift market equals the joint gain. In the second period, society loses j, an amount which increases with supply elasticity and demand inelasticity. The buffer fund destabilizes consumer surpluses since the gain occurs in a period of high surplus and the loss in a period of low surplus. A corresponding line of reasoning will show that in the demand shift market of Figure 4.1b, both producers and consumers suffer a loss in surpluses while stability is increased. (See also discussion on surpluses Section 4b of this chapter, p. 144).

Buffer funds, notably those in what was formerly 'British' West Africa, have come under criticism for lapsing into negative price policies and accumulating excessive stabilization reserves. A so-called buffer fund device which fixes producer price below the lowest world price is in effect an extreme case of the progressive export tax device. In its formal aspects it may remain a buffer fund, but funds are transferred from producers on a continuing basis and may be invested in forms which do not provide the liquidity needed by a true stabilization reserve. Historically, accumulated funds have been invested in the equity of private and government enterprises, particularly those involved in processing and marketing of the commodity, loaned to the government on a long term basis or appropriated outright by the government. This type of device could perhaps be more realistically viewed as an export tax structured to give producers a fixed price which is largely unrelated to world price. When the tax is set so that the producer price of the export is held at a fixed target price whatever the world price, it is called an 'equalizing export tax'. A rise in world price leads automatically to an equalizing rise in the export tax. In this way countries in which other forms of self-financing are expensive enjoy the advantages of export taxes discussed in the preceding chapter. With reference to Figure 4.1b, the effects of the alternative fixed price, P_{1a}^*, representing this price policy, is to restrain output in all periods and to raise average world price. The effect on world price stability and export earnings cannot be generalized within the assumptions of the model. Determination of the extent of the device's influence on the market can be approached along the lines taken with export taxes in the preceding chapter. One outstanding advantage of this price policy from the government's vantage point is that it avoids the risks of commitment of funds and holding of stocks which arise under true buffer fund and national buffer stock devices. Where funds and stocks are not used for price support, there is no possibility of their being exhausted. Problems arising from an excess accumulation of stocks and costs associated with storage are bypassed as well.

c. Voluntary Buffer Funds

Bauer and Yamey (1964) have suggested a voluntary counterpart to the compulsory buffer fund scheme which would overcome limitations cited above in applying it to a domestically produced and consumed commodity. Producers would contract individually and voluntarily to supply a fixed agreed volume to the fund in all periods, regardless of fluctuations in their volume of output, and in turn receive a controlled price designed to stabilize incomes or price. Unlike the compulsory buffer fund discussed above, the voluntary scheme would offer to individual producers a choice of control provisions designed to meet the needs of producers in, for instance, different yield risk categories. As it is voluntary, producers who might be disadvantaged by a compulsory scheme, such as high yield risk producers in a supply shift market, need not be affected. Those whose concern over the risks of the free market is nominal, that is, rich producers who can easily absorb fluctuations in price or income, could also choose not to be affected by the scheme. In order to attract participation, a formula for the determination of the controlled price would have to be established beforehand and publicized. (Under compulsory schemes the government as a monopsonist-buyer can set price arbitrarily without producer approval.) In sum, such a scheme is voluntary, does not require any control over production, sales, exports or imports of the commodity and does not directly influence price. In contrast, the compulsory buffer fund affects the total output of the commodity unless supply is perfectly inelastic, the domestic market price, domestic consumption through price and, thus, the volume of exports and export earnings. The favourable aspects of voluntary schemes also hold if the fund does not handle the commodity but merely accepts or pays producers the difference between the fixed price and the market price for the participation quantity. This arrangement would broadly resemble the insurance scheme discussed in the preceding chapter, or a savings bank in which deposits are made by the producer during periods of high income and withdrawn during those of low income. Members who wished to withdraw from the scheme would receive the amount of a positive balance in their account or be obliged to make good a deficit. Like voluntary insurance schemes, however, personal contact with the producer is necessary and wide participation is not assured. Operated on an international scale between governments, such a scheme would not require an international monopoly or the control of the import or export of the commodity and would not directly affect the supply or price. It would be akin to multilateral contracts discussed in Chapter 5.

3. MULTIPLE EXCHANGE RATE SCHEMES

Frequently buffer funds are administered by a board established for that purpose; export taxes and tariffs may come under the auspices of the customs department. On the other hand, all three devices can be integrated within the existing exchange control machinery. The latter approach may be preferred where the monetary authority is affected by a more convenient set of international obligations and institutions than conventional tariffs and export taxes or if exchange rate adjustments do not require the same parliamentary legislation. When not part of an exchange rate scheme, export taxes and tariffs generally go through the government budget and buffer funds entail the establishment of a statutory body. Under a buffer fund operated through the exchange rate, the effective exchange rate applied to the exported commodity is less favourable than the rate for imports during a period of high world market prices; prices accruing to producers in local currency will be lower than otherwise. A more favourable rate during a period of low world prices supports producer prices in terms of the local currency. For example, world prices over two periods may move from $1 to $2. If in the period of low price, exporters receive one unit of local currency (LC) for each $1 earned from exports on the international market, and during the period of high price they receive $LC1$ for each $2, the price to the producer in local currency will remain unchanged. If the exchange rate at which importers buy foreign exchange is fixed at $LC1$ for $1.50 over the two periods, the government will make a gain in the period of high world price and a loss in that of low price in the manner of the buffer fund discussed above.

In a supply shift, demand inelastic market, high output brings low export earnings during a period with a favourable export rate, and low output brings high export earnings during a period with a penalty export rate. The consequent increased fluctuation in foreign exchange availabilities under a dual rate system, with producer price and income stabilized in local currency, may also necessitate a controlled fluctuation in the import exchange rate. If importers are offered the same fluctuating rate as exporters, expenditures of foreign exchange on imports would be discouraged in periods of low world prices for the exported commodity and encouraged in those of high. In this event a buffer *fund* would not operate since the monetary authority is selling foreign exchange at its purchase price in both periods. This variation provides an advantage over buffer fund control by avoiding commitment of government funds to price support and the risk this entails. Also it can be initiated in a period of low prices since price support does not depend on a previous accumulation of funds. Under a 'mixed' system, such as those that have been used in the Philippines, two basic rates may operate, say $\$1 = LC1$ and $\$4 = LC1$, with foreign exchange earnings from the primary export being converted partly at one rate and partly at the other. If world price fluctuates from $\$1$ to $\$2$, conversion by exporters of all currency at $\$1 = LC1$ in the first instance and 67 per cent at $\$4 = LC1$ and 33 per cent at $\$1 = LC1$ in the second would achieve complete stability in producer price at $LC1$.

Where a multiple exchange rate scheme appreciates the export rate above a unified rate during an export boom it serves a twofold purpose: it siphons off excess income and captures some of the monetary expansion in the form of exchange profits by giving a lower value to the import rate. The anti-inflation effect may be increased if the exchange profits are used to retire government debt. Habits of high import consumption, which are difficult to reverse when earnings and the export exchange rate return to normal, may nevertheless be generated if the revalued export rate allows some of the increased earnings to be passed on to producers. When the source of inflation is domestic, rather than international, a devaluation of the import rate below the export rate will raise the price of imports, and, compared to a general devaluation, will increase government revenue and preclude a windfall increase in export producers' incomes—especially where export supply is inelastic for the periods of the partial devaluation. The operation of this multiple exchange rate scheme during a period of domestic inflation is similar to an export tax accompanied by a general devaluation of a like magnitude. Partial devaluations are desirable when a general devaluation would raise the price of a vital import, a staple food or a raw material such as cotton for clothing, above acceptable levels. In this case the import rate for these items would remain unchanged or only slightly devalued while that for all exports and other imports is devalued by a greater amount.

A miasma of exchange regulations may disguise any tax or tariff aspect of exchange manipulation compared to the overt operation of an export tax or tariff or a buffer fund which does not release its 'stabilization reserve'. Maintenance of export exchange rates that overvalue the domestic currency is, in effect, an *ad valorem* tax on exports. The exporter receives less local currency for foreign currency earned than otherwise. The effect on the level and stability of export earnings, producer income, prices and profits will be the same as with the fixed *ad valorem* tax discussed in Chapter 3, Section 7a (p. 88), if the export rate is held constant over the two periods of the model. Those utilizing foreign exchange, whether government or private importer, will acquire foreign exchange cheaply in terms of the local currency since the exporter must sell it cheap. Under an overvalued unified rate for exports and imports, income is transferred from those who export to those who import. If exports are largely from the primary sector while imports are to the industrial sector, the terms of trade will be turned against the primary sector. Without the market incentives provided by an equilibrium exchange rate for primary exports, a diversification program to other exports may be inhibited. The development of import substitution industry may likewise be restrained if the low price of competing imports is not offset by the low cost of imported equipment and raw materials used in production.

The tax function of a multiple exchange rate may be eroded over time in an internal inflationary situation if exchange control authorities depreciate the export rate to offset declining competitiveness of exports in international markets. On the other hand, if the spread between the import and export rate becomes considerable, a black market might well emerge and undermine the device's revenue raising abilities. Where the aim of a multiple exchange rate device is in part to raise revenue, a balance must be struck between the decrease in revenue as the spread narrows and the decrease in revenue through black market operations as it is widened. Controlling the spread is a delicate process as a reduction may lead to a devalued export rate unjustified in terms of costs of production, ability to expand production or diversification goals. As was the case under export taxes, revenue generated through the difference between the import and export exchange rates can be put to uses which indirectly benefit exporters. Revenue collected by the Brazilian and Columbian governments from the penalty rate on coffee exports, for instance, has been used in part to finance national buffer stocks designed to raise and stabilize world coffee prices.

Where one aim of development policy is to encourage export diversification (or import substitution) without jeopardizing the traditional primary commodity export base, it may be necessary or convenient compared to alternative methods to differentiate the rate between different export commodities (or to differentiate the export rate from the import rate) so as to assign a more depreciated rate to new or minor exports than to major exports. The exchange rate at which world price covers the costs of producing major exports may be inadequate for encouraging the growth of new or minor exports (or for restraining import demand and encouraging import substitution). A decline in production of traditional exports will not follow so long as the export rate for these is not changed and so long as the rate differential is developed gradually such that expanded production of minor exports is created with newly generated investment. Multiple export rates of this type can also be used when a boom in the major export market causes the costs of minor exports to become uncompetitive. In the absence of a flexible differential, a favourable rate for minor exports in normal periods may be an unattractive one when costs are periodically raised by a boom in the major export markets. Although governments have occasionally used devices which fix an overvalued rate for major exports and permit export earnings from minor exported commodities to be exchanged at lower free market rates, such an arrangement might allow minor exports to receive a higher average price only at the cost of greater price instability. This will occur where free markets are destabilized by speculative and volatile capital movements or frequent policy changes regarding control over imports and other exports. To circumvent this, it may be necessary to isolate all primary producers from the free market by pegging the rates for both minor and major exports, one below the other.

When compared to import quotas with licences that are not auctioned, two tiered multiple exchange rate schemes are attractive because they distribute the use of foreign exchange according to importers' ability to pay rather than their ability to obtain licences through historical share of the market, bribes, political influence and the like. That is, they minimize arbitrary decisions and reduce the pressure on licensing authorities by political and commercial interests. When the number of exchange rates is not limited or when there is not strict enforcement of rules regarding which of two rates apply to different commodity categories, however, pressure may be brought to bear on authorities to give specific commodities more favourable treatment than is called for by the scheme's objectives. Despite possible abuses, a further argument in favour of multiple exchange rates is that wide and prolonged use of quotas and tariffs can in the course of time bring an overvalued currency which discourages exports. If dismantling or changing the quota or tariff machinery is difficult, these devices may have to be supplemented by a devaluation of the export rate. Finally, multiple exchange rate devices, like tariffs, assure that windfall gains that might otherwise accrue to importers or foreign exporters under quotas are captured by the government.

Multiple exchange rates appear attractive *a priori* because they can raise revenue, relieve balance of payments difficulties and prevent or reduce inflation and otherwise perform many of the functions of progressive export taxes, export subsidies, import quotas, tariffs, and buffer funds. This they do by means which are less politically and administratively cumbersome and less expensive compared to the alternative methods. Frequently, however, tax, balance of payments and inflation goals are difficult to achieve simultaneously. Balancing payments may be difficult, for instance, in a situation of domestic inflation, where those rates which have become overvalued are maintained in order to hold down exporter income and the price of importables. Furthermore, multiple exchange rate schemes designed to raise revenue may increase imports if income is transferred from those with a lower propensity to import than the government. (This, however, occurs under other revenue raising devices as well.) The ease with which exchange rates are able to alter price compared to control by other conventional devices has caused wide and frequent *ad hoc* price changes to the detriment of the primary producer and consumer. Indeed, devising a rate structure to serve these multiple objectives may be too ambitious an undertaking. In attempting to make a multiple exchange rate device achieve both tax and balance of payments functions, especially under conditions of strong domestic inflation, a complex and cumbersome system which serves neither end is likely to evolve. Administrators might try to offset failure with adjustments that over time produce a multiplicity of rates and ever more roundabout and complicated applications that divorce trade from market realities, with consequent unfavourable effects on export earnings, import substitution, and resource allocation. Perhaps a combination of or all the unfavourable reasons cited above account for the declining popularity of multiple exchange rates in recent years.

4. BUFFER STOCKS AND EXPORT QUOTAS

Buffer stocks would appear to be the earliest form of price stabilization device. In 110 B.C., for instance, we find a Chinese economist organizing a government department to stockpile when produce was abundant and to sell in times of shortage. In more recent times the buffer stock device has been found to complement the export quota device in a number of useful ways which has accounted for their combination in the International Tin Agreement and International Cocoa Agreement. In these agreements, buffer stocks are considered the first line of defence with the slower responding export quota device in reserve for situations with which the buffer stock cannot cope alone. Sales and purchases of a buffer stock are largely at the manager's discretion while export restriction may involve a meeting of the council (which under the Tin Agreement occurs only after the equivalent of 10,000 tons of tin-in-concentrates has been accumulated by the buffer stock). Although buffer stocks respond more readily to market conditions, the export quota device may be stronger for its resources are not dependent on pre-financing while those of buffer stocks frequently are. Member countries tend to be less willing to contribute funds before a crisis than during one and thus the prescribed strength of the buffer stock may be limited. Export quotas can be used to mitigate the effects of fluctuations on the supply side of the market, leaving the buffer stock to absorb demand fluctuations. If exports are stabilized with export quotas and the demand facing exporters stabilized with a buffer stock, export earnings will be stabilized as well, although producers' income may not be.

Constraint under export quota schemes lies entirely with the exporting countries. These suffer in two ways that make them reluctant to negotiate strong export quota devices; they must finance the storage of stocks in their own countries if export restriction is not implemented through production control and they must forego export earnings in periods of restriction. Even if exports are withheld at the floor price in the face of an inelastic demand, more would be earned under a strong international buffer stock operating alone since the volume of exports would be maintained or increased and the price would be supported at the floor. Where export quotas are implemented through production restriction, however, the problems associated with financing and risk of loss on stocks held is avoided. If domestic stocks are withheld from a demand elastic market in periods of low prices, the loss in income may be recovered by the subsequent sale of stocks at high prices, providing the difference between the floor and ceiling and the frequency with which transactions are reversed are sufficient to cover costs associated with storage.

The effects of a national buffer stock for an exported commodity will be similar to those of an export quota device implemented through domestic storage, although the elasticity of demand faced by a single country operating a national buffer stock will be greater than for a group of countries operating an international export quota scheme. National buffer stocks for commodities produced and consumed locally will have producer income effects similar to those of an international or national buffer stock for an export or an export quota device implemented through domestic storage. These may meet welfare criteria in stabilizing the price to the consumer providing this favourable effect is not undone by increased consumer real and money income instability for the reasons covered in Chapter 3, Section 4 (p. 78).

a. THE ROUTINE

Unlike buffer funds, buffer stocks and export quotas influence the market through restriction and release of stocks or through restriction of production. For effective defence of the price limits the volume of stocks accumulated or released must be equal to the difference between what is demanded and supplied at the limits. Furthermore, if an excess of stocks is to be avoided, stocks accumulated at the floor price should, over time, equal those sold at the ceiling. In order to permit the scheme to break even in terms of stocks, the price range must approach being symmetrically distributed between the uncontrolled market equilibrium prices if demand and supply elasticities are assumed not to vary substantially with the level of prices. The floor price will then be reached about as frequently as the ceiling price and for a similar volume of support. This assumes, of course, that the stock is managed with a somewhat atypical rigidity. Given sufficient latitude, the manager could sell before the price reached the ceiling if the quantity in stock appears to be excessive, so long as the amount sold does not drive the price below the floor. Conversely, he could buy before the price reached the floor if the quantity in stock appears insufficient for the device to stabilize price effectively in the future.

In Figure 4.3 the price range $P_1^* P_2^*$ is symmetrically distributed between the uncontrolled market prices P_1 and P_2. Because the supply function S is linear, and demand functions D_1 and D_2 linear and parallel, $\hat{Q}_1 Q_1^* = Q_2^* \hat{Q}_2$. These two expressions represent the difference between the volume demanded and supplied at the price limits. Thus, in terms of stocks, the buffer stock or export quota scheme shown breaks-even over the two periods. In the first period of floor price support the difference between supply and demand at the floor price, $\hat{Q}_1 Q_1^*$ is bought by the buffer stock or stored by exporting countries under an export quota scheme. Removal of this amount from the market re-

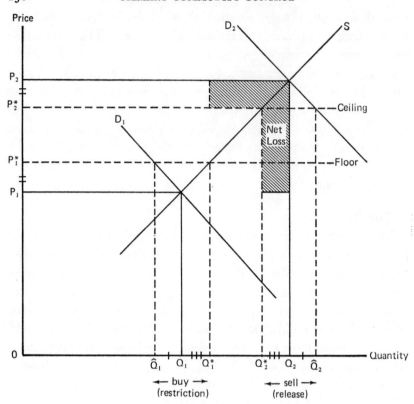

FIGURE 4.3

THE ROUTINE AND POSSIBLE EFFECT OF BUFFER STOCKS AND
EXPORT QUOTAS IN A DEMAND SHIFT MARKET

duces supply to the amount demanded, $\hat{Q}_1$, at the floor price. In the
second period a like amount is sold such that the amount available to
consumers corresponds to that which they demand at the ceiling price.
In contrast to a buffer fund operating in such a market, these two
devices stabilize world price since world market supply is increased
in periods of high price and decreased in those of low price. Assuming
demand increases to D_2 because of an investment boom in importing
countries, defence of a ceiling price (and thus cheaper raw materials for
importers) may serve to hinder attempts to curb the boom.

The international buffer stock causes more to be exported in the low
price period and less in the high price period than without control. In
the low price period the larger volume is exported at a higher price,
and in the high price period the lower volume is exported at a lower
price than without control. Thus, buffer stock control stabilizes producer income and export earnings in a demand shift market. A buffer

fund, as previously illustrated, may not have a stabilizing effect on export earnings in a demand shift market. In a supply shift demand elastic market, producer income and export earnings under a buffer stock may be destabilized for in the low price period of high income the buffer stock will increase volume and price and, in the high price period of low income, volume and price will be further reduced. On the other hand, if demand is inelastic, buffer stock control will increase stability (subject to the qualifications regarding the width of the price range, the amount of shift in the supply function from one period to the next, and the elasticities of supply and demand discussed in Chapter 3, Section 4, p. 78).

In a demand shift demand elastic market controlled by an export quota device implemented through domestic storage and release of stocks rather than through production control, export earnings will be destabilized. Earnings in the low price and earnings period will be further reduced with restriction and increased with release in the high price period. Producers' income, however, will be stabilized as price and volume are stabilized. In a supply shift demand inelastic market stock releases in periods of high prices and earnings and restrictions in periods of low prices and earnings will stabilize export earnings. The converse will occur in a supply shift demand elastic market. Producer income will be destabilized in a supply shift demand elastic market, for control further reduces the low income in high price periods and increases the high income in low price periods. If demand is inelastic in a supply shift market, the effect on the stability of producers' incomes will depend on the price range and market functions.

Periods of high prices will be unaffected by control if the export quota scheme operates through production restriction. In periods of low prices producer and export earnings will be increased if demand is inelastic and reduced if it is elastic. In a supply shift demand inelastic market export earnings and producer income will be stabilized since income in the low income period is increased. Similar reasoning indicates that producer income would be destabilized in a supply or demand shift demand elastic market.

These and the above observations derived from two period models are to be accepted only with extreme caution. As amplified in Chapter 3, control or the anticipation of control may alter market parameters and the conclusions reached here. Moreover, this short-term analysis cannot be transposed to the long-term without qualification since short-term price stabilization can affect long-term demand and supply. In the case considered here, for instance, the reduced threat of periodical supply shortage could lead the producer of the end product to shift to a technology favouring the controlled commodity and consequently bolster the competitive position of the commodity for a long period.

National buffer stocks which are designed to stabilize the price of a product produced and consumed domestically would also have to stabilize world price in the absence of a mechanism that would insulate the domestic market from the international market. Quotas may be used concurrently to restrict imports in periods of floor price support above international price or exports in periods of ceiling price support below world prices. Alternatively, if the country is normally a net importer of, for example, rice, the volume of imports can be controlled by tying them to compulsory purchases by importers of rice from the national buffer stock at the stock's ceiling price. In Malaysia a variable ratio of compulsory rice buffer stock purchases to imports assures that imports are discouraged in periods of domestic abundance. (See Chapter 3, Section 7b, p. 97.) As the domestic price approaches the buffer stock ceiling, the ratio is gradually reduced until at the ceiling it is suspended altogether. When the domestic price is below the buffer stock ceiling price, importers lose on compulsory purchases from the buffer stock at the ceiling price. They make gains, however, on imports if the world price is below the domestic price. If both sets of transactions give a net gain to importers, rice will be imported. Should the government find that a high volume of imports is eroding the domestic price, the ratio is increased. The advantage of such a system is that it avoids the inequities, temptation to buy favour, and friction created when an import quota is divided among importers.

Buffer stock and export quota price support may occur at other than the price limits. In the post-war period proposals have ranged from support only at the limits to intervention anywhere within the price range. Under the Tin Agreements and the Cocoa Agreement, for instance, the buffer stock manager may, at his discretion, buy when the world price is in the lower third of the price range and sell when it is in the upper third. He is compelled to buy when the world price reaches the floor and sell when it reaches the ceiling until the stock's resources are exhausted. By allowing operation within the outer thirds of the price range, price movements may be more readily controlled, for they will not be likely to gain as much momentum in a single direction before reaching the limits. Export quotas under the Tin Agreement are imposed only after the buffer stock has accumulated an established amount of stock. Thus, they may become operational only as the world price reaches or falls below the floor. Under the Cocoa

Agreement export restriction would be accompanied by national stock accumulation. Such accumulation would, however, be delayed for the buffer stock under the proposed arrangements must, up to an established volume of transactions, buy the amount restricted. Whether a buffer stock or export quota operates within the outer thirds of the price range or only at the limits is not a determining factor for the general conclusions reached here. The operational range will influence the magnitude of the effect of these devices on the variables considered, however, because purchase and sale within the price range has the effect of narrowing the price range for some transactions.

The effects of buffer stocks and export quotas when market functions assume a logarithmic linear formulation are illustrated in Appendix 3. Tables 9 and 10 relating to these two devices should be compared to Tables 1 and 2. If export quotas are accompanied by production restriction, the figures for the second period in a demand shift market and the first period in a supply shift market under control will be the same as those in the uncontrolled market given in Tables 1 and 2. A summary of effects with linear functions is given in Tables 4.1 and 4.2 of this chapter (pp. 125 & 126). The favourable and unfavourable effects indicated will diminish as the price limits approach the uncontrolled market prices.

b. Possible Net Producer Income Loss

The net loss to the producer under a buffer fund in a demand shift market will also occur for the same reasons under an international or national buffer stock or an export quota scheme. In Figure 4.3 this net loss over the two periods is represented by the cross-hatched area. Under an international buffer stock, the loss to the producer will represent a loss in export earnings as well. Such a loss may be recovered entirely or in part by the buffer stock buying $Q_1 Q_1^*$ at the floor price and selling a like amount at the ceiling unless the difference gained is taken up by brokerage, handling, storage, deterioration, insurance and interest charges on stock held. Where demand is elastic and returns under a buffer stock or export quota are smaller but more certain, producers may increase their output in the long run, depressing world price but expanding income. Under national or export control schemes, any gains from stockholding would accrue directly to the exporting country. If the national buffer stock or export quota device uses a single price at the mean of the uncontrolled market prices in a demand shift market, a net loss in export earnings would occur for reasons cited in the discussion surrounding Figure 4.1b above. As the price range spread is widened, however, this and the producer income loss would be re-duced. It is worth repeating from the previous subsection that the application of this line of analysis may be limited by the assumption that demand and supply are functions of current price only. A major advantage of a stabilization scheme might, for instance, be the increased competitiveness with substitute products. Should average demand increase with reduced price risk, the possible losses indicated above will be reduced or turned into gains. On the other hand, if price stabilization increases producer income risk, supply may decline for any given price and resources flow out of the industry into less remunerative alternative uses.

The loss indicated by cross-hatching in Figure 4.3 may not arise if, for reasons given in Chapter 1, the elasticity of demand is greater at high prices than low, as shown in Figure 4.4a. For simplicity it is assumed that the buffer stock or export quota supports a single fixed price P^* instead of a price range. $\hat{Q}_1 Q^*$ must equal $Q^* \hat{Q}_2$ if the device is designed to break even in stocks. The fixed price needed to accomplish this, P^*, will be above the mean of the uncontrolled market prices. If P^* is above the mean by a requisite amount with D_2 sufficiently more elastic relative to D_1, the loss $P^* P_2 . OQ_2 + OP^* . Q^* Q_2$ will be cancelled by the gain $P_1 P^* . OQ^* + Q_1 Q^* . OP_1$. The loss could also be avoided by a low price range that precludes successful ceiling price support. Under the International Tin Agreements the possible loss has been reduced by a price range the mean of which is below the mean of world prices. Although consumers urged the adoption of a low price range, this has meant that insufficient stocks have been accumulated at the low floor price to defend the low ceiling price. (The complementary use of a strong export quota device and less than generous buffer stock funding has also contributed to inadequate stock accumulations at the floor.) Under the so-called 'food aid' buffer stock schemes that defend a ceiling price but not a floor in the recipient country, the local farmers may make no gains to offset their losses. Such programmes have been useful in alleviating situations of critical shortage of food staples but have been accused of reducing domestic prices to such an extent in periods of low harvest that self-sufficiency programmes are thwarted. Disposal of surplus strategic stocks (e.g. those of copper, rubber and tin held by the United States) generally during periods of above average prices has acted to dampen world price increases and possibly caused a producer loss of the sort envisaged here. However, by raising prices during their accumulation following the Second World War, they provided in effect an interest free long term loan to

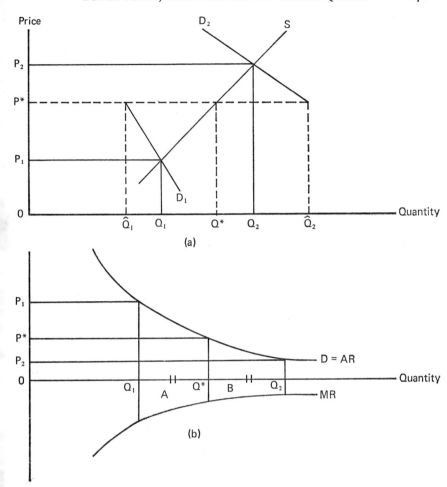

(a)

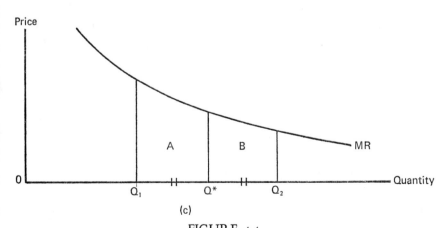

(b)

(c)

FIGURE 4.4

POSSIBLE EFFECTS OF BUFFER STOCKS AND EXPORT QUOTAS
UNDER ALTERNATIVE MARKET SITUATIONS

developing exporters—repayable in terms of lower prices when disposed.

Bateman (1965) has shown that under some circumstances the exporting country operating a national buffer stock or member to an international export quota scheme may lose in a supply shift market as well. If we assume a logarithmic-linear demand function of the form $D = KP^n$ used in Appendix 3, the marginal revenue function will be negative and increasing, as shown in Figure 4.3b, when demand is inelastic. Price stabilization through the stabilization of exports at Q^*, midway between outputs Q_1 and Q_2 over two periods, would reduce export earnings by A when Q_1 is produced and increase them by B when Q_2 is produced and supply is perfectly inelastic. $(P_2 P^* \neq P^* P_1.)$ Since B is smaller than A, a net loss in export earnings will occur. On the other hand, if the marginal revenue is positive and falling, in the manner of Figure 4.4c, such schemes would increase earnings in a supply shift market. That is, the gain during a period of disposal, A, would exceed the loss, B, during a period of restriction. This would also hold if marginal revenue became negative between Q_1 and Q_2. These observations will apply if supply exhibits a positive elasticity and shifts parallel to itself and if supply and demand are linear. Losses in earnings would occur if restriction at low prices took place in a demand elastic market and release at high prices in a demand inelastic market. Possible reasons for such a demand function are covered in Chapter 1. Demand may, for instance, become elastic at very low prices if the price reaches a carrying charge threshold. In this case, losses in export earnings may occur with wide shifts in supply but not with small. The possible effects on net income have been considered in the discussion of Porter's argument in Section 5, p. 83, of the preceding chapter.

One approach to analyzing the effect of a national buffer stock or export quota scheme on export earnings can be made through the total revenue function. This approach may also be taken with international buffer stocks if all gains made by the stock are assumed to be distributed to exporting countries. Since each of these devices reorders the pattern of sales to consumers, we may ask what quantities $Q_1, Q_2, \ldots Q_i, \ldots Q_n$, sold during periods $1, 2, \ldots i, \ldots n$, maximize total export earnings in a supply shift market if a given quantity, Q_t, is available for redistribution. With reference to Figure 4.5a, if unequal quantities are sold during each period, the average earning is the ordinate of the gravity centre G of points $O_1, O_2, \ldots O_i, \ldots O_n$, of which the abscissa is $Q_a = \dfrac{Q_t}{n}$. However, if the same quantity is sold each period, the average

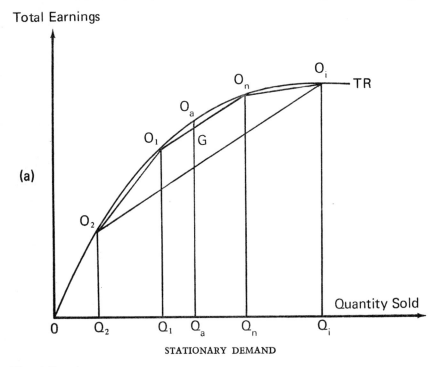

STATIONARY DEMAND

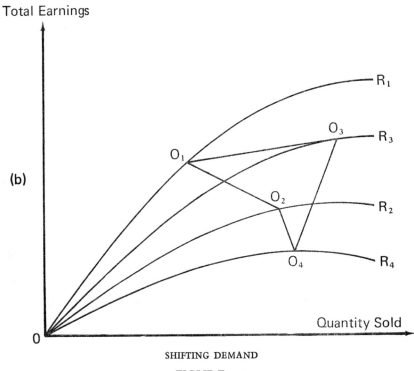

SHIFTING DEMAND

FIGURE 4.5

THE EFFECT OF REDISTRIBUTED SALES ON AVERAGE EARNINGS

earnings obtained, $\left(Q_t = \dfrac{Q_t}{n} \right)$, is the ordinate of point O_a on the

total revenue curve of which the abscissa is $\dfrac{Q_t}{n} = Q_a$, the quantity

sold in each period. Since the curve is convex and has its convexity turned upward, G, which is inside the convex polygon $O_2 O_1 \ldots O_n O_i$, is below O_a. Thus, whatever the unequal quantities $Q_1, Q_2 \ldots Q_i \ldots Q_n$, the average export earning is less than when the same amount is sold each period. Any equalization of a given quantity of sales through an export quota or buffer stock scheme would lead to an increase in export earnings. Conversely, when the total revenue curve has its convexity turned downward (i.e. when the second derivative of total revenue function is positive—cf. Appendix 2, Section 5, p. 252), the maximum earnings are obtained by selling the total available quantity, Q_t, in one period. In a market characterized by demand shifts this reasoning does not hold since the revenue curves change with each shift. In Figure 4.5b, for instance, the earnings polygon has no defined position in respect to any given curve whatever the convexity of the revenue curves $R_1, R_2, \ldots R_i, \ldots R_n$.

Buffer stocks and export quotas, unlike sliding-scale export taxes and buffer funds, stabilize the consumer's price as well as the producer's and thus will have different effects on surpluses. With reference to Figure 3.3a of Chapter 3, p. 81, consumers realize a net gain from price stabilization in a demand shift market since $a < c+d+e$, while their expected surplus in the supply shift market is reduced by $\frac{1}{2}(a+b-c-d)$ as depicted in Figure 3.3b. Buffer stocks and export quotas with stocks stabilize producer surplus in demand shift markets since they increase it in periods when it is low and decrease it when it is high. The converse is true of consumers' surplus, namely, it is increased in periods when surplus is high and decreased when surplus is low. In supply shift markets, on the other hand, consumer surplus is decreased in periods when it is high and increased in periods when it is low. Where control is directed at a domestically produced and consumed product, a buffer stock in a supply shift market may be acceptable on strictly cost-benefit grounds since the gain to the producer exceeds the loss to the consumer. If we subtract consumer loss, $c+d$ in Figure 3.3b, Chapter 3, from producer gain, $c+d+e$, and producer loss, a, from consumer gain, $a+b$, the result is a net gain of $b+e$: $(c+d+e-a)+(a+b-c-d) = b+e$. Welfare and Pareto cost benefit criteria may both be met if the cost of providing compensation for the net loss to consumers does not negate the after compensation gain to producers. A corresponding argument will show a net gain of $b+e$ to producers and consumers jointly in the demand shift case (Figure 3.3a). (Howell and Lovesy (1945) have additionally demonstrated how price may be fixed in order to confer specific gains on consumers, or, by implication, on producers —e.g. consumers will make net gains if price is stabilized at or below the weighted average, $\dfrac{P_1 Q_1 + P_2 Q_2}{Q_1 Q_2}$, of uncontrolled market prices in a supply shift market.) Since producers gain with supply shifts and lose with demand shifts, we could expect (as Massell (1970) has shown) that when both functions shift simultaneously, producers are more likely to gain if the supply variance is larger than the demand variance. Per contra, consumers gain the larger the demand variance is relative to that of supply. In the limiting case of either a perfectly inelastic supply or no demand shift, producers cannot lose surplus from price stabilization under our assumptions, while consumers cannot lose with a perfectly inelastic demand or when there is no supply shift.

Under a production control scheme (e.g. an export quota device with no stocks and thus no ceiling price support) a net loss in surpluses will occur to producers and consumers considered jointly. With reference to Figure 4.2b, if $P_1{}'$ is a floor price, producers gain $a-d$ and consumers lose $a+b$. If demand is inelastic, producers will always gain by restriction regardless of the elasticity of a normal supply curve. If production control entails restricting only one input (e.g. land) such that marginal costs increase, producer surplus gains would be diminished. Producer surplus (profits) will be maximized under an export quota device if output is limited to that quantity at which marginal revenue is equated with marginal cost for the industry. Alternatively, if the supply function shifts downward as a result of, say, a productivity increase, limiting export volume to its historical magnitude in the face of a static elastic demand may increase producer surplus (bearing in mind that under some common conditions no welfare significance attaches to long run industry supply curves—cf. Mishan, 1968). With reference to Figure 4.2a, p. 124, for instance, restriction of output to OQ_1, after a productivity increase shifts supply from S_1 to S_2, provides surpluses $P_2 P_1 . OQ_1$ (i.e. $a+b+c+d$) that would be lost if output were allowed to expand to OQ_2 and price drop to OP_2. If S_2 is sufficiently elastic, this loss could exceed surplus gain h. Limiting output to OQ_1 under an export quota or export tax device when demand is unity or inelastic would always bring surplus gains since $P_1 P_2 . OQ_1 \geqslant OP_2 . Q_1 Q_2$ while surplus losses from restriction will, with a positively sloped supply, be less than $OP_2 . Q_1 Q_2$.

c. LIMITS ON PERIODS OF INITIAL USE AND RESOURCES

Buffer stocks and export quotas cannot be implemented in a period of ceiling price support since such support through the disposal of stocks presupposes a previous accumulation of stocks. An export quota device which operates through production restriction in periods of low price is incapable of supporting a ceiling price as no stocks are held. When stocks are held, the strength of support at a ceiling price is pre-determined by the volume previously accumulated. The strength of support at the floor price is not so rigidly determined since it will depend upon the amount of funds which are allocated or may be mobilized for this purpose. Once the stocks or funds are exhausted the market reverts to an uncontrolled market.

Buffer funds entail no net costs other than those for administration and may earn income if the stabilization fund is invested in periods when it is not being used for price support. (If invested, however, the investment would have to be in short term assets to allow liquidation at short notice.) In contrast, the stock holding activities of buffer stocks and export quotas entail brokerage, handling, storage, interest and de-terioration charges, in addition to the normal administrative expenses. These must be weighed against earnings from the short term invest-ment of any stabilization fund under their control. If the period be-tween low and high prices is very long the unit storage costs could become greater than the difference in the price limits. The difference can be increased with a wide price range but transactions will be reversed less frequently than under a narrow price range.

A narrow price range requires a stronger buffer stock or export quota scheme than a wide price range. As we narrow the price range around the mean of the uncontrolled market prices in Figure 4.3 (p. 136) for example, the difference between supply and demand at the controlled price increases. At the floor price a greater volume must be purchased than with a wider range and it must be purchased at a higher price. If there is a high floor price for a coarse grains buffer stock, for instance, the differential between supply and demand at that price would increase because there would be substitution of oil cake and other non-grain feeds such as fodder crops on the demand side of the market. On the supply side there would be substitution of coarse grains production for alternative crops. If exporters under an export quota scheme with-hold stocks rather than restrict production in periods of low prices, the burden of stockholding to support a given floor price may become particularly heavy if consumers reduce their stocks because they feel an increase in demand will be met by releases of exporters' stocks.

Stockholding schemes which stabilize price, however, may reduce destabilizing movements in commercial stocks, increasing the underlying price stability and reducing the minimum strength needed for effective control at the price limits.

A related limitation is the likely restriction of storage schemes to commodities which are not highly perishable. If the costs of storage are high, these may not be covered from periods of low to periods of high price, even in the absence of price limits. Some perishable commodities, however, can be processed into less perishable forms. Liquid milk, for instance, could be processed into butter or powdered milk and pineapples can be tinned. Alternatively, quality deteriorations may be avoided by rotating the stock. Although, as a general rule, storage schemes will be limited to commodities which have a high value in relation to bulk, and thus low unit storage costs in relation to unit value, this is not a necessary condition. Water, for instance, both bulky and cheap, is a primary commodity with a long history of buffer stock control.

d. The Price Range and Trend

In attempting to devise buffer stock and export quota schemes that are equitable to producers and consumers, equity may not be achieved and the viability of the agreement itself may be threatened if the trend is not correctly anticipated. When the price range is low in relation to the trend of prices, as under the Tin Agreements from 1963–1966, less will be accumulated at the floor than needed to support the ceiling. The ceiling price will be defended only partially and consumers will consequently forego benefits which they anticipated in the negotiation of the agreement. Ironically, consumers frequently bargain for a low price range that reduces the chances that the ceiling price will be successfully defended. The lower the range, the less will be accumulated at the floor and the more will be needed to defend the ceiling. Consumer interest in a low floor price implies that gains from a low price (with consequent weak ceiling price support due to insufficient stock accumulation) are seen to outweigh the gains from price stability when the ceiling price is successfully defended (due to a floor price sufficiently high to allow adequate stock accumulation). Conversely, if the price range is too high, more will be accumulated at the floor than can be sold at the ceiling. Where bargaining is between developing producer countries and developed consumer countries, and where supply is concentrated and demand derived, the representatives of consumers may make concessions to producers that are not in their strict economic interests. Concessionary prices may be given through a high price range in the conviction that trade and aid are not complete substitutes for one another, especially if producers are unable to expand exports. (Consumers may, of course, agree to a high price range without providing facilities for its maintenance: a strong buffer stock capable of controlling the trend or subsidized surplus disposal.) On the other hand, the producer may give in to pressure from consumers because he is in a more tenuous position than the consumer in that a large proportion of his income is dependent on the commodity under consideration while only a small proportion of the consumer's income is spent on its purchase. The questionable advantages of directly controlling the trend with price support by a buffer stock do not necessarily hold under less direct methods. The idea of price *stabilization* around the trend is, in fact, often to indirectly alter the trend which, because of irreversible substitution on the demand side of the market due to price fluctuations, would otherwise be downward; stabilization aims to influence the trend by retarding unfavourable technological progress.

If negotiators on both sides of the market attempt to arrive at a price range mean centered on the trend, schemes involving the holding of stocks could nevertheless disrupt the market if the forecast of the trend upon which the price range is based is erroneous and the price range inflexible. Such a situation is depicted in Figure 4.6. The trend forecast is assumed to be over-optimistic. Up to time period A in the life of the agreement the forecast finds support in the council administering the agreement since one period of buying is balanced by two of selling. From A to B, however, the device's resources are exhausted supporting the floor price and the scheme collapses at B causing price to drop precipitously to P. Although the device may have stabilized price up to B, its effect including the period of decline to P may be destabilizing. Moreover, the stocks accumulated up to time B may be stored at increasing loss, in terms of deterioration and storage costs, in the futile hope that prices will rise to the ceiling in the future. Alternatively they may be destroyed, a solution used for surplus coffee and cocoa national stocks in the 1950's and early 1960's, or they may be disposed of at low prices through non-traditional channels (e.g. cocoa for school lunch programs in needy countries or as cattle feed). Sales of surplus stocks in traditional channels would perpetuate and increase the unfavourable situation created by a declining trend of prices. But so long as surplus stock remains unsold it will overhang the market and depress prices. If a new price range is created around the correct trend at P'_c and P'_f, surplus stock would be sold at a loss at C.

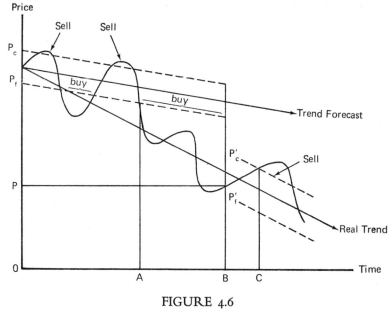

FIGURE 4.6

THE POSSIBLE EFFECTS OF AN INACCURATE FORECAST OF PRICES ON CONTROL

Improved forecasting could have allowed this collapse to be avoided and perhaps precluded the need for a buffer stock or reduced the strength required for, if prices are reliably projected, producers will respond in a stabilizing manner by changing production and investment plans. (See Chapter 1, Section 5b and c, p. 12.) In the above market the price at which stocks are bought may be higher than that at which they are sold, even though the trend is correctly projected from the outset, given a sufficiently narrow price range which declines with the trend to avoid collapse of the scheme. If a loss at the ceiling is anticipated or if more stocks are accumulated than reasonably needed to defend the ceiling, stocks may be sold when the market price is within the price range providing such sales do not drive the price below the floor. Although the device illustrated was slow in responding to the trend, it may be undesirable to allow the price range to respond too readily to movements in the short or medium term equilibrium price if speculators are strong relative to the control device. They could exhaust accumulated stocks by purchases at the ceiling price with the assurance that the price range would be adjusted upwards and their risk of loss on speculative purchases reduced.

e. CONCESSIONARY TRADE

Because primary commodity exports of the developing countries tend to be absorbed by the developed countries, international buffer stocks, export quotas or multilateral contracts may, as mentioned above, include elements of aid. The history of post-war international commodity agreement negotiation suggests that developing countries expect agreements to serve this end. The usual medium is a high price range. Developed countries, however, have not generally been receptive to this form of aid largely because of its lack of selectivity. Aid is limited to those countries exporting the handful of primary commodities which are exported only by developing countries. Some of these countries, moreover, may be relatively prosperous and in less need of aid while others may not have the absorptive capacity for aid or they may be in political disfavour with the major importing countries. This form of aid provides no assurance that the aid will be spent wisely even if needed or that it will go to those who need it in the recipient country. If the higher world prices are passed on to producers in the exporting countries, producers will benefit equally, whether they are relatively rich or poor. On the demand side, higher prices are paid by all consumers regardless of their economic well-being. Aid through concessionary trade may merely allow a higher level of consumption in exporting developing countries while supervised direct aid by the donor country could be channeled into activities which promote external equilibrium and economic growth. Where supervised direct aid permits the recipient country to reduce the tax burden, direct aid, like concessionary trade, may be dissipated on increased consumption. Higher average world prices under the 1968 International Coffee Agreement as a result of the export tax used to finance the diversification fund do not represent a form of indiscriminate aid since the fund's resources are allocated to development projects.

f. Possible Loss of Market Share

National schemes which increase world prices by withholding stocks or restricting production in periods of low prices tend to encourage production in other countries. The long run effect of increased production elsewhere is to leave the country that imposes restrictions with a smaller share of the world market and possibly no long run increase in prices. If other countries expand production and the country restricting exports does not reduce production capacity, long run prices could be lower than otherwise. Post-war attempts by Brazil and Columbia to restrict coffee exports, for example, led to expansion of Central American and African output. This expansion reduced price and left Brazil and Colombia with large stocks which could not be disposed of without further lowering price. Prevention of dislocation by stock accumulation rather than production restriction and diversification increased potential instability since Brazil and Colombia gained singular control over nearly all the world's coffee stocks. Several attempts by them to sell these stocks eroded market price and necessitated further accumulation to regain the former price position. Pre-war rubber production restriction schemes in Malaya failed from Malaya's point of view because, by raising prices, they stimulated output in Indonesia and Thailand and left Malaya with a predominance of old trees and a smaller market share. Pakistan's more recent attempt to raise world prices by restricting the planting of jute stimulated Indian production and the use of synthetic fibres.

g. Difficulty of Production Control

Regulation of production on a world-wide basis in a situation of chronic oversupply constitutes an attack on the disease, rather than the symptom, but is normally too slow in operation for short run adjustments and may be resisted because of the possible dislocation caused. Direct controls over production (or income) entailing detailed regulation often require elaborate record keeping and close supervision. These are expensive and burdensome, even if desirable results are obtained, and the favourable effects may be neutralized by a multiplicity of exceptions and instances of uneven administration. The specific nature of direct control implies the fragmentation of control authority, with its consequent opportunities for conflict and inconsistencies between outcomes and goals. Direct production control of numerous dispersed smallholds may, in the extreme, be administratively unfeasible. Moreover, once an annual crop is planted or a perennial reaches maturity it could be politically unwise to prevent its harvest. Products like cattle, tea, rubber and tin which are produced continuously are more amenable to short run adjustments without creating friction, since production restriction would not cause the total loss of investment which occurs when the harvesting of an annual is prohibited. Short run production control can also cause long run loss in production capacity. Export control under the first International Tin Agreement (1956–1961) was to a large extent responsible for the subsequent shortage of tin supplied under the second Agreement (1961–1966) because of the difficulties and expense in rehabilitating unused mines.

In order to assure that production is restricted under an export quota scheme, a limit may be placed on the volume of stock which an exporting country may hold in a period of restriction. As this limit is approached, exporting countries would be expected to take measures to limit production. Under the International Sugar and Tin Agreements, for example, stocks were not to exceed 20 per cent and 25 per cent, respectively, of a country's annual production. The Coffee Agreement contains provisions for production goals for each member country which remain free, however, to adopt whatever policies they see fit to achieve them. During periods of export restriction under the Tin Agreements, Malaysia has issued individual production quotas based on historical share of exports to each of over a thousand mines in the country. Since these quotas may be bought and sold, marginal mines may sell their quotas and shut down completely while those mines which purchase additional quotas may continue operating as before.

h. Price Control over the Business Cycle

If, over the business cycle, the price of primary commodities tends to fluctuate more than those of manufactured imports of exporting countries, price control can be used to eliminate the consequent fluctuation in relative prices over the cycle. Too narrow a price range, however, may replace the relative price changes of the uncontrolled market with changes in the opposite direction. With such a reversal of cyclical price relationships primary producers would find their real income increased during the troughs of the cycle and decreased during the peaks. This would hold particularly if the business cycles in the importing countries are transmitted without significant lag to the exporting countries. Because of the reversal in price relationships, control instruments would have to be stronger than when reversals do not occur. A buffer stock, for instance, would have to cope with reduced demand, resulting from the commodity's relatively high price in a depression, as well as increased supply as resources are attracted into the commodity's production by its relatively high price. In order to accommodate these changes, a buffer stock would have to increase purchases and an export quota scheme increase restrictions by the sum of the increments of decreased consumption and increased production. Diagrammatically this could be illustrated in Figure 4.3 (p. 136 above) by shifting D_1 to the left and S to the right at price P_1^*. Floor price P_1^* could only be defended in this case by a volume of purchases or restriction larger than $\hat{Q}_1 Q_1^*$.

i. The Residual Market

A residual market will be created under export quota schemes if provision is made for consumer discrimination against non-members in periods of export restriction. The Draft Sugar Agreement of 1965, for example, stipulated that during a period of quota restriction imports from non-members could not exceed the largest amount imported in any of the three years 1962/64. Any amount could be imported from non-members if quotas became inoperative due to high world prices. Below a certain price, imports of sugar from non-members were prohibited altogether except under conditions of extreme hardship. One alternative provision offered by the Draft Sugar Agreement asked for no non-member imports if quotas were in effect. Under the Cocoa Agreement of 1973, each member importer undertakes not to import between the price limits more from non-members than its annual average for the years 1970-2. When the world price falls below the floor, this quantity is reduced by half. When quotas operate on both sides of the market such that a residual market with a price largely independent of the agreement price limits does develop, the scheme acquires aspects characteristic of a multilateral contract. The effects of such arrangements on the residual market are considered further in the following chapter (p. 172). One advantage of discrimination against non-members is that price may be controlled among consenting countries without wide participation in the scheme. Where provision for discrimination is not made, non-members will enjoy the advantages of price control without paying the cost in terms of export restriction. This could discourage participation and increase the burden of restriction on the reduced number of exporting countries which do participate.

j. Freezing of the Pattern of Trade

Allocation of basic quotas to exporters, for the purpose of determining benefits or obligations in periods of price control, is customary under export quota schemes, as well as with multilateral contracts. These may either be fixed for the duration of the agreement or altered only by the two-thirds distributed majority vote considered in the next chapter. As pointed out there, this voting procedure provides a disincentive to alterations in the original distribution of basic quotas. (Under the Cocoa Agreement, for instance, basic quotas may be altered after two years of operation and only with the formidable two-thirds distributed majority vote.) Under export quota schemes, basic quotas derived from an historical period fix share of the market during periods of restriction. Such *pro rata* reduction in output implies discrimination against exporters who have a larger potential for expanding output than do others. Freezing of the pattern of trade works contrary to efficiency objectives if it serves to preserve the position of the high cost producer. The alleged uneconomic production of robustas in Africa encouraged by coffee producer cartels in the 1950's was, for example, frozen in the 1963 and subsequent international export quota schemes which allowed African producers to retain their share of the market. Share of the market, however, is open to competition during rene-gotiation of an agreement and periods of no restriction. Although the same historical period is used for all exporters in determining their basic quotas, individual countries will press for an historical period in which their market share was particularly large. In the inevitable dispute that arises over the choice of period and the strength of the export quota device, the exporting country may find itself impaled on the horns of a dilemma if it manoeuvres to keep the world's supply as small as possible and to maximize its own share in that supply.

The Tin Agreements have provided for an annual one-twentieth cor-rection in the distribution of export quota percentages between coun-tries on the basis of efficiency or need. But what the efficient producer may deserve the inefficient one may need and both have a claim on the amount redistributed. Moreover, if actual exports in the period of low prices (upon which the potential for expanded low cost exports is indicated) are based on the original quotas, it would be difficult to determine which countries were most capable of low cost expansion of production. The expressed objective of avoiding 'premature aban-donment' of mines in times of low price so that their output is available in times of high prices may work to preserve the existing distribution. Again, even with the floor price above the costs of all producers, the high cost producers might not permit a continuing redistribution against themselves without threatening to withdraw from the agreement. One partial solution to the problem adopted by the 1962 Coffee Agreement is to allow exports to countries having a low level of consumption per head to proceed without restriction. Habits of consumption in these countries may be developed with low prices which can be met only by the low cost producers. Low cost sales for humanitarian projects may be excluded as well as certain special varieties or qualities of the commodity if they do not significantly influence the general market. For instance, certified seed is excluded in the Wheat Agreements and flavour cocoa in the Cocoa Agreement.

The fixed basic quota allocations in an export quota scheme are gener-ally determined by costs of production, balance-of-payments position, current trading position or past performance. In the 1956 sugar nego-tiations, quotas were distributed by past performance, and Peru, a low cost producer who could not obtain a quota that was higher than 15 per cent below her 1937 quota, declined to join. Producers may be given large quotas regardless of past performance, efficiency or ability to fill them if the agreement would not be effective without their participation. Bolivia, a high cost tin producer, was given a quota in the first Tin Agreements which was not representative of her declining output. Thus, a given percentage restriction on her basic quota in a period of low prices would have a smaller proportional effect on her output than on the output of countries whose exports in periods of no restriction were above their basic quotas. Indonesia's basic quota in the first post-war Tin Agreement based on her pre-war position in the market could not be met with the reduction in her capacity with invasion during the war. In an effort to win the support of Indonesia and Thailand for the pre-war rubber cartels, large quotas were granted to these countries at Malaya's expense. If a country is a large supplier, like Brazil is of coffee, and possesses large stocks as a result of past attempts to raise the price, its bargaining position for a large basic quota is enhanced. Such a country will receive a quota that allows her to dispose of her stock and satisfies her in other respects since she could disrupt the market and undermine the agreement if she declined to join because the conditions of her participation were not favourable to her. Such inequities point up a major shortcoming of export quota schemes; success will depend largely on the participation of the bulk of producers. This need for wide participation makes concessions to some exporters, at the expense of others, almost inevitable. Under multilateral contracts, by comparison, freezing of the pattern of trade is relieved by the opportunity to sell on the residual market and there is no need for wide participation.

Export quota schemes perpetuate the initial pattern of trade only during periods of restriction and the apparent rigidity of *pro rata* reductions in exports under the schemes in periods of restrictions may be severely limited by a stipulated maximum restriction. In 1961, the last year of the first series of International Sugar Agreements, the special reserve and basic quota of the Sugar Agreement amounted to 6,545,000 tons and of this the Sugar Council had control over 1,266,000 tons, because of a limit placed on export restrictions. Net imports were about 20 million tons compared to production of 55 million tons. Since 1964 the Coffee Council has been permitted to alter quotas by only 6 per cent of the basic quota.

Although buffer stock devices cannot control the long run trend unless they are accompanied by provision for surplus disposal, export quota agreements will control the trend if they prevent expansion of low cost production or encourage the restriction of production. This

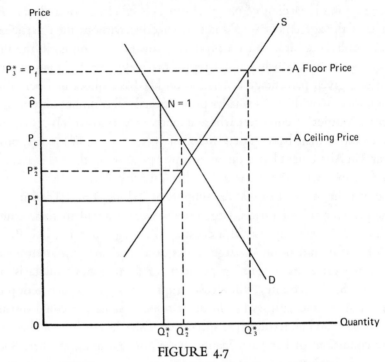

FIGURE 4.7

BUFFER STOCKS AND EXPORT QUOTAS WITH BUFFER FUNDS

aspect of their operation conflicts with the avowed purpose, expressed in the Havana Charter and GATT, to assure adequate supplies to consumers at prices that provide a reasonable return to producers. A long run equilibrium between supply and demand can be met if production restrictions are temporary and designed to eliminate a past accumulation of national stocks or facilitate reduction in output in a situation of chronic over-capacity.

k. BUFFER STOCKS AND EXPORT QUOTAS WITH A BUFFER FUND

Conditions for maximizing export earnings will alter if a buffer stock or export quota scheme is imposed on a national buffer fund which maximizes export earnings in the manner described in Chapter 3, Section 3b (p. 65). The Cocoa Agreement for instance will operate a buffer stock and export quota device in a market already characterized by various types of buffer funds, notably those which stabilize inter-year prices in former 'British' West Africa, the *caisses de stabilisation des prix* of former 'French' West Africa, and the multiple exchange rate schemes of Brazil.

Figure 4.7 illustrates the possible effect on the export earnings maximizing price when such a juxtaposition of devices occurs. If demand is of unit elasticity at price $\hat{P}$, the export earnings maximizing producer price will be P_1^* when the buffer fund operates alone. With the introduction of international buffer stock ceiling price control at P_c, below world price $\hat{P}$, the export earnings maximizing price will become P_2^* and export earnings will be reduced. Producer price P_2^* allows the world price to move as far as possible toward $\hat{P}$, given the constraint on its rise imposed by the ceiling price, and consequently maximizes earnings. The national device, in effect, makes the international device redundant, for with producer price P_2^* no international support is needed. If previously accumulated national stocks $Q_1^* Q_2^*$ are available for release, export earnings continue to be maximized with fixed producer price P_1^*. In a period of floor price support, with world price $\hat{P}$ below a floor price P_f, export earnings under an international buffer stock would be maximized by the highest possible producer price. If producers are not subsidized, the optimal producer price P_3^* will equal the floor price P_f.

5. SUMMARY

Buffer stocks and export quota devices stabilize producer and market prices by withholding supplies in periods of low prices and selling from stock in periods of high prices. This is in contrast with national buffer funds which stabilize producer price by withholding export earnings in periods of high price and supporting producer price out of stabilization funds in periods of low price. In doing so they destabilize market price by reducing output in periods of high and increasing it in periods of low price.

In a demand shift market under conditions of positive supply and negative demand elasticity, devices which stabilize producer price stabilize income. In a demand shift market an international buffer stock will stabilize export earnings because volume and price are reduced during periods of ceiling price control and increased during those of floor price control. Under the assumptions surrounding Figures 4.1 and 4.2 above, national buffer stocks and international export quota devices will destabilize export earnings in a demand shift demand elastic market and stabilize them in a demand shift demand inelastic market. Export quotas accompanied by production restriction will have a like effect. Efforts to stabilize price according to a price range symmetrically distributed between the equilibrium prices will lead to a net income and export earnings loss to producers which will diminish in magnitude as the controlled prices approach the uncontrolled market prices. Devices that hold stocks may recover losses by buying at the floor and selling at the ceiling price providing the difference is not accounted for by costs associated with the transactions and storage.

Price control devices which do not control the trend will destabilize producer earnings in a supply shift demand elastic market because volume and price will be increased in periods of high income and decreased in those of low income. Export earnings will be destabilized under national buffer funds, whether in a demand elastic or inelastic supply shift market. Net losses to exporters will occur under a national buffer stock or export quota scheme in a supply shift market if marginal revenue is negative and increasing, while gains will be made if it is positive and decreasing.

Although some risk to the price control authority is inevitable regardless of the device chosen, the total sum of risks appears greatest when control entails stockholding. Buffer funds involve no stocks and consequently avoid the risk of excessive stock accumulation and the costs associated with transactions and storage. Although stockholding devices may cover costs by buying at low and selling at high prices, the wider the price range is the less frequently will transactions be reversed while the narrower the range the stronger the device must be. Stockholding under an export quota scheme can be avoided by production restriction. The risk that funds under a buffer fund may be insufficient to support the floor price may be averted by a producer price below the lowest market price or by operating through a fluctuating exchange rate scheme that offers importers and exporters the same exchange rate. Stockholding devices can be initiated only in periods of low prices and depend for success in periods of ceiling price support upon the volume of previously accumulated stock. National buffer funds and the multilateral contracts and compensatory finance schemes to be discussed in the following pages may be initiated at any time.

Export quotas and international buffer stock devices are frequently considered to be necessary complements to one another. Buffer stocks react more readily to unexpected price movements while export quotas provide greater strength because they are not limited by the amount of prefinancing. However, a low permitted maximum percentage *pro rata* reduction on basic quotas in periods of export restriction may limit strength. Export quotas are considered a second line of defence because of their lagged reaction to market changes and inconvenience to exporting countries. If export quotas operate through production control, reaction may be further delayed if it is administratively difficult to implement restriction. Moreover, it may be undesirable for political and welfare reasons to prohibit harvest of a short crop that has already been planted. In periods of export restriction exporters must finance stocks held, or administer production control programmes, as well as forego foreign exchange earnings in a low price period. International buffer stocks, in contrast, support both the price and the volume of exports in periods of low price.

Export quotas and national and international buffer stocks run the risk of creating an excessive burden on producers if consumers reduce their stocks in the assurance that an increase in demand will be met by releases of exporter or international stocks. However, movements in commercial stocks may be reduced with price stabilization, reducing in turn the underlying instability that must be controlled. If the device controls the market price over the business cycle, and replaces the relative price fluctuations of manufactures and the primary commodity with changes in the opposite direction, the disparity between supply and demand at the price limits would be increased necessitating a stronger device than one which eliminates relative price fluctuations.

In order to break even, rather than collapse or accumulate excessive funds or stocks, buffer funds, buffer stocks and export quotas rely on an accurate projection of the trend and a flexibility that permits smoothing of fluctuations around the trend without control of the trend itself. Failure of a price control device to defend a price limit, because the range is too narrow relative to the device's capacity or because of an error in the trend projection, can cause a precipitous change in price at the point in time at which the market reverts from the controlled to the equilibrium price. Disruption can be particularly severe under a stockholding device which unsuccessfully defends a floor price, for accumulated stocks may overhang the market, incur mounting storage fees and perpetuate and aggravate an unfavourable situation with their eventual disposal on the market.

Where trade is between developed and developing countries correct projections of the trend, if available, may not be followed in establishing price limits. Developed importing countries may see concessionary trade through a high price range as a constructive means of allowing transfers in wealth between the rich and not-so-rich. Although they may consent to a high price range, they may not take the more difficult step of providing facilities for its maintenance. A buffer stock with a high price range would need, for instance, considerable financial resources to support a large volume of floor price purchases and to subsidize disposal of stock which was not sold in periods of ceiling price support. Aid through concessionary trade is unpopular among some donor countries because of the lack of selectivity. No discrimination is made between countries or individuals within recipient countries and the aid may foster a higher level of consumption, rather than a higher level of investment in activities which promote external equilibrium and economic growth.

National export restriction schemes can reduce market share by raising the world price and, consequently, encouraging production elsewhere. If local capacity is not reduced with restriction and output elsewhere increases, price could decline below previous levels when the restriction is lifted. Under international export restriction schemes market share may be frozen through a fixed allocation of basic quotas. In the freezing of the pattern of trade those countries which are capable of expansion of output at low prices are restrained in the interests of high cost marginal producers who would not survive in a competitive market and of the consumer who is assured that production capacity in the high cost producing countries is maintained. Fixing of the trade pattern, discrimination against non-members, production restriction, and surplus disposal of buffer stocks over the long run will raise the trend of prices. If demand is elastic in the long run, export earnings will decline. Production restriction and surplus disposal of stocks on a temporary basis may occur without threatening long run consumer interests if they are used to reduce a previous accumulation of stocks by exporting countries or chronic overcapacity.

The magnitude of net gains or losses to producers from international commodity control is elusive both before and after the fact. Even if the costs and benefits cited above could be identified and quantified, it would also be important to know the extent to which fluctuations in export earnings are transmitted to the economy and the effect this has on the rate of economic growth and the distribution of income before a meaningful policy judgement could be reached.

Readings

Ali, L., 'The Regulation of Trade in Tea', *Journal of World Trade Law*, Vol. 4, No. 4, July–August 1970, pp. 565–85.

Baer, W., & Herve, M.E.A., 'Multiple Exchange Rates and the Attainment of Multiple Policy Objectives', *Economica* (*N.S.*) Vol. 39, 1962, pp. 176–84.

Bateman, D.I., 'A Further Comment', *Journal of Agricultural Economics*, Vol. 17, September 1966, p. 201.

————, 'Buffer Stocks and Producers' Income', *Journal of Agricultural Economics*, Vol. 16, December 1965, pp. 573–75.

Bauer, P.T., & Yamey, B.S., 'Organised Commodity Stabilisation with Voluntary Participation', *Oxford Economic Papers*, (N.S.) Vol. 16, No. 1, March 1964, pp. 105–13.

Beringer, C., 'Real Effects of Foreign Surplus Disposal in Underdeveloped Economies: Comment', *Quarterly Journal of Economics*, Vol. 77, May 1963, pp. 317–23.

Bilder, R.B., 'The International Coffee Agreement, a Case History in Negotiation', *Law and Contemporary Problems*, Vol. 28, No. 2, 1963, pp. 328–91.

Blau, G., 'International Commodity Arrangements', *Monthly Bulletin of Agricultural Economics & Statistics*, Vol. 12, No. 9, September 1963, pp. 1–9. Also in *Agriculture in Economic Development*, ed. Eicher, C., & Witt, L., 1964, Ch. 20., and *Problems in Economic Development*, Ed., Robinson, E.A.G., MacMillan, 1965, pp. 553–71.

————, 'International Commodity Arrangements and Policies', *Commodity Policy Series No. 16*, FAO, Rome 1964.

Brown, C.P., 'International Commodity Control through National Buffer Stocks: A Case Study of Natural Rubber', *Journal of Development Studies*, Vol. 10, No. 2, 1974.

————, 'Short Run Static Price & Income Effects of Cocoa Control', *Journal of Development Studies*, Vol. 6, No. 3, April 1970, pp. 267–81.

————, 'Some Implications of Tin Price Stabilisation', *Malayan Economic Review*, Vol. 17, No. 1, April 1972 pp. 99–118.

Campbell, K.O., & Powell, A.A., 'Revenue Implications of a Buffer Stock Scheme with an Uncertain Demand Schedule', *Economic Record*, Vol. 38, No. 83, September 1962, pp. 373–85.

Cordon, W.M., 'The Exchange Rate System and the Taxation of Trade', in Silcock, T.H., (ed.), *Thailand: Social and Economic Studies in Development*, Canberra, 1967.

Courtenay, P.P., 'International Tin Restriction and its Effects on the Malayan Tin Industry', *Geography*, Vol. 46, 1961, pp. 223–31.

Cracknell, M.P., 'The Slippery Path to an Oilseeds Agreement', *Journal of World Trade Law*, Vol. 4, No. 6, Nov.–Dec. 1970, pp. 743–69.

D'Amico, S., Eastwood, S.T., & Tyszynski, H., 'New Proposals for the Stabilization of Incomes of Primary Producers', *FAO Monthly Bulletin of Agricultural Economics & Statistics*, Vol. 11, No. 7, July 1963, pp. 7–14.

de Vries, M.G., 'Multiple Exchange Rates: Expectations and Experiences,' *IMF Staff Papers*, Vol. 12, 1965, pp. 282–311.

Duloy, J.H., 'More on Buffer Stocks and Producers' Incomes', *Journal of Agricultural Economics*, Vol. 17, September 1966, pp. 197–201.

————, 'On the Variance Effects of a Buffer Stock Scheme: A Simulation Study of a Floor Price Plan for Wool', *Australian Economic Papers*, Vol. 4, 1965, pp. 79–92.

————, 'Some Variance Effects of a Floor Price Scheme for Wool: A Two-Period Analysis', *Australian Journal of Agricultural Economics*, Vol. 8, No. 1, June 1964, pp. 74–80.

Edwards, J., 'The International Tin Agreements', *Journal of World Trade Law*, Vol. 3, No. 3, May–June 1969, pp. 237–50.

FAO, 'Observations on the Proposed International Sugar Agreement', *Commodity Policy Series No. 4*, Rome, June 1953.

Falcon, W.P., 'Real Effects of Foreign Surplus Disposal in Underdeveloped Countries: Further Comment', *Quarterly Journal of Economics*, Vol. 77, May 1963, pp. 323–6.

Fisher, F.M., 'A Theoretical Analysis of the Impact of Food Surplus Disposal on Agricultural Production in Recipient Countries', *Journal of Farm Economics*, Vol. 45, November 1963, pp. 863–75.

French-Davis, R.M., 'Export Quotas & Allocative Efficiency under Market Instability', *American Journal of Agricultural Economics*, Vol. 50, No. 3, August 1968, pp. 643–59.

Galloway, L.T., 'The International Coffee Agreement', *Journal of World Trade Law*, Vol. 7, No. 3, May/June 1973, pp. 354–74.

Gerhard, H.W., 'Commodity Trade Stabilization through International Agreements', *Law and Contemporary Problems*, Vol. 28, No. 2, 1963, pp. 276–93.

Grubel, H.G., 'Foreign Exchange Earnings and Price Stabilization Schemes', *American Economic Review*, Vol. 54, No. 4, June 1964, pp. 378–85.

Heymann, H., 'The International Tin Scheme', *Problems in Economic Development*, ed., Robinson, E.A.G., MacMillan 1965, pp. 599–614.

Howell, L.D., 'Does the Consumer Benefit from Price Instability?' *Quarterly Journal of Economics*, Vol. 59, February 1945, pp. 287–295.

Kanesa-Thasan, S., 'Multiple Exchange Rates: The Indonesian Experience', *IMF Staff Papers*, Vol. 13, No. 2, July 1966, pp. 354–68.

Khatkhate, D.R., 'Some Notes on the Real Effects of Foreign Surplus Disposal in Underdeveloped Economies', *Quarterly Journal of Economics*, Vol. 78, November 1964, pp. 653–8.

Knorr, K.E., *Tin Under Control*, Stanford, 1945.

Longworth, J.W., 'The Australian Wheat Industry Stabilization Scheme: An Analytical Model', *Economic Record*, Vol. 42, June 1966, pp. 244–55.

Lovasy, G., 'Further Comment', *Quarterly Journal of Economics*, Vol. 59, February 1945, pp. 296–301.

Mason, E.S., *Controlling World Trade*, McGraw-Hill, 1946.

Massell, B.F., 'Some Welfare Implications of International Price Stabilization', *Journal of Political Economy*, Vol. 78, No. 2, March/April 1970, pp. 404–17.

McKinnon, R.I., 'Futures Markets, Buffer Stocks & Income Stability for Primary Producers', *Journal of Political Economy*, Vol. 75, No. 6, December 1967, pp. 844–61.

Meade, J.E., 'International Commodity Agreements', *Proceedings of UNCTAD*, Vol. 3, New York, 1964, pp. 451–57.

Ojala, E.M., 'Some Current Issues of International Commodity Policy', *Journal of Agricultural Economics*, Vol. 18, No. 1, January 1967, pp. 27–51.

Olson, R.O., 'The Impact & Implications of Foreign Surplus Disposal on Underdeveloped Economies', *Journal of Farm Economics*, Vol. 42, December 1960, pp. 1042–5.

Pincus, J., 'Commodity Agreements: Bonanza or Illusion?', *Columbian Journal of World Business*, Vol. 2, 1967.

Porter, R.C., 'The Optimal Price Problem in Buffer Fund Stabilization', *Oxford Economic Papers*, Vol. 16, No. 3, November 1964, pp. 423–30.

Radetzki, M., *International Commodity Market Arrangements*, C. Hurst, London, 1970, pp. 86–102.

Riefler, W.W., 'A Proposal for an International Buffer Stock Agency', *Journal of Political Economy*, Vol. 54, December 1946, pp. 538–46.

Robertson, W., 'The Tin Experiment in Commodity Market Stabilization', *Oxford Economic Papers*, Vol. 12, October 1960, pp. 310–35.

Rowe, op. cit. pp. 120–55 and 169–208.

Schmidt, W.E., 'The Case Against Commodity Agreements', *Law and Contemporary Problems*, Vol. 28, No. 2, 1963, pp. 313–27.

Sen, S.R., 'The Impact & Implications of Foreign Surplus Disposal on Underdeveloped Economies—the Indian Perspective', *Journal of Farm Economics*, Vol. 42, December 1960, pp. 1031–42.

Snape, R.H., & Yamey, B.S., 'A Diagrammatic Analysis of Some Effects of Buffer Fund Price Stabilization', *Oxford Economic Papers*, (New Series), Vol. 15, July 1963, pp. 95–106.

Southgate, J., 'World Trade in Sugar', *Journal of World Trade Law*, Vol. 1, No. 6, November–December, 1967, pp. 595–631.

Swerling, B.C., & Timoshenko, V.P., *The World's Sugar*, Stanford, 1965.

Swerling, B.C., 'Problems of International Commodity Stabilization', *American Economic Review*, Vol. 53, pp. 65–74.

———— 'Current Issues in Commodity Policy', *Essays in International Finance No.38*, Princeton, June 1962.

———— 'The Free Market and the International Sugar Agreement of 1953', *American Economic Review*, Vol. 44, December 1954, pp. 324–51.

UNCTAD, *The Development of an International Commodity Policy Study*, TD/8/Supp.1, New Delhi, 14 November 1967.

Wassermann, U., 'International Cocoa Agreement 1972', *Journal of World Trade Law*, Vol. 7, No. 1, January/February 1973, pp. 129–34.

———— 'Towards an International Cocoa Agreement', *Journal of World Trade Law*, Vol. 2, No. 5, September–October 1968, pp. 521–43.

Wickizer, V.D., *Coffee, Tea & Cocoa*, Stanford, 1951.

——————— 'International Collaboration in the World Coffee Market', *Food Research Institute Studies*, Vol. 4, No. 2, 1964.

Yates, P.L., *Commodity Control: A Study of Primary Products*, Jonathan Cape, London, 1943.

Yip Yat Hoong, 'Domestic Implementation of the 1953 International Tin Agreement', *Malayan Economic Review*, Vol. 5, No. 2, October 1960, pp. 59–65.

Yong Shu-Chin, *Multiple Exchange Rate System: An Appraisal of Thailand's Experience 1946–1955*, University of Wisconsin Press, 1957.

Waugh, F.U., 'Reply', *Quarterly Journal of Economics*, Vol. 59, February 1945, pp. 301–303.

Zaglits, O., 'International Price Control through Buffer Stocks', *American Journal of Farm Economics*, Vol. 28, No. 2, May 1946, pp. 413–43.

See also articles on buffer funds-cum-export taxes in Chapter 3, Readings.

V
Multilateral Contracts, Compensatory Finance and Demand Expansion Schemes

1. INTRODUCTION

MULTILATERAL contracts and compensatory finance are among the least used conventional international devices. To date the multilateral contract has been confined to the post-war Wheat Agreements while compensatory finance for fluctuations in the export earnings of individual primary commodities has been introduced only recently on a limited scale by the International Monetary Fund (IMF). They are considered together here because the two tend to have like effects on the economic environment in which they operate when administered in a similar manner. The chapter includes a brief consideration of monetized and non-monetized multi-commodity buffer stocks in order to give the reader a taste of some of the proposed but as yet untried devices that lie on the fringes of thought about commodity control. International actions designed to raise demand through new markets, new uses and sales promotion, although not as prescribed as the international devices of this and the preceding chapter, are discussed since they are receiving increasing attention and may as effectively accomplish some of the control objectives because they directly attack the underlying problem of a lagging growth in demand relative to supply. In conclusion, important aspects of voting in council, escape clauses and the means of effectuating a new or renegotiated international agreement are considered.

2. MULTILATERAL CONTRACTS

In most of the literature on multilateral contracts and in practice in the Wheat Agreements the importer is committed to buy not less than an established minimum amount of the controlled commodity at not less than a floor price. The producer is required to supply not less than a minimum amount at not more than a ceiling price. Where such commitments are met by intergovernmental payments equal to the difference between the world price and the price limits for the contract volume the device amounts to a form of compensatory finance. The intergovernmental transfer aspect predominates as well when governments of exporting and importing countries trade the contracted amount at the price limits without passing on the losses or gains to producers and consumers. Multilateral contracts and compensatory finance as commonly understood are differentiated by the actual, and perhaps unnecessary, government intervention on both sides of the market with the former and the emphasis on export earnings rather than a specific volume and price with the latter.

In contrast to buffer stocks and export quotas, multilateral contracts do not specifically aim at maintaining the world price at a pre-determined level, and their strength is not dependent upon wide support. Unlike buffer funds, which can be introduced only in periods of high prices if there is no pre-financing, or buffer stocks and export quotas which can be introduced only in those of low prices, multilateral contracts and compensatory finance schemes which include obligations and benefits to both producers and consumers may be introduced at any time. Where transfers are to be made only to developing exporting countries however, such schemes will begin only in periods of low prices or incomes.

a. THE ROUTINE

A diagrammatic rendering of the multilateral contract routine is given in Figure 5.1a, illustrating a demand shift market. In perfect anticipation of the uncontrolled market prices, negotiators of the contract place price limits at P_f and P_c such that P_1P_f equals P_cP_2. The contract is for OC. It is assumed that contracts are not made larger than the lowest equilibrium output, Q_1. If they were, benefits would be unequally divided as exporters would not be able to meet the full contract in a period of low price and thus would receive less from consumers than given in return in a period of high price. In the period of low price, the amount denoted by a is transferred to exporters and in the period of high price a like amount denoted by b is transferred from exporters to consumers. These transfers stabilize export earnings in a demand shift market since they move inversely with uncontrolled

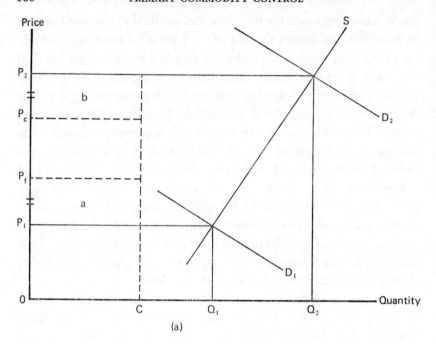

(a)

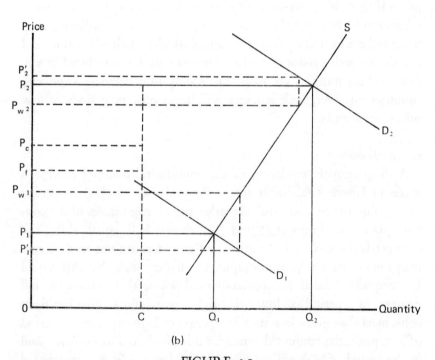

(b)

FIGURE 5.1

THE ROUTINE AND EFFECTS OF A MULTILATERAL
CONTRACT IN A DEMAND SHIFT MARKET

market earnings. If producer price remains unaffected no net change in export earnings or producer income will occur over the two periods. In a low price and export earnings period the device works in the right direction but does not provide the stability of an international buffer stock because it compensates for the fall in price but not in volume. If the price elasticity of supply were small, however, most of the change in earnings might be countered.

The possible stabilizing effect of a multilateral contract in a supply shift market will depend on the elasticity of demand. If demand is elastic, periods of low producer income and export earnings will coincide with transfers to consumers while receipts from consumers will occur in periods of high producer income and export earnings. In a supply shift demand inelastic market earnings may be destabilized (through a reverse instability) if the price range is sufficiently narrow and/or the size of the contract a sufficiently large proportion of total exports (i.e. if in Fig. 5.2b, p. 170, $P_1 Q_1 - P_2 Q_2 < (P_2 Q_2 + b) - (P_1 Q_1 - a)$).

The above observations would hold if the weighted average price received by the exporting country under the contract is passed on to the producer only after production and export have occurred and if producers do not anticipate sharing in the transfer. Once either of these two conditions are not met, the effect becomes contingent upon a number of less tangible factors. If the producer, say, anticipates receiving the weighted average of prices P_1 & P_c, that is P_{w1}, in Figure 5.1b or actually receives it at the time of sale, output would expand as shown, with price P_1' being realized on sales in the residual market; P_{w1} would no longer be the weighted average of free and controlled prices. If some attempt is made by the exporting government to pass on some of the benefits to producers in a low price period, output will expand and residual market price decline. Depending on the increase in producer price above P_1, the gain under the contract may be lost to sales on the residual market. Likewise, attempts in periods of high price to pass some of the obligations under the contract on to the producer will reduce output and increase residual market price and some or all of the cost of the obligations may be recovered in the residual market. The effect over the two periods is to destabilize the residual market price. Such instability can be avoided by concurrently operating a buffer stock which, say, keeps residual market price at the weighted average prices P_{w1} and P_{w2}. Since under the assumptions of the diagram more would be bought at the floor than sold at the ceiling ($P_1 P_{w1} > P_{w2} P_2$), a production restriction scheme would also be needed to insure that purchases and sales by the buffer stock were balanced. In this event, however, the contract would become superfluous as the market would be fully controlled by the buffer stock and production control scheme. McCalla (1966) and others have maintained that under the Wheat Agreements world price has been controlled by such producer buffer stocks and production control. The contract has been seen by some as window dressing since producers have exercised their power to fix world prices at levels that suited their interests.

b. No-volume Schemes

One suggested variation of the above type of contract is a no-volume guarantee under which funds equal to actual volume traded times the price difference would be transferred. In Figure 5.2a illustrating a demand shift market, producers would receive $OQ_1.P_1P_f$ in the low price and income period and forego $OQ_2.P_cP_2$ in that of high price and income. If the price limits P_f and P_c are symmetrically distributed between the uncontrolled market prices, producers would suffer a net loss of $Q_1Q_2.P_1P_f$. An alternative that has been suggested is to pay compensation on an established volume even though a lesser amount is traded. With reference to Figure 5.2a, if the established volume were Q_2 the gain to producers in the high price period would equal the loss in the low price period and a net income transfer would be avoided. Schemes involving a guaranteed volume of transactions within the price limits, like this one and the one covered in the previous section, have the advantage over no-volume schemes of insuring that the loser in any period does not redirect trade so as to avoid the loss. Under both types of schemes concessionary trade objectives with producing countries as the beneficiaries would be met by a contract without a ceiling price and with the highest possible proportion of guaranteed transactions at the highest negotiable floor price.

The treatment of obligations under the Wheat Agreements has varied considerably. The early agreements conformed to the classical model by specifying contracted volumes with price limits which applied only to those volumes. The 1959 and 1962 Agreements stipulated that if world prices were at or above the ceiling price, the obligations of exporters would continue to be defined in terms of pre-established quantities while those of importers were to be determined as a percentage of imports of wheat from all sources. Moreover, importers' commitments were applied throughout the price range and not only at the floor as previously. The 1967 Wheat Trade Convention has further required that members on both sides of the market are obliged to observe the price limits when trading with non-members. These new obligations

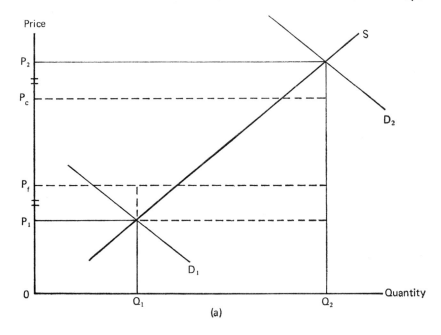

(a)

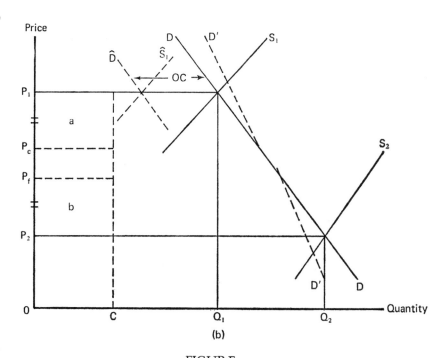

(b)

FIGURE 5.2

NO–VOLUME CONTRACTS AND POSSIBLE EFFECTS
OF CONTRACTS ON THE RESIDUAL MARKET

do not prevent member exporting countries from making sales at prices above the ceiling so long as certain ancillary obligations are observed. Commitments relating to guaranteed quantities still essentially apply only to members.

c. The Residual Market

It has already been shown that if producer price is stabilized by the contract, world price will be destabilized (for the same reasons that apply under a national buffer fund). Some early commentators feared as well that supply or demand fluctuations would have a greater proportional impact on the residual market than on the market as a whole and therefore further destabilize residual market price. A 20 per cent fluctuation of 90–110 in total supply or demand would be doubled in relative magnitude if the market was halved by a multilateral contract such that residual market supply or demand fluctuated from 40–60. This argument, however, failed to allow for the fact that the change in one of the residual market functions would be accompanied by an identical change in the other function. If the contract is for OC, as shown in Figure 5.2b, residual market supply and demand is derived by a horizontal subtraction of OC from aggregate supply and demand. An equal horizontal leftward shift of D and S_1 by OC to $\hat{D}$ and $\hat{S}_1$ has no effect on the equilibrium price.

Johnson (1950) has argued that the income effect of multilateral contract transfers will destabilize residual market price. That which is saved by consumers in periods of ceiling price support increases their income and their demand if the commodity is a normal good. The converse occurs during periods of floor price support. The effect on the demand function is illustrated in Figure 5.2b. Demand becomes increasingly greater for prices beyond the ceiling price since the higher the uncontrolled market price relative to the ceiling the greater are consumer savings. Thus, above the ceiling demand develops according to D'. The reverse occurs below the floor price limit and the net effect is to decrease demand elasticity for extreme prices and increase price fluctuations on the residual market. Effects on the residual market, however, will be determined by the way participating countries administer their obligations under the contract. Were governments to agree to pay the difference in prices to each other annually and to pass these changes on to the general taxpayer, there would be no short run effect on the residual market. On the other hand, if they buy and sell the contracted quantity at the price limits, importing governments would have to administer the price so that some consumers were not paying the floor or ceiling price and others the residual market price. To do this, they could establish a stabilization reserve in high price periods, allowing consumers to pay the residual market price and using funds accumulated to finance obligations in low price periods in which case the scheme would have no effect on demand. Where import quotas exist, as they do most notably for cane sugar, consumers may not be in a position to spend additional incomes on imports of the commodity.

If the income effect is lagged and the price range is such that the average price is within it, the effect on income may be felt within the acceptable range of prices. Any long run effect might be neutralized by increases in the demand and supply elasticities due to reduced risk of trading under control. Even if there is a short run income effect it may be nominal. If the disposable income of North America, for instance, is, $1,000 billion and consumer savings under a contract in a period of ceiling price support is $10 million, the change in the quantity demanded would be 0.0002 per cent if the short run income elasticity of demand were 0.2. Savings or losses to consumers due to a multilateral contract may go unnoticed if they are not reflected in retail price changes, if the retail price changes but marginally, or if habits of consumption change gradually.

One of the principle advantages of the multilateral contract device is that it preserves the free market mechanism as an indicator of the underlying equilibrium position. Under the buffer stock and export quota devices the equilibrium position is indicated only by the volume of support at the price limits. It may be estimated if the supply and demand elasticities and the volume of support are known. If, however, the residual market under a multilateral contract is narrow and subject to the magnitude of speculative forces that existed on the wider uncontrolled market, residual market price may not be a reliable indicator of the equilibrium position. The residual market did not indicate the equilibrium under the Wheat Agreements because exporters controlled residual market prices with national buffer stocks. Residual market prices would have been driven below the floor of the contract in 1953/54 by exceptionally large harvests in exporting countries. In order to avoid the embarrassing spectacle of developing importing countries making transfers to the developed exporting countries, world price was held above the floor by national buffer stock activities. Although a transfer under the contract was avoided, developing consumer countries paid more per unit of wheat imports than they would have done if the residual market price had been allowed to seek its own level and they had met their obligations under the contract.

d. Purchase Guarantees

Demand for primary products imported by developed countries could be stabilized by unilateral or multilateral purchase guarantees operated by single or groups of importing developed countries. Unlike the multilateral contracts discussed above, the developed countries alone would have obligations. If the developed countries are exporters the procedure could work in reverse, as it has in fact for wheat, with exporters unilaterally stabilizing export supply. Purchase guarantees could operate through a national buffer stock or series of co-ordinated national buffer stocks in importing countries. All sales and purchases would continue to be at market prices. In periods of low demand, importing governments operating a buffer stock would undertake to purchase any shortfall in the volume of private imports while in periods of high demand private importers would buy some of their needs from domestic buffer stocks. Alternatively demand could be stabilized by standby temporary tariff reductions, liberalization of quantitative restrictions or temporary withdrawal of subsidies or price support for domestic producers when import demand declined. Purchase guarantees would stabilize export earnings of developing countries in a demand shift market but could disrupt those in one of supply shift demand inelasticity since attempts to maintain import volume in a period of low export volume and high price and earnings would further raise price and earnings and reduce consumption. Stocks accumulated in high price low volume periods would be disposed of during low price high volume periods, further reducing world price. Losses would be made by the buffer stock, world price would be destabilized and, if demand is inelastic, export earnings would be destabilized.

Benoit (1959) has suggested a form of import guarantee to assure developing countries a fixed share in domestic demand expansion over the long run. Barriers to trade would be reduced when the ratio of imports to domestic production fell below a pre-established level so that domestic production would not be substituted for imports; imports would thus be assured as rapid a growth as that of domestic production. These conditions are most nearly met in the United States' meat-sharing plan which assures participation of imports from developing countries in market growth. Under the plan imports from developing countries have increased faster than domestic production and imports from other developed countries. In the sugar and other long established preferential arrangements, by contrast, imports are regarded as a residual used to meet needs after all domestic production has been absorbed and domestic price goals attained. More recently under the General System of

Preferences endorsed by UNCTAD hundreds of tariff positions of the developed countries have been reduced or eliminated for imports from developing countries. This action has elevated these imports from a strictly residual status by providing for their possible substitution for domestic production.

3. COMPENSATORY FINANCE

a. USES OF COMPENSATION

Compensatory finance schemes provide compensation for shortfalls in export earnings from a base period, moving average of earnings, trend estimate or immediately preceding period. Compensation can be for the full amount of the shortfall or for some proportion of it. If compensation is reciprocal or in the form of a loan, producers would forego earnings in normal and/or favourable periods. Conventional quantitative devices, such as those discussed in the last chapter, may, like compensation schemes, stabilize export earnings and producer income in demand shift markets but they may also reduce earnings and in supply shift markets destabilize them. Price control schemes more-over, aggravate the problems which arise from fluctuations in output of individual countries which are not in the same direction as for all countries and they frequently introduce undesirable forms of discrimination against members and non-members. These undesirable effects can be avoided in compensatory schemes specifically directed to the maintenance and stability of export earnings.

A major advantage of the device is the generality of its application. It can be used for all exports regardless of homogeneity and perishability and it applies without distinction to fluctuations in earnings whether these originate on the demand or supply side of the market. In contrast to the multilateral contract and other conventional devices, compensatory finance allows consideration of volume as well as price. Neither demand shift markets or other specific conditions are requisites for the device's stabilizing effect. Like multilateral contracts, the arrangement may operate between a few or many countries without effect on its viability and without discriminating against those who do not participate. Some of the stumbling blocks in negotiation experienced with other devices—such as fixing price limits and distribution of export quotas—are avoided. However, where compensatory finance aims at compensation for changes in the income terms of trade, negotiations may falter on matters of index construction and the usefulness of this criterion as a measure of welfare. Moreover, it is sometimes difficult to induce developed countries to contribute toward export earnings shortfalls which result from internal factors such as expanded domestic consumption, political crises or inflation. Compensatory finance does not pretend to cope with the efficiency aspects of price changes, for it avoids interference with market forces. These tend to be specific to commodities and individual producing countries, and their solutions may best be left to national devices. Compensatory finance is generally agnostic to the effects of the market on individual producers in exporting countries since its purpose is to prevent short run reduction in export earnings from impeding economic growth, either as a result of reduced aggregate domestic income or foreign exchange.

Because it stabilizes export earnings, a compensation scheme is complementary to devices which are weak or detrimental in this respect. National buffer funds in supply shift demand inelastic markets, for instance, would be augmented since export earnings as well as producer income would be stabilized. With external funds available to support producer income in low income years, a buffer fund could be initiated in a period of floor support. Compensatory funds could serve as an external source of financing national buffer stocks or stocks accumulated under an export restriction scheme and consequently eliminate the instability in export earnings experienced under these devices. The arrangement could further be used to moderate the reduction in export earnings which occurs under buffer funds, buffer stocks and export quotas in periods of demand shift. In those circumstances in which these three devices stabilize export earnings they would support compensatory finance action in that actual payments of compensation would be smaller than otherwise. Finally, compensation schemes can be used to right individual wrongs when conventional controls are applied *pro rata*, as they nearly always are, and thus overlook exceptional circumstances. If, for instance, one exporting country in a demand inelastic world market does not share an increase in income enjoyed by others in a low output period (because her proportional decrease in output is greater than the proportional increase in price) but is forced under a multilateral contract to make a transfer to consumers, her export earnings could be stabilized by a compensatory transfer.

In weighing the advantages of compensatory finance against the disadvantages one detraction is that only part of the balance-of-payments problem is considered. Compensatory finance for shortfalls in export earnings would not, for instance, be available if the shortfall arose from excessive imports or debt repayments in the face of stable export earnings. Where compensatory finance takes the form of short or intermediate term financing of a self-liquidating nature, in contrast to grants or contingent loans, repayment could aggravate shortfalls if the long term trend is downward. In addition, automatic and unconditional rendering of compensation provides no assurance that useful steps will be taken to remove the cause of the deficit or that the assistance will be used generally for investment activities designed to promote external equilibrium and economic growth. For this reason it may be more desirable to make funds available under a programme of managed assistance. If attaching strings to compensation is likely to be resented as undue interference in the domestic affairs of developing by the developed countries, the scheme may be most appreciated and effectively administered if managed by an independent international agency such as the IMF. Automatic compensation by grants is unwise if recipient countries adopt policies which result in a decline in export earnings with the assurance that such decline will be automatically compensated by a transfer of funds which do not have to be returned. The premium placed on instability would be reduced if the recipient was required to repay the compensation should the shortfall be succeeded by gains in the short or medium run but not required to do so if the recovery was incomplete or delayed, and it was shown that the shortfall was beyond its control. Inequities also arise if a uniform system of contributions to the international agency making payment is applied. Under the proposal for a United Nations Development Insurance Fund, all members would pay a premium related to GNP or export earnings regardless of their degree of risk; even if risks are identical, some countries are better able to absorb shortfalls in export earnings than others. (This fund would permit developing countries to draw more than they contribute and thus, unlike a true insurance scheme, would also be a vehicle for the distribution of aid.)

Where compensation for a decline in export earnings is available according to an automatic formula, compensation may have little relevance to a particular country. Discretion is reduced by the automatic application of rules which are common to all participants. If, for instance, compensation is made for shortfalls in export earnings from a three year moving average and earnings develop 80, 100 and 120, giving an average of 100, and if in the fourth year they fall to 100, no compensation would be forthcoming on the 18 per cent decline. If the proportion of the shortfall to be compensated is fixed such that shortfalls of five per cent would go uncompensated, earnings in the fourth year would have to decline below 95 before compensation began. If the series were 120, 120, 120, and 100, the exporting country would be compensated for nearly three-fourths of its shortfall in the fourth year. Compensation could be made according to an agreed normal volume and price. This would avoid dependence upon earnings in the previous years but would bring its own inequities. If, for instance, the agreed volume and price placed earnings at 100, no compensation would occur for either of the fourth year shortfalls given above. It would seem more reasonable to compensate according to the shortfall from the previous year or not relate compensation to shortfall at all but rather to overall balance-of-payments position. Those who support the rule that, whatever the system upon which a shortfall is determined, there should be some established minimum decline before compensation begins argue that shortfalls should to some extent be supported with drawings on the country's foreign exchange reserves, for this is the purpose of reserves. Automatic compensation would have unequal effects since funds would go primarily to those with large and fluctuating export earnings, not necessarily to those who need it most. Prosperous countries like Malaysia with ample reserves but subject to volatile export earnings would benefit more than others like India whose level of export earnings is relatively stable but small. Where incomes are particularly low and/or compensatory monetary and fiscal facilities inadequate, even moderate fluctuations in earnings can cause hardship and retard growth. Unfortunately, no satisfactory measure exists for determining the level below which reserves cannot fall without threatening a crisis. For this reason automatic compensation as well as the rule of a minimum decline before compensation loses much of its cogency. The proper amount and timing of compensation will depend on the individual case.

Like the other control devices discussed in this and the preceding chapter, a compensatory finance device designed to break-even in the short or medium run does not assure a solution to long run problems. Long term loans and grants may be needed to enable a country to make the structural readjustments discussed in Chapter 3 that combat declining or unstable export earnings. Long term projects should not depend for their financing on short term increases in export earnings. It takes time to evaluate and initiate projects and specific projects must be fitted into the priorities, timing and complementarities of the collection of projects of which long term development plans are made. Development assistance agencies interested in long term growth might, however, provide supplementary financing at short notice for projects which were in danger of being delayed or eliminated by unforeseen shortfalls in export earnings.

b. International Monetary Fund Compensatory Schemes

The IMF is the principle agency dealing with short term compensatory finance. The World Bank together with a large number of national and international agencies are more concerned with longer term efforts to reduce instability. (Tinbergen (1959) has envisaged an International Treasury that would perform both functions. It would also serve to correct cyclical fluctuations, in the manner of a central bank, by inflationary financing of its stabilization expenditures during a depression and deflationary action during a boom.) The World Bank provides support to members who have long term financial commitments to commodity stocks, but such compensatory support is provided only in an indirect manner. When development loans are being considered account will be taken of requirements for foreign exchange arising from participation in approved commodity stock schemes. The Bank will also provide direct long term support by financing, for example, a commodity control storage facility, as well as less direct support of projects that reduce the effects of external disequilibrium.

i. *The Compensatory Facility*

In addition to the gold and credit tranche drawing facilities (which themselves provide a form of compensatory finance, the gold tranche representing a largely automatic drawing right) the IMF operates three facilities which aim primarily at the stabilization of foreign exchange availabilities to developing countries. Under the compensatory facility the availability of foreign exchange is stabilized by loans made on a temporary basis during periods of low export earnings compared to the medium term trend with the understanding that the transaction will be reversed in three to five years, or sooner if export earnings exceed the medium term trend. After the end of the four years following a drawing, members are encouraged to repay an amount of approximately one half of any excess of export earnings over the medium term trend.

Payment under the compensatory facility is not automatic. If export earnings over the latest twelve month period for which the Fund has statistical data have fallen short of the estimated medium term trend, defined as the five year moving average centered on the shortfall year, the Fund will consider requests for drawings. The determination of the trend itself would seem to be open to varying interpretation for it is based partly on a forecast of earnings. Moreover, in order to qualify for a drawing on the facility, the shortfall must have occurred for circumstances beyond the exporting country's immediate control, it must be the cause of the balance-of-payments problem and the exporter must have taken or pledge to take corrective action, which meets the Fund's approval, to forestall a repetition of the problem. These eligibility tests, however, are less searching than those applied to credit tranches under the tranche policies. When the appropriate conditions are met payment can be for the full amount of the shortfall. However compensatory drawings outstanding cannot increase by more than 25 per cent of the member's quota in any twelve month period except if the Fund is especially pleased with the member's cooperation in finding solutions to underlying problems or under exceptional circumstances such as a national disaster. The total amount outstanding cannot exceed 50 per cent of quota. Therefore, large requests exceeding 25 per cent of quota may not be met in full while smaller requests are more likely to be.

Drawings under the compensatory facility can occur only after a shortfall has occurred since a shortfall must be shown to exist. In anticipation of a drawing on the facility, exporters may make ordinary drawings which are later reclassified under the facility if the above conditions are met. Drawings on the facility are considered additional to and separate from ordinary drawing rights. Thus, when reclassification occurs, ordinary gold and credit tranche drawing rights are restored. In making the ordinary drawing to *avert* a shortfall, conditions of eligibility will become increasingly severe with the size of the drawing and outstanding drawings.

ii. *The Buffer Stock Facility*

The Fund offers short run compensation for contributions to an international buffer stock since these may be substantial and an important source of short run shortfalls in foreign exchange. Such compensation can reduce drawings under the compensatory facility for if the buffer stock operates in a demand shift market or a supply shift demand inelastic market (subject to the conditions covered in Chapter 3, Section 4, p. 78), price stabilization may stabilize export earnings. Unlike the compensatory facility, which aims to offset shortfalls, this facility is designed to avert them.

Financing of international buffer stock commitments is provided to members indirectly because direct lending from the Fund to a commodity agency would require amendment of the articles of agreement and possibly reduce the Fund's power to deny access to the facility to countries which clearly do not need assistance. The facility is only available to those who can show they have a balance-of-payments need. If the controlled export is a minor product, a need to draw would probably not arise. As with the Fund's other facilities, those who draw must agree to co-operate with the Fund in an effort to find solutions to any balance-of-payments difficulties.

The buffer stock to be indirectly financed by the Fund must fit into the Fund's objectives. Among other things, it should not be operating in a supply shift demand elastic market for here the buffer stock would destabilize export earnings and thus work contrary to Fund objectives. It should not attempt to control the long term trend. If it does it must be with the consent of member and non-member consumers and not likely to result in the collapse of the scheme. Since the Fund will not finance a long term debt to the buffer stock with short term loans, what is bought by the buffer stock at the floor must be sold at the ceiling within three to five years unless the buffer stock acquires an alternative source of funds within this period. Although the Fund will provide initial financing through participants, it will encourage negotiators to make provision for the buffer stock agency to build up its own reserves, out of a levy on exports for example, so that Fund assistance can be repaid without disrupting buffer stock activities. The buffer stock agreement must conform to the widely accepted tenets of control laid out in the Havana Accords and GATT on voting, representation, and publicity, and the price stabilization activity of the buffer stock must serve to stabilize export earnings of participating exporters as a whole. Where individual exporting countries find their export earnings destabilized because they experience supply shifts which the other exporters do not, the Fund would nevertheless approve the scheme if its aggregate effect on all exporters was beneficial. The disadvantaged country would be offered Fund assistance from the compensatory facility to compensate for the disruption to its export earnings.

Although gold and credit tranche rights are unaffected by a drawing under the compensatory facility, a member who drew on the buffer stock facility at a time when it still had automatic gold tranche drawing rights at its disposal would lose these to the amount of the drawing. It would not lose its credit tranche, however. Access under the buffer stock facility, like that under the compensatory facility, is limited to 50 per cent of quota making assistance under the facility restricted since quotas of developing countries are generally small. As pointed out in Chapter 2, Section 2c (p. 45), however, reserves to trade ratios tend to be high for developing compared to developed countries. The requirement that drawings outstanding cannot normally be increased by more than

25 per cent of quota in any twelve month period might discourage the adoption of a useful buffer stock agreement if applied to the buffer stock facility. Drawings on both facilities together can amount to the equivalent of 75 per cent of quota provided that under neither facility does the amount outstanding exceed the equivalent of 50 per cent of quota.

iii. *The National Stock Facility*

A third facility is designed to assist the financing of stocks held in the exporting country. Presumably these include national buffer stocks for exported commodities as well as stocks resulting from export quota restriction, but there is some uncertainty as this device is still in its formative stages. Export quotas, as shown in the preceding chapter, can be a necessary adjunct to international buffer stocks. Unlike international buffer stocks, they will have a stabilizing influence on export earnings in a supply shift market, but they may destabilize export earnings in a demand shift demand elastic market. Under the national stock facility the Fund would provide assistance for export quota schemes which complement buffer stocks. (Since it agrees to finance buffer stocks in markets in which demand shifts predominate, it would appear that support may be given to a quota device which in such a market destabilizes export earnings.) Drawings would be available under the usual conditions: if the national stocks are not of a long term nature, if the drawing country is taking or pledges to take steps to mitigate export earnings fluctuations, and if the national stocks do not create important disruptive repercussions on other member or non-member countries through, for instance, the possible unsettling effects on the market when national stocks are disposed. The typical export quota system fixes the pattern of trade between members and discriminates against non-members during periods of restriction. Although the Fund is specifically empowered to discourage discrimination in payments arrangements between its members, its attitude to the forms of discrimination against member and non-members of export quota agreements is not clearly expressed. As with the compensatory facility, the national stock facility is available only after the country has run into balance-of-payments difficulties as a result of national stock accumulation.

4. MULTIPLE COMMODITY BUFFER STOCK SCHEMES

One of the more intriguing variants on the theme of multi-commodity buffer stock price control schemes is that put forward by Hayek (1943) and others. He has argued that the monetization of such a scheme would not only serve to stabilize commodity prices but diminish the importance of conventional international reserve mediums and their undesirable aspects. If a volume of primary commodities in fixed proportions to one another were to be substituted for gold or reserve currencies, or to complement these as a means of international exchange, money could be defined in terms of commodities. This commodity currency, Hayek maintains, could be issued in exchange for a fixed combination of warehouse warrants for a number of price leading storable commodities and be redeemable in the same units. Storage would remain in private hands; brokers would collect warehouse warrants in their established proportions and exchange them for the commodity currency. Those who stored would be compensated by a margin between the price at which the currency was bought and sold.

Since money would be issued only against the total collection of primary commodities in their fixed proportions to one another and would be redeemable in the same proportions, the aggregate price of the collection would be fixed in terms of money in the same way values are tied to gold. A multi-commodity buffer stock would respond to an increase in demand for liquid assets with an accumulation of stocks of raw materials and thus provide demand for the primary commodities in periods of recession. During a recovery stocks would be exchanged for money, the money supply would decline and economic activity would be dampened. As a reserve medium, commodities avoid some of the undesirable aspects of the gold exchange standard, most notably, the slowness and irreversibility with which gold responds to increased demand. The commodity reserve currency scheme would also satisfy those who object to expenditure of considerable resources on an item which is unproductive. On the other hand, it might work contrary to national full employment policies as it implies a restriction of the money supply during an upswing. Moreover, production of some of the commodities necessary to back the scheme, such as copper, oil and tin, would be no more responsive to increased demand than gold.

The multi-commodity buffer stock might destabilize the relative prices of commodities and manufactures if these move together over the business cycle, regardless of whether or not it is monetized. The scheme would also destabilize individual commodity prices if proportions of the commodities in the currency unit are fixed. Sales from the buffer stock in periods of recovery would occur because aggregate demand for the commodities in the stock increases. But if the demand for a single commodity lagged behind the rest, its forced sale on the market could depress its price. Likewise, on the supply side of the market cyclical patterns and annual fluctuations may differ between commodities. Thus' individual producing and consuming countries may be subjected to the kind of external disturbances for which the gold exchange standard is criticized. Commodities should be given individual treatment if the stabilization of export earnings is a primary objective.

5. DEMAND EXPANSION

As mentioned in Chapter 1, the expansion of supply of a number of primary commodities is related to the rate at which producers become aware that a market exists and productivity is increased with research and education. That is, output expansion will be largely unrelated to price. If the product is in income inelastic demand, as many are in their major markets, a significant gap may develop between the rate of growth in demand and supply. This situation may be further aggravated by the development of technological and economical substitutes. Production restriction is usually difficult when output is on numerous widely scattered producing units and can be detrimental unless it occurs among the bulk of producing countries. A corollary to the problems of supply reduction is demand expansion.

a. New Markets

One possible approach to the need to expand demand is the intrusion into new markets where for economic or cultural reasons habits of consumption of the primary commodity have not developed. The possibility of opening up new markets occurs where per capita consumption is low and trade barriers high. The socialist countries would offer such an opportunity for some of the tropical food products that are considered luxuries in these countries despite their relatively high per capita income. Opening up of new markets could be most effectively accomplished through international action. A body representing a united front of all developing exporting countries would be capable of exerting more pressure on barriers to entry than any single exporting country acting alone.

The development of new markets should not be confused with disposal of surplus production at a loss in non-traditional markets. Non-traditional markets that offer a below cost price are new only in the sense that commercial sales have not been made there because of the loss involved. Such sales must be subsidized while sales in the new markets referred to above need not be.

b. New Uses

Finding a new use for which there is a demand at a competitive price is another way of expanding aggregate demand for a commodity. For example, natural rubber is now seen as a feasible technological and economical substitute for some inputs used in metalled roads. If this new use is exploited, it can serve not only to alleviate rubber's secular decline in price, but also to dilute the high end use concentration of demand. Efforts to discover new uses are most effectively organized through international co-operation if these involve research with attendant economies of scale. Individual countries may not undertake research into new uses because of the expense involved and the diffusion of benefits.

c. SALES PROMOTION

Finally, demand can be expanded through sales promotion in new and old markets. Again this is most effectively accomplished through international action since no one country is likely to incur the expense if demand is not selective among sources of supply. The costs of raising demand by a given amount through sales promotion can be recovered by increased returns to producers as a whole, but if one country bears the cost the returns to that country may not justify the expense since it shares in only a proportion of the aggregate increase in demand. In this respect sales promotion is analogous to a national buffer stock. If one exporting country wishes to create a given increase in its price with a buffer stock it must raise the price to all producers. The cost may be prohibitive for one country to bear. The highest returns to investment in sales promotion in consuming countries are likely to occur where the product is not already well established. If entry has been unrestricted, per capita consumption relatively high and expenditure on the commodity a small part of the consumer's normal budget, a situation of saturation may already exist. The income elasticity of demand and the rate of increases in income may be higher in developing countries than in those that are developed.

6. THE FRAMEWORK FOR INTERNATIONAL CO-OPERATION

Formal international control of commodity markets falls roughly into four categories. Emphasis in this and the preceding chapter has been on agreements conducted in the spirit of the Havana Accords and GATT. The body of regulations which they advocate has the sanction of the United Nations and most of the agreements which conform to them have been negotiated under United Nations auspices. The most notable point of difference in comparing this type of agreement to other categories is the avoidance of discrimination in the market place and, as far as possible, the avoidance of direct intervention in commodity markets. In contrast the commodity agreements of the socialist bloc are characterized by long term bilateral contracts which provide assurance of market outlets for exporters but frequently require a bilateral balance of trade between the two countries in exchange. This can be a disadvantage to the exporting developing country where the socialist country has a limited range of goods to offer or is not the lowest priced producer. Trade agreements between metropolitan powers and former colonies or spheres of influence are largely in the form of preferential quota and tariff structures that discriminate against non-members. Finally, formal or tacit collusion is occasionally practised among exporters to raise world price through export restriction. Such cartels have existed for coffee and cocoa in the post war period and were the predominant form of control before the war. In 1972, for instance, 90 per cent of the world's coffee exporters decided independently of the importing members of the International Coffee Agreement to maintain the 1971–2 global export quota rather than compromise with importers who sought to have it raised. Similar one-sided restrictions are currently being practised by the petroleum exporting countries.

The Havana Charter and GATT aim specifically at abolishing the last three categories of international control. International discrimination in the form of preferential arrangements, closed bilateral contracts and collusion among exporting countries against importers is disapproved. Unilateral national trade distorting activities such as price support programs and export subsidies as well as restrictive business practices of private enterprise are also condemned. The guidelines do permit discrimination against non-members under export quota and multilateral concessionary trade agreements and in the freezing of the pattern of trade among members under export quotas and multilateral contracts. In the latter case, however, the disadvantaged producer or consumer would have an option to withdraw, if the disadvantages appeared to outweigh the advantages, and sell or buy on the uncontrolled residual market. Any attempt at concessionary trade through a high price range under a buffer stock or export quota device would have the consent of the participating consumers but possibly not that of non-member consumers.

The principles of the Havana Accords and GATT, under which buffer stock, export quota, multilateral contract and International Monetary Fund compensatory finance schemes have been conducted, provide for consumer participation, publicity as to the terms of the agreement and international study groups for commodities being considered for control. Study groups to date include those for citrus fruit, cocoa, coconut, coffee, cotton, grains and oilseeds, non-ferrous metals, rice, rubber and wool. Although only six commodity agreements conforming to these standards have been successfully negotiated in the post war period (wheat, tin, sugar, coffee, cocoa and olive oil), less formalized international action under these regulations has also been achieved, particularly in the field of co-ordination of national policies through the study groups or other bodies. For instance, developed countries have reduced numerous tariff positions in the rounds of tariff reduction negotiations held in GATT conferences since 1947. International measures calling for adjustment of commercial and fiscal policies in importing countries also form part of the network of international action, for international action includes all efforts that are more than unilateral.

a. The Division of Interests

An equal distribution of votes to members on both sides of the market has insured that the rule that producer and consumer interests be equally represented in international commodity agreements is practised. Normally each side receives 1,000 votes which are then divided roughly according to market position. All participants no matter how small their market share may be entitled to some minimum number of votes. In the Cocoa Agreement, for example, no member exporter holds less than about ten votes since 200 votes are distributed democratically. Strict democratic representation, however, is not attained as the remaining 800 votes are distributed according to position in the market. Under this proportional representation each member has a percentage of the remaining votes based on the proportion that his historic imports or exports bear to the total import or export market represented by the participants in the agreement. A country's vulnerability to the influence of the agreement on total export earnings is not taken into account. Countries which were dependent upon the non-preference market controlled under the Sugar Agreements, such as Peru, the Dominican Republic and Taiwan, had no more strength in votes collectively than South Africa, France and Australia which were only nominally dependent on the partial market but major contributors to it. A limit may be set on the number of votes that one country can hold in order to curtail the power of any one exporter or importer; a common limit is 300 votes. Considering that the distributed two-thirds majority decision discussed below may be blocked by 333 votes on either side of the market, the importance of this rule is apparent.

The council which administers the agreement is composed of representatives of all participating countries, with their respective allotments of votes to exercise. Decisions are reached by a variety of vote counting methods. They may be based, for instance, on a simple majority of all votes together, making no distinction between producer or consumer votes. Under this system, all producers and one consumer holding the minimum number of votes would be capable of carrying a decision, even if a plurality of consumers dissented. The simple majority vote is generally not used for important decisions since a dissenting majority on one side of the market might threaten the viability of the agreement. More important decisions are carried by a distributed majority vote. Under this system a majority must be reached on both sides of the market considered separately. Although used for somewhat more important decisions than the former tally, it is not generally used for decisions which are likely to cause disruption should one of the minority members on one side of the market dissent.

In such circumstances a 'special vote' may be taken. This vote requires a two-thirds majority on each side of the market considered separately. Most decisions regarding export quota reallocations, *pro rata* export restrictions, and price range adjustments are subjected to the special vote. Frequently a specification is made in the articles of agreement that a decision on these matters may only be reached with this vote. This assures individual participants that the terms of agreement are not likely to be turned against them after they have given their consent to participate. It also means that any group of members holding one-sixth of all votes can block any change of significance once the agreement has become operative. In the 1953 and 1958 Sugar Agreements, for example, the United States and the United Kingdom controlled nearly a majority of all votes held by importers. They could control distributed two-thirds majority decisions and with one other importer holding the minimum of 15 votes, control simple distributed majority decisions. Although the council usually has the power to alter by vote almost all control provisions, this apparent flexibility should be regarded with some qualification if alteration requires the special vote. Change will occur during renegotiation (which under the GATT rules would occur every three to five years to avoid trend control), when the agreement itself is at stake.

In distinguishing two separate interests, those of the producer and consumer, each member is assigned to one or the other side of the market. Post-war agreement history suggests, however, that such strict division of interests may not be realistic. Some nations, like Italy, Mexico and Spain under the Wheat Agreements and the Soviet Union and India under the Sugar Agreements, are net importers in some years and net exporters in others. Developed countries which are consistently on one side of the market may, nevertheless, show some ambivalence, for reasons mentioned earlier, if their trade is with developing countries. For example, although the price of wheat had long been above the ceiling of the agreement price range, developed exporters accepted new importing countries into the 1953 agreement and a ceiling price under the new agreement which was below the world price that had ruled for the duration of the preceding agreement. In 1954, developed exporters did not test the market assurances of the 1953 agreement despite large harvests, which if not stored by exporters would have driven the world price below the floor. The developing importing nations were relieved from their obligations because the exporting nations did not wish to accept transfers from developing importers. Agreements between developed and developing countries may not be a preferred arrangement if the economic interests of the developed country producer or consumer are to be upheld. The developing countries are assured of compliance with the provisions of the agreement by the developed countries while the developed countries may be reluctant to press economically weak countries to meet their commitments.

Under the Sugar Agreements France, both an importer and exporter, maintained a policy of low world prices to discourage expanded competition. The United Kingdom, an importer, had an interest in negotiating a floor price in 1953 that was above the price she paid for stock accumulated at high prices. The United States, although an importer, favoured high cane sugar prices. Support of a high price cost her little since her internal price was also high, and earned her political dividends with developing exporting countries. When influential consumers vote as producers for high prices, a price range above the trend is likely to result. Consuming countries which are less capable or willing to provide this form of aid are nevertheless compelled to against their wishes.

The division of interests may be further obscured if consuming countries have financial interests in the commodity's production in the exporting countries. The Malaysian tin smelters and many of the mines, for example, are owned by English firms. These firms represent an element in a consuming country which might benefit by higher tin prices. Foreign owned rubber estates in South-East Asia might give rise to a similar anomaly in the proposed international rubber agreement. The influence of investors in consuming countries will depend on how well they are organized compared to consumers and their access to the circles of power.

Important aspects of an agreement, such as the positioning of the price range, depend largely upon guesses about the future, and thus involve a margin of error. As a result, large producer and consumer countries without whom the agreement could not function effectively may play upon the uncertainty about the future and the importance of their participation in order to manoeuvre provisions to their advantage. The relative bargaining strength of producers and consumers will also be dependent upon their supply and demand elasticities. If consumers need the commodity and have no substitute, their bargaining position will be weak. If producers can vary production easily without dislocation, their position will be strong. Producer strength is likely to be stronger for short crops than long if, in each case, alternative crops are available.

b. Escape Clauses

All post-war agreements negotiated under the Havana and GATT principles could be accused of providing an excessive number of escape clauses. The burden of control, however, has remained largely with the developing exporting countries. They have been required to finance domestic stockholding, administer production restrictions, and, in the case of the Tin Agreements, finance the international buffer stock. The escape clauses release members from these obligations during periods of hardship such as a poor harvest, war or balance-of-payments difficulties. Expulsion of members for not meeting obligations because of circumstances beyond their control would either increase their hardship, if there are strong provisions for non-member discrimination, or allow them to enjoy the benefit of control without the prospect of further contribution to its maintenance.

c. Effectuating the Agreement

Most agreements have provided members three opportunities to change their minds. These have occurred when negotiators sign the agreement, again when their governments ratify the agreement and, finally, when members meet in council to decide whether to put the agreement provisionally or permanently into operation. In the last case, after a percentage of provisional or definite ratifications have been received, the council will decide whether the agreement is viable for control of trade by those represented. At this point members who do not believe it is have an option to withdraw. This flexibility may be fortunate in that it prevents the agreement having to limp along with only a part of the original participants adhering to its provisions. If a maximum vote holder declined to ratify an export quota agreement, for instance, those countries which did ratify might then want a chance to negotiate a multilateral contract, a form of control which is unaffected by the proportion of the market represented.

7. SUMMARY

The multilateral contract is a producer- consumer agreement to trade a contracted volume at or between established price limits. The compensatory finance device, on the other hand, is a scheme for providing partial or complete compensation for shortfalls in export earnings from some established norm, base period or other point of reference. Both devices provide a more direct and specific transfer between producers and consumers and are viable with a smaller number of participants than the price control devices of Chapter 4. When the multilateral contract operates through inter-governmental transfers the two types of devices become indistinguishable. In general, however, multilateral contracts differ from compensatory finance devices because their administration may involve government intervention on either or both sides of the market and they entail predetermined control of price for an established volume of trade. Both devices are indifferent in their influence on the economic environment of individual producers. Benefits and obligations under the devices may or may not be passed directly on to producers by the governments of participating exporting countries. Producers are unlikely to be involved because this would entail additional control measures. Under compensatory finance in the form of loans or externally administered grants recipient governments may be reluctant or unable to involve individual producers. Both devices minimize the types of discrimination among members or against non-members found under export quotas. Quotas are allocated under multilateral contracts but exporters are free to sell additional output on the residual market. Compensatory finance further avoids the discrimination against non-member importing countries found in price control agreements which conspire to raise world price. Unlike devices involving storage, multilateral contracts and compensatory finance can be applied to all commodities regardless of their spoilage properties, and the latter may also be applied to non-homogeneous products since price and volume control is not involved.

Multilateral contracts are committed to an established volume and

price for all participating producer countries and thus they reflect in-
difference to hardships which are not shared by the bulk of producers.
If a single exporter has, for example, a greater proportional reduction
in output than increase in price, the country may nonetheless be called
upon to make a transfer to consumers if the residual market price is
above the contract ceiling. Export earnings will be destabilized with
price control in periods of a supply shift demand elastic market. Moreover, price control on a fixed volume of trade may limit the export
earnings stabilizing effects in periods of a demand shift or supply shift
demand inelastic market, relative to an international buffer stock. Compensatory finance for shortfalls in export earnings will have no effect on
shortfalls due to excessive imports or debt repayments with stable
export earnings and may unwisely correct for shortfalls in earnings
resulting from foreseeable internal factors such as increased domestic
consumption, political crises and inflation unless there is an element
of discretion in making disbursements.

The two devices may be useful substitutes and complements for each
other and the devices of Chapter 4. Compensatory finance would be
preferred to a multilateral contract in a predominantly supply shift demand elastic market and serve as a complement in a predominantly
demand shift market which experiences periods of supply shift or in
which there are individual countries which are disadvantaged. Where
wide support for an export quota or buffer stock scheme is not obtainable, negotiators may turn to a multilateral contract or compensatory
finance device. Compensatory finance can be used as a complementary
device to buffer funds, buffer stocks and export quotas where these
devices reduce or destabilize export earnings. Where they stabilize export earnings compensatory finance would play a supportive role.

The residual market price under a multilateral contract in a demand
shift or a supply shift market will be destabilized if benefits and obligations are passed directly on to producers, since more would be produced
in low price periods and less in high than without control. Residual
market price might be further destabilized if the importing country's
prescribed gain or loss is passed on to the consumer, without a significant lag, because demand would increase in high price periods and
decrease in those of low price. When the product is in income inelastic
derived demand, however, the effect could be negligible. The scheme
would have no effect on demand if governments of importing countries established a reserve fund out of transfers in periods of high prices
and met obligations out of the fund in periods of low prices. Even if
neither supply or demand are affected in these ways, the residual mar-

ket may not be preserved as an indicator of the equilibrium position f the volume of speculative activity is the same on the narrow residual market as it was on the total market before control or if exporters operate supportive buffer stocks and production controls which allow them to determine the level of world prices.

An automatic and unconditional rendering of compensation in the form of grants will not assure that useful steps are taken to remove the causes of the shortfall or that assistance will be used generally for investment activities designed to promote external equilibrium and economic growth. Automatic payment would also be undesirable if it is likely to result in recipient countries adopting policies which result in a decline in export earnings. For this reason it may be desirable to provide funds either in the form of loans or under managed assistance. One possible compromise between ready assistance and avoidance of misuse would involve automatic provision of short term credit which could be converted into a grant or long term loan if the shortfall is shown to be beyond the exporting country's control, if the disbursing agency obtains the country's co-operation in efforts to overcome external instability, or if recovery is delayed or incomplete.

Compensatory finance as practised by the IMF is designed to meet short term shortfalls in export earnings that might prevent or delay development projects or otherwise disrupt the economy of the recipient country. Longer term action to lessen dependence on specific commodity exports or to reduce the influence of external disequilibrium is met by the World Bank and a plethora of other international financial institutions. The short term compensation of the Fund is exercised through the compensatory, international and national buffer stock facilities. Loans under these facilities must be repaid three to five years after receipt and are contingent upon demonstration that there is a need to draw upon the facility, co-operation of the recipient country with the Fund in finding solutions to the country's external disequilibrium, and the size of the country's outstanding and requested drawings. Drawings on a facility cannot increase by more than 25 per cent of the member's quota in any year and the total amount outstanding is limited to 75 per cent of quota. The restrictive character of these rules is underscored by the small size of the quotas of many developing countries which are heavily dependent on export earnings. Drawings on the compensatory facility can occur only after the shortfall while drawings to finance buffer stock obligations can be used to avert a shortfall. The actual shortfall might be avoided in the former case, however, if the country is eligible to make an ordinary drawing on the Fund. Drawings on the buffer stock facilities may be made only for approved buffer stock programes. In line with its general objectives and repayment pattern, the Fund tends not to approve long term restrictive schemes or those that are detrimental to some exporters unless the benefit to the remainder is considerable. Moreover, approval would not be given for drawings to finance an international buffer stock in a supply shift demand elastic market since the resulting instability in export earnings would be contrary to the Fund's objectives.

With the steady expansion of supply of a number of primary commodities in response to non-price factors, it is likely that growth in supply will outpace that of demand. One producing country alone is unlikely to undertake control of supply and it may be difficult to solicit the co-operation of the bulk of producers. Moreover, actual control could be administratively unfeasible if production is by widely scattered small units. An alternative approach in narrowing the gap between supply and demand is the expansion of demand through reduction of trade barriers to new markets, research into new uses, and sales promotion. Each of these approaches could be most effectively made through international co-operation. Power lies in numbers; pressure in the form of moral suasion to reduce trade barriers to new markets will carry more weight if developing countries act as a group. Sales promotion and research require international action because of the expense involved and the inability of individual countries to capture all the benefits for themselves.

International agreements and other less formal international action have increasingly been conducted according to the principles of the Havana Accords and GATT. These aim to reduce discrimination in the international market place and specifically condemn other popular forms of international control: closed bilateral contracts, preferential arrangements, and producer cartels. Although designed to discourage the forms of discrimination and trend control practised under these devices, the Havanna Accords and GATT do allow discrimination under producer-consumer agreements. Trade patterns may be fixed against the interests of low cost producers, concessionary trade arrangements that raise world price may be made without the consent of non-member developed consuming countries, and production restriction in periods of low prices may be used to raise the trend of prices. Equality between producer and consumer interests is given practical expression through an equal distribution of votes on each side of the market while minority interest among those that participate is preserved with the 'special vote'. Although nearly all important control provisions of these agreements are subject to change in council, the use of the special vote limits their apparent flexibility.

Readings

Benoit, E., 'Purchase Guarantees as a Means of Reducing Instability of Commodity Export Proceeds of Underdeveloped Countries', *Kyklos*, Vol. 12, 1959, pp. 300–56.

Burgess, C., 'The International Wheat Agreement', (Symposium), *International Journal of Agrarian Affairs*, Vol. 1, No. 3, September 1949, pp. 51–65.

Farnsworth, H.C., 'Imbalance in the World Wheat Economy', *Journal of Political Economy*, Vol. 66, No. 1, February 1958, pp. 1–23.

————, 'The International Wheat Agreement and Problems, 1949–1956', *Quarterly Journal of Economics*, Vol. 70, May 1956, pp. 217–48.

Fleming, J.M., et. al. 'Export Norms and Their Role in Compensatory Finance', *IMF Staff Papers*, Vol. 10, No. 1, March 1963, pp. 97–149.

————, & Lovasy, G., 'Fund Policies and Procedures in Relation to the Compensatory Financing of Commodity Fluctuations', *IMF Staff Papers*, Vol. 8, 1960, pp. 1–76.

Food Research Institute, *International Commodity Stockpiling as an Economic Stabilizer*, Stanford, 1949.

Golay, F.H., 'The International Wheat Agreement of 1949', *Quarterly Journal of Economics*, Vol. 64, August 1950, pp. 442–63.

Gold, J., *The Stand-By Arrangements of the International Monetary Fund*, IMF, Washington, 1970.

Grubel, H.G., 'The Case Against an International Commodity Reserve Currency', *Oxford Economic Papers*, Vol. 17, No. 1, March 1965, pp. 130–5.

Harbury, C.D., 'An Experiment in Commodity Control—The International Wheat Agreement, 1949', *Oxford Economic Papers*, Vol. 6, February 1954, pp. 82–97.

Harmon, E.M., *Commodity Reserve Currency*, Columbia University Press, New York, 1959.

Hart, A.G., 'The Case for and against an International Commodity Reserve Currency', *Oxford Economic Papers*, Vol. 18, No. 2, July 1966, pp. 237–41.

————, Kaldor, N., & Tinbergen, J., *The Case for an International Reserve Currency*, Contributed Paper No. 7, E/CONF. 46, February 17, 1964.

Hayek, F.A., 'A Commodity Reserve Currency', *Economic Journal*, Vol. 53, September 1943, pp. 176–84.

Hazlewood, A., 'Stabilization and Development, A Proposal', *Kyklos*, Vol. 12, 1959, pp. 307–15.

Henderson, A.M., 'A Geometrical Note on Bulk Purchase', *Economica* (New Series), Vol. 15, No. 57, February 1948, pp. 61–9.

Hodan, M., 'Economic Aspects of the International Wheat Agreement of 1949', *Economic Record*, November 1954, pp. 225–31.

IMF, *Compensatory Financial Measures to Offset Fluctuations in Export Income of Primary Producing Countries*, E/CN.13/58, 7 March, 1963.

————, *Compensatory Financing of Export Fluctuations*, First Report, Washington, 1963.

————, *Compensatory Financing of Export Fluctuations*, Second Report, Washington, 1966.

————, *The Problem of Stabilization of Prices of Primary Products*, Washington, 1969, Part II.

————, 'Some Problems of Developing Countries', *Annual Report*, IMF, Washington, 1966, pp. 21–32.

Johnson, H.G., 'The Destabilizing Effect of International Commodity Agreements on the Prices of Primary Products', *Economic Journal*, Vol. 60, September 1950, pp. 626–29.

Journal of World Trade Law, 'The International Grains Agreement, 1967', Vol. 2, March–April 1968, pp. 233–9.

Kaldor, N., 'Stabilizing the Terms of Trade of Underdeveloped Countries', *Economic Bulletin for Latin America*, Vol. 8, No., 1, March 1963, pp. 1– .

————, Assisted, 'A Reconsideration of the Economics of the International Wheat Agreement', *Commodity Policy Series No. 1*, FAO 1952.

Lovasy, G., 'Survey and Appraisal of Proposed Schemes for Compensatory Finance', *IMF Staff Papers*, Vol. 12, No. 2, July 1965, pp. 189–223.

McCalla, A.F., 'A Duopoly Model of World Wheat Pricing', *American Journal of Farm Economics*, Vol. 48, No. 3, August 1966, pp. 711–27.

Meade, J.E. 'International Commodity Agreements', *Proceedings at UNCTAD*, Vol. 3, New York, 1964, pp. 451–457.

Mikesell, R.F., 'Commodity Agreements and Aid to Developing Countries', *Law and Contemporary Problems*, Vol. 28, No. 2, 1963, pp. 294–312.

————, 'International Commodity Stabilization Schemes and Export Problems of Developing Countries', *American Economic Review, Papers & Proceedings*, Vol. 53, No. 2, May 1963, pp. 75–91.

Morgan, D.J., 'International Compensatory Financing Applied to the Federation of Malaya and Singapore', *Malaysian Economics Review*, Vol. 7, No. 2, October 1962, pp. 64–76.

Reynolds, op. cit. esp. pp. 101–2.

Rowe, op. cit. pp. 56–66, 155–69 and 209–20.

Silard, S.A., 'The Impact of the International Monetary Fund on International Trade', *Journal of World Trade Law*, Vol. 2, No. 2, 1968, pp. 121–61.

Spitzer, E.G., 'Stand-By Arrangements: Purposes and Form', *International Monetary Fund, 1945–1965*, Vol. 2, Ch. 20, IMF Washington, 1969, pp. 468–91.

Stern, R.M., 'International Compensation for Fluctuations in Commodity Trade', *Quarterly Journal of Economics*, Vol. 77, May 1963, pp. 258–73.

Swerling, B.C., 'Current Issues in Commodity Policy', *Essays in International Finance No. 38*, Princeton, 1962.

————, 'Financial Alternatives to International Commodity Stabilization', *Canadian Journal of Economics and Political Science*, Vol. 30, November 1964, pp. 526–37.

————, 'Income Protection for Farmers: A Possible Approach', *Journal of Political Economy*, Vol. 67, No. 2, April 1959, pp. 173–86.

Tinbergen, J., 'International Coordination of Stabilization and Development Policies', *Kyklos*, Vol. 12, 1959, pp. 183–89.

Tyszynski, H., 'Economics of the Wheat Agreement', *Economica*, Vol. 16, February 1949, pp. 27–39.

UN, Department of Economic & Social Affairs, *International Compensation for Fluctuations in Commodity Trade*, E/CN 13/40, New York, 1961.

Walker, H., 'The International Law of Commodity Agreements', *Law and Contemporary Problems*, Vol. 28, No. 2, 1963, pp. 392–415.

Westerman, P.A., 'Changes in the World Wheat Situation and the 1967 International Grains Arrangement', *Quarterly Review of Agricultural Economics*, Vol. 22, No. 1, January 1969, pp. 20–34.

VI
The Choice of a Control Device

I. INTRODUCTION

EVERY control device, indeed every economic activity, in altering the economic environment will change the balance of wealth and risks. The preceding chapters have demonstrated the ambiguity of effects of single control devices and the disparity of effects on given variables between devices. They have not, however, suggested a precise method by which devices might be ranked in accordance with single or multiple objectives. As we have seen, more of one social good, for example price stabilization, can usually only be obtained at some sacrifice of another social good, say full employment. Although the members of society might unanimously agree that both are to be desired, few would be able to suggest a rational method by which to weigh the net benefit to society of more of one and less of the other. Social cost-benefit analysis provides a tool for evaluating and reaching rational decisions in the choice of commodity control mechanisms. The conceptual framework and application is much the same here as with other types of public projects, such as transport and communication, with one notable difference in that benefits and costs of commodity control are largely indirect and in the form of so-called 'spillovers' or 'externalities'. Cost-benefit analysis of primary commodity control does not, at this early stage in its development, require meticulous simulation techniques and statistical methods, although some knowledge of these is likely to be necessary. The overriding constraint in applying the techniques to commodity control is the inadequacy of tools to measure the sorts of indirect effects encountered. Even where we are unable to assign magnitudes to these effects, it is nonetheless enlightening and profitable to expose clearly our areas of ignorance. The present chapter delineates the areas of indirect effect in primary commodity control and illustrates the use of cost-benefit analysis in the choice of a control device.

2. DISTRIBUTIVE EQUITY AND THE PARETO CRITERION

The approach taken in the following paragraphs may strike the reader as incongruous, given the earlier preoccupation with distributive equity (particularly in Chapter 3, Sections 3a and 4, p. 63), since the ranking of control devices followed below largely ignores the distributive effects of an outcome. A device which satisfies the cost-benefit tests given here can properly be rejected on grounds of equity. Distribution effects and the efficiency effects tested in cost-benefit analysis are perhaps best kept separate because of the difficulty or unfeasibility of devising a system of distributional weights and the problems arising in effecting the distribution. In dealing with the problem of distributive equity a frequently recommended alternative approach incorporates distributive weights in the net benefit stream. In this approach it is necessary to delineate the groups to which the costs and benefits flow. Weights are then attached to the flows (before discounting) according to considerations of equity. For simplicity of exposition and application, the efficiency and distributional effects may be kept separate so long as the importance of both is kept in mind. In the short run one might justifiably de-emphasize the distributional effects since those disadvantaged by a device will over time share in the ensuing benefits of the increase in output that a device brings if chosen on cost-benefit grounds.

The approach taken here as applied to international trade is slanted toward the developing country, and so it is feasible to analyse the efficiency and distributional effects of control solely in their relation to the developing country rather than the world at large. From this point of view favourable or unfavourable spillovers in developed countries are only important in-so-far as they affect the actual negotiation of producer-consumer agreements. A national buffer fund which increases export earnings and stabilizes producer price, for example, is acceptable within our narrow framework because it benefits the developing exporter even though it results in a loss to developed importers which exceeds that gain.

The potential Pareto improvement criterion provides that a contrived change in the economic environment should occur if the gain *can* be distributed so as to make everyone in the community under consideration better off than before. That is, if those who gain were to compensate those who lose, at least one person must be better off and no one put in worse straits. It is not necessary that the redistribution actually occur as long as it is possible that it can occur. In other words, a device which satisfies an adopted cost-benefit criterion does not assure that everyone is made better off, but only that conceptually it is possible to make everyone better off by the amount of the excess benefit if the necessary redistribution is costless. Thus, in a scheme chosen purely on potential Pareto improvement grounds, one can envisage a situation where the rich are made better off by $2 million, at the expense of the poor who are made worse off by $1 million. The device is nonetheless acceptable on a cost-benefit basis because the excess of costs over benefits is $1 million. For this reason, a potential Pareto improvement may be considered an inadequate measure of social gain.

Although single communities might be satisfied by such an improvement, as described above, successful bargaining between communities requires an improvement to all sides. In international commodity negotiations importers may, for instance, gain with any degree of increased price stability and initially ask for a device with a narrow price range, the mean of which is on the trend. Producers stand to gain with any amount of increased income stability and therefore might counter by suggesting a wide price range or a higher one if price control destabilizes income. Consumers will be willing to accept a higher range in exchange for their preferred price limits providing the range remains narrow and consequent losses do not exceed gains. Given the price range spread, if the high price range conceded by consumers is sufficiently high to more than compensate producers for the increased income instability which comes with price control, agreement will be reached. If not, agreement will not occur. Moreover, if the concerned parties are aware beforehand that what consumers are willing to pay for a narrower price range is less than what producers will accept for the consequent income instability, bargaining will not be initiated.

The disparity between a potential Pareto improvement and an actual Pareto improvement, in which the redistribution is in fact made, may be expected to be small where income taxes are progressive and competition intense. A producer price stabilization scheme that benefits the rich low yield risk farmers at the expense of poor high yield risk farmers might be chosen if increases in the wealth of the low yield risk beneficiaries are taxed sufficiently and the tax revenue finds its way to the high yield risk farmers in the form of input subsidies, extension education, irrigation schemes or the like. In the absence of a tax or other transfer device, price stabilization measures may satisfy the dual welfare criterion (potential Pareto improvement and distributive equity) if, for example, they stabilize the income of poor food deficit producers while, *ceteris paribus*, destabilizing that of the rich food surplus producer, so long as the gain to the former exceeds the loss to the latter. If a narrower criterion, requiring that no change be instituted unless one party is made better off and no one worse off is adopted, then any device which cannot make some better off without making even one individual worse off would not be chosen. The optimum outcome in this situation is the *status quo*.

3. COSTS AND BENEFITS

In commodity control, costs and benefits refer to direct disbursements and receipts by the control authority and to indirect losses and gains to others. These comprise social benefits and costs or, if expressed in terms of money and set against one another, simply net excess benefit, a positive or negative figure. The economist's quantification of various views and hunches about costs and benefits that appear plausible *a priori* will allow the correct to be sorted out from the incorrect and the important from the unimportant, permitting eventual decisions to be better informed and open to intelligent discussion. What is quantifiable should be quantified since their is no other basis for a rational allocation of resources.

Indirect effects for which individuals offer to buy or sell a quantity for a given price are more readily measured than those upon which people place only a subjective price. For instance, income changes resulting from price control can be estimated with some confidence in the manner illustrated in the preceding chapters and appendices, but the value attached by producers to a given degree of price stability presents a greater problem. In the former case one can assume that the estimated collective income change is a measure of the valuation of the loss or gain, but it is impossible to directly observe the subjective valuations placed on the latter.

Information of the quantities offered or accepted at certain prices gleaned from past experience is useful in estimating income changes and the like if there is reason to suppose that the conditions which existed in the past will recur in the future. Since international commodity agreements run for 3–5 years, and have a certain flexibility in any case, statistical forecasts based on past records may be useful over the likely period of the analysis. If not, an arbitrary cut-off period may be invoked. The more uncertain the future, the nearer to the present the cut-off would be. Alternatively, most probable excess benefits may be bracketed by optimistic and pessimistic limits for which the differential increases as the projection moves forward through time.

Where direct observations are not possible, one may have to resort to a survey of opinion of those affected. This may provide a basis for an intelligent guess as to the value of the anticipated benefit or disservice. If not, then after arriving at the excess benefit over costs of those items which are measurable, one can spread the excess benefit over those individuals who will be adversely affected by the indirect effect which is unmeasurable. The resulting *per capita* excess benefit will show how much excess benefit is available per disadvantaged person to offset the total measurable excess benefit. Thus, if a measurable excess benefit is $1 million and the unmeasurable disservice will disadvantage one million people, the excess benefit of $1 million when spread over one million people implies that if each is willing to put up with less than $1 by way of compensation, the scheme will show an excess benefit. One then decides whether $1 per disadvantaged person is a reasonable compensation for the likely magnitude of the disservice. $1 may be so small in relation to the disservice as to demand consideration of another scheme or waiting until a more accurate estimate of the effect is carried out. Conversely, the per person benefit might be so large in relation to the disservice each victim suffers that no doubt remains that the scheme will produce an excess benefit. When to proceed this far is impossible, say, because the number of individuals affected cannot be estimated, the area of ignorance should be described in detail and included in the final listing of costs and benefits without any money value attached.

In measuring or considering the costs and benefits of a device, expediency may require restricting the analysis to a partial context in which secondary, tertiary and further reverberations of control are ignored if there is reason to believe that these are of minor importance or that the cost of their enumeration and quantification appear to be out of proportion to their likely significance. Not all of the incidental effects on the prices of other commodities and factors resulting from the contrived change in the price of the commodity under consideration are likely to be known, measurable or important. Even if they are measurable, the costs of taking the measurement and the possible marginal effect on the total outcome might not warrant the effort. Limiting consideration of indirect costs and benefits to those which are ethically acceptable in terms of the society's moral norms is academically acceptable as well. On purely utilitarian grounds we might measure as a benefit the perverse pleasure the low yield risk farmer derives by seeing his high yield risk neighbour suffer because of income instability resulting from a price stabilization programme. But this benefit would hardly be admissible on ethical grounds, whereas the benefit the low yield risk farmer derives from increased income stability would be.

a. Money Outlays and Receipts

Among the most apparent costs and benefits of a commodity control scheme are the actual money disbursements and receipts of the control authority. Money costs are associated with the negotiation of an agreement, cost-benefit surveys, capital outlays on physical plant and the costs of administration, including losses on stock held. Receipts, on the other hand, occur in the collection of levies by the authority, grants from government and income from the sale of stock. As elucidated earlier in the text, running costs or benefits to the authority may be considerable when the controlled price does not follow the trend of prices or the price range mean does not, in the shorter run, approximate the mean of the uncontrolled market equilibrium prices. Where attempts are made to directly control producer income or production, administrative costs can be large if production is on numerous widely dispersed production units. When investment in administrative buildings, warehouses and other facilities are part of a general improved marketing scheme, they are not legitimately attributable to the price control device. On the other hand, extensive marketing facilities such as a network of collection depots and transportation equipment may be installed not to improve marketing efficiency *per se*, but rather to insure that the producer receives the controlled price. Initial and running costs could be nominal if the device does not entail the storage of stocks and is operated by an already existing national or international organization. A progressive export tax, for example, may easily be fitted into an existing customs machinery.

Where bargaining on a national or international level plays a part, costs associated with the negotiations should be entered as an initial investment, along with outlays on fixed assets, against which future net benefits are compared. Negotiation should not occur if no excess benefit is likely to remain after the cost of negotiation has been accounted for in the cost-benefit calculations. The side initiating the negotiation might be expected to incur the largest initial costs, particularly if expensive public relation and other persuasive devices are needed to cajole the other side to sit down to the bargaining table. The initiator may indeed have to carry out the cost-benefit analysis for both sides, even if the other side is a foreign country, in order to show the other party that it has something to gain through commodity control. In making the assessment, the victims or benefactors must be identified and contacted. Fellow developing exporting countries may have to be persuaded to agree to the idea of making a common offer to importers, by way of a concession, in order to induce the importers to support a proposed measure. They must, moreover, bargain among themselves on how the benefits or concessions are to be shared. If a fairly high degree of accuracy is sought, the cost-benefit analysis itself can represent a significant cost, especially in light of the risk that subsequent action will not necessarily be justified. Costs of calculating the optimum device or combination of devices will be related to the degree of accuracy rather than to anticipated benefits.

It may be argued that neither persuasion nor cost-benefit calculation is needed if the costs of negotiations are less than the potential Pareto improvement, in which case agreement would be sought and reached automatically. Both sides will want to bargain if each stands to gain and believes that the other side will see gains to itself that will bring negotiations to fruition. But the argument that negotiations will occur automatically without a cost-benefit study disregards our frequent ignorance of the magnitude of the excess benefit until the impetus of bargaining induces further analysis.

Costs of negotiation will increase the greater the numbers of individuals or parties to be contacted and the more spurious the nature of the benefits. If the costs and benefits affect only commercial profits and the decision is to be taken by private enterprise, the acceptance or rejection of a control proposal will be straightforward. The costs of persuading the less economically minded public to make or accept an offer involving intangible spillovers may be considerably higher. Bargaining between parties and the costs of compensation measures to those disadvantaged can be avoided in control of domestically produced and consumed products provided it is agreed that any device which makes some worse off will be acceptable so long as the loss is less than the gain to those whose lot is improved.

One should not be content to regard money payments as a measure of benefits where the public pays for the service, for example, through a levy on exports to finance an international buffer stock or premiums on a crop insurance scheme. Even if the service is sold at a price that covers cost, the revenue collected will most likely be less than that which recipients would be willing to pay rather than do without the service. The full benefit to the beneficiaries of a service provided by a control device is equal to the area under the demand function for the service, rather than the price at which the service is being sold. Taxes on benefits under a device, such as benefits in the form of increased export earnings under a progressive export tax scheme in a demand inelastic market, are not deducted from the total benefits to society. Rather they should be regarded as transfer payments, means of spreading the benefits to other members of society. Similarly, if interest free funds are provided by the government to finance the device, the free funds are not an additional benefit; they are a transfer from general revenue to those who benefit from the device without paying the full cost.

b. Valuation of Indirect Effects

In the valuation of indirect effects of the device one can distinguish between those which are within the scope of the device and those which are external. Whether an effect is internal or external will depend on the objectives sought. Thus, if the device is set up solely on the producers' behalf and is designed to stabilize their income, increased income stability may be seen as an internal effect while benefits to consumers an external or spillover effect. Since the term 'spillover' normally connotes an incidental or unintentional effect, any unintended effect of the device on the producers whom it serves would be considered external as well. If the device is given the broad objective of increasing society's welfare, then all effects are internal so long as they are anticipated. In cost-benefit analysis it is necessary to assign money values to those internal and external effects which cannot be ignored. As mentioned above, losses and gains can sometimes be valued by reference to market prices. The money value placed on stable farm income, for instance, can be indicated by the popularity and the premiums paid for crop insurance while that which miners place on stable prices may be roughly indicated by the use and costs of hedging. Without a market mechanism that allows a price to be placed on losses and gains, no objective means of measuring them exists. Politically determined weights (premiums), for instance, may have to be assigned to benefit streams accruing to labour brought into employment by a device, to reflect the value of human dignity and political stability gained by this employment, and to income received by the poor to reflect the relatively high value poor people attach to marginal income. Similarly, governments may wish to indicate the benefits to society of greater production of nutritional pulses and less of rice and wheat by placing a favourable weight on the market value of the former since the superior dietary value of pulses is not usually reflected in the relative market prices of the two types of food.

i. *Compensating Variations*

Most indirect effects will ultimately have to be evaluated by reference
to the subjective estimates of those affected. An individual who is the
victim of an unfavourable effect is assumed to be willing to receive
some minimum sum, known as a compensating variation, in order to
tolerate it. This sum measures the 'value' of the disservice to him and
enters the cost-benefit calculation as a cost, even if no effort is made
to provide the compensation. (However, unanimous agreement between communities to implement control implies an understanding
that compensation is to be made to those communities disadvantaged
with benefits to the others exceeding the amount of the compensation.)
For those made better off, the compensating variation measures the
maximum sum an individual or community will pay rather than do
without the device. The compensating variation of buying a service
or product at a different price will be the loss or gain in consumer's
surplus and that for selling a factor at a different price will be the
factor rent lost or gained. The compensating variations individuals
place on the price risk may be ascertained by asking them, for instance,
what certain price they would accept if it is known that the average
future price would be $20 with an equal chance of it being $10 or $30
in any given period. If their answer is, say, $15, then the value of the
risk, or risk premium, is $20–$15 or $5. Again, if it is known that a
producer's income will decline by $50 with control, his compensating
variation, the minimum sum of compensation needed to make him
feel as well off as before, will most likely be $50. In the calculations
of the following sections we will assume that it is.

In commodity control foreknowledge as to which persons will be
affected or by how much they will be affected cannot be taken for
granted. Indeed, in some periods an individual may be a beneficiary
and in others a victim of the device while other individuals will remain
totally unaffected. The preceding chapter illustrated, for example, how
a single exporting country might be required to make a transfer to
consuming countries in a low earnings period if under a multilateral
contract its production declined more than proportionately with a
price increase during a period of ceiling price support. At the time of
negotiation no one may know which country will experience this unfavourable phenomenon. Thus, the relevant cost here is not the compensating variation of the disadvantaged country in this predicament,
but the compensating variation of the risk to all countries that any of
them will find themselves in it. The individual (or country), however,
tends to underestimate the value of the risks he assumes (especially

when the statistical risk is small) in the sense that if he does become the victim of the device, the value he attaches to his hardship is more than the periodical valuations placed on the risk. In other words, if in a poor crop year the poor uninsured farmer was asked whether the savings on not paying fair crop insurance premiums was worth the hardship of a poor crop year, he would reply in the negative. A beneficiary of a device may in fact deliberately understate his need for a benefit of the device in the expectation that he would thereby be relieved of a part or all of his share of the cost without affecting the gain he received. The logical extension to this line of reasoning is that a commodity control device may be accepted, on the basis of undervalued individual compensating variations, that will bring widespread hardship and political crisis. Risks can go unnoticed or be improperly evaluated by the individual, no matter how great an effort is made to disseminate information on the device. However, if we are to maintain that the individual is the best judge of his own interest, it is *his* compensating variation that is used in the cost-benefit calculation. Acceptance of his judgement is consistent with the belief that he should determine the quantity of a commodity or service he will buy at the market price.

The compensating variations of the risks attached to commodity control proffered in the political debate surrounding acceptance or rejection of a proposed device are not to be confused with the actual compensating variations individuals themselves would assign. Every risk to which the politician can assign a value might be more accurately estimated by directly surveying those affected. A public fully informed as to the various effects of a device might be able to indicate the net excess benefit or loss through a referendum. Although this method may improve upon a purely political decision, it is not to be preferred over the survey since it offers those who are greatly affected by the device no more influence individually than those marginally affected or unaffected.

ii. *Surpluses and Rents*
The optimum degree of control is determined at that point where the subjective price or sum which recipients are willing to pay for the service is equal to the social costs. At this point the marginal social valuation should equal marginal social cost in a manner discussed with reference to Figure 3.1c in Chapter 3 (p. 68). In line with this principle the optimum reduction in uncontrolled market income fluctuations, given the functions of Figure 6.1, would be 30 per cent. If the device has only one objective as far as the exporting country is concerned,

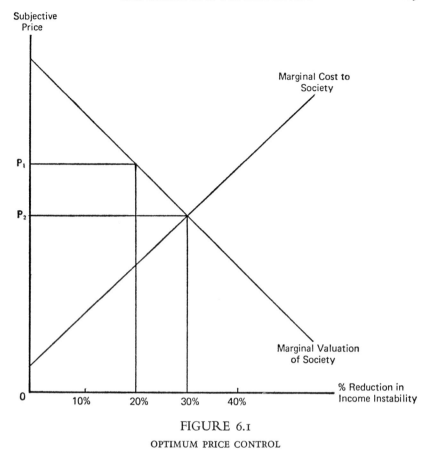

FIGURE 6.1

OPTIMUM PRICE CONTROL

namely, producer income stability, and the only favourable effect is a reduction in income instability, then the marginal valuation curve for society would measure what producers in aggregate are willing to pay for various degrees of income stability. If there is no 'objective' measure of this curve, it could be estimated by asking producers what they are willing to pay for, say a 10 per cent reduction in income instability, 20 per cent and so forth. The demand margin from 20 to 30 per cent for Figure 6.1 delineates the maximum amount producers would be willing to pay to see their income instability reduced by 30 per cent instead of 20 per cent. If producers do not pay the cost of the device, their gain is the entire area under the marginal valuation curve from 20 to 30 per cent. However, it is likely that they will pay some of the costs in the form of reduced profits with price stabilization, for instance (cf. Chapter 3, Section 5, p. 80), or reduced income (cf. Chapter 4, Sections 2b, p. 122 and 4b, p. 139). Other costs to producers may arise from loss of market share, a freeze on the pattern of trade, export earnings instability, and loss on stocks held. Since most devices produce joint services or services and disservices, it is necessary, when inquiring as to the value of a device to a producer, to obtain net valuations. Thus, a producer might be asked the value to him of a 50 per cent reduction in income instability with a 5 per cent decrease in income, a 40 per cent reduction in income instability with a 4 per cent decrease in income, and so forth. Valuations of different effects cannot be determined separately for the value he places on a single effect will be influenced by the other effects.

Benefits estimated from surveys of existing producers of the primary commodity being considered for control should be augmented where important by the sum of prospective benefits to those who switch from alternative outputs to the income stabilized commodity, the sum of additional quasi-rents to those who continue producing the alternatives at higher prices which come with reduced production, and the costs to existing producers of the controlled commodity in the form of reduced prices as production expands. Production will expand with the reduction in costs (i.e. reduction in risk premiums) and with the influx of producers switching from alternative employments. Where the primary commodity is partly or entirely consumed domestically, the benefits and costs to domestic consumers will also enter the assessment. With a fall in the price of the controlled commodity as costs decline, consumers will benefit by the amount of this decrease and in the reduction in price of close but imperfect substitutes from which consumers switch their purchases. Consumers' surplus for the close substitute of the controlled commodity is reduced as demand for that commodity shifts to the left, but this is countered by an increase due to the reduction in its price. In order to elicit the switch, however, there must be a net gain in surplus. The importance of consumers' surplus for a single commodity will likely diminish with increases in the number of close substitutes and the income of the consumer. In developing countries, low income and a frequently limited variety of goods implies a need for greater stress on this aspect than in developed countries.

The cost of factor movements out of production of the close substitute into new occupations as a result of reduction in the demand for the substitute should where perceptible enter the calculus as a cost. In the short run these factors may also suffer a reduction in their prices as they move to lower paying employment. On the other hand, factors shifting to the production of the income stabilized commodity would experience an increase in their factor prices that is entered as a benefit. If unemployed factors are brought into employment by the device, the price attached to those factors is the price needed to induce them to forego leisure for work. Normally, any price above zero can be expected to be sufficient inducement for non-human factors, unless owners of land and capital derive some enjoyment from their non-use. Human factors, however, can be expected to place a value on unemployment. Only when an individual has no preference for leisure is his opportunity cost zero. If account is to be taken of non-pecuniary factors, the opportunity cost to society, according to one view, can be seen as the minimum wage the unemployed would be willing to accept in the new occupation, less any tangible or intangible benefits he receives from his family or government when unemployed.

The rise in wage of those who were producing the controlled commodity before control was introduced is a benefit insofar as factors are being paid more than is necessary to maintain them in the production of that commodity. For those factors that switch to the production of the controlled commodity, an increase in factor surplus would occur if the rise in income is more than sufficient to induce the switch. If surplus is defined as the amount paid a factor above what it would receive in its next most lucrative employment, surplus (rent or quasi-rent) can be considerable in the short run if the factor is specific to a certain function or is in oversupply.

The consumer can switch between a variety of products and only spend a portion of his budget on any single type of good; his welfare may not be severely affected by a pronounced change in the price of a single good. The individual who can supply only one type of labour is more exposed to change in his price. Thus, changes in producer surplus can be of relatively greater importance than changes in consumer surplus in a cost-benefit calculation. On the other hand, control devices are likely to have more influence on the price of the controlled commodity than on the price of its factors where factor prices are determined on a wide national or international market. Care should be taken to avoid double counting where factors are also consumers. A price stabilization scheme which stabilizes the real income of food deficit farmers, for example, also stabilizes their real expenditure. Likewise, care must be taken not to count any perceptible increase in consumers' factor rents when consumers' surplus is increased. An increase in consumers' surplus as a result of a price decline, for instance, will mean consumers are willing to demand more for a given amount of work because of the income effect.

Any summing up of effects on individuals should, where relevant, include effects to those individuals who do not produce the product in question but who regard its control as a form of insurance should they at some future date choose to produce it, thereby raising their opportunity value. If the device under consideration encourages other types of control that produce unfavourable effects, these are also included in the cost-benefit calculation. For example, an export quota device might be supported with a production control scheme (rather than national stockholding) which produces unemployment. Again, financial commitments to an international buffer stock may induce an inequitable tax in participating countries. In the latter case, although the cost of financing the stock will already have been included in the assessment of the device, a regressive tax should prompt qualification of results obtained on strictly cost-benefit terms.

A calculation of costs and benefits over time should be prefaced by an estimate of the growth rate of relevant independent variables and of the population likely to be affected. The magnitude of the social benefit or cost can increase merely because the same device is affecting a greater number of people as the population expands. With a static society, the sizes of affected groups of people within it may change. If, for example, a land reform programme or settlement scheme exists causing a movement of production from plantations to smallholds, the aggregate costs and benefits, and certainly their distribution will be affected. The percentage fluctuation in income may remain unchanged over time under a particular device, but a net loss in income with price control in a demand shift market will increase with the volume of trade. As per capita income increases, so will the ability to stabilize yields through irrigation and plant protection measures. If the price is stabilized, then the benefits accruing through income stability will increase with per capita income where this is accompanied by greater ability to control output. An increase in consumer income implies a wider variety of purchases and a smaller proportion of all purchases dependent on any single commodity. Moreover, as income increases, the ability to absorb risks rises. Increased income and the consequent greater ability to pay for a service, however, will call for an increased valuation on non-pecuniary gains and losses to individuals.

Once consumer surplus or factor rent has been estimated with and without the prospective control, further deductions or additions for changes in risks and wealth are not necessary since these are presumably already included when the individual shapes his supply or demand function for the service to be rendered by the device. However, risks may be encountered which he cannot anticipate at the time of the estimate. For instance, risks under an export quota device or international buffer stock will be dependent upon the number of participants, a fact which is not known until the signed agreement is ratified by individual governments. The original estimates will have to be modified in the light of the number of participants if this number differs from that upon which the estimates are made.

iii. Valuation of Production

One approach in valuing the benefits and costs of changes in output as a result of a control device, the OECD (Little & Mirrlees) approach, relates these to the earnings, savings or use of foreign exchange. Since a) everything produced and consumed domestically has an effect on the balance of payments, b) we can value any good in terms of foreign exchange because of substitution possibilities and c) foreign exchange itself can be used to satisfy almost any want, world prices are seen as the appropriate accounting prices. World prices express the real cost or benefit of using or producing a good to the country in terms of foreign exchange. They may not be more 'rational' than domestic prices, but they do express the actual terms on which a country can trade. In the valuation (costing) of outputs (inputs), all goods and services are classified according to whether they are traded or non-traded or are domestic resources such as land and labour. If the country has no perceptible influence on world prices of a traded good (is a price-taker), then all exportables are valued in terms of f.o.b. prices while all importables are accorded c.i.f. prices. Where the country has some influence on world prices, then exportables are valued in terms of the marginal export revenue they generate and importables according to the marginal import cost.

Since non-traded goods and services use up traded inputs in their production and, thus, are likely to affect the balance of payments, their traded components should be valued according to the above principles. The residual non-traded components, as well as non-traded goods which cannot be broken down into their components in this fashion and domestic resources are valued according to their marginal social cost. For instance, unskilled labour is valued by its shadow wage rate:

$$\text{SWR} = c - \frac{1}{s}(c - m) \text{ where } c \text{ is the wage rate or the earnings of}$$

a smallholder for his labour services, m the marginal product in alternative employment (e.g. subsistence agriculture) and s the value of a unit of savings or investment in consumption units. $s = 1$ so long as savings and investment are in equilibrium or already high or if taxes can be readily increased or money put to no more valuable use by the government than by the producer. The latter would not be true (and $s > 1$), for instance, if the government redistributed income to persons poorer than those gaining employment as a result of the control device. If $s = 1$ then $SWR = m$. In full employment $m = c$. The SWR and other costs or benefits which are expressed in domestic currency (e.g. compensating variations and the direct costs or benefits to the control authority) are aligned with world prices by a so-called 'standard conversion factor' which corrects for any over or under valuation of the domestic currency such that all costs and benefits are in terms of their foreign exchange equivalent (i.e., in world prices).

The OECD approach has been challenged on a number of grounds. For instance, it seems to suggest that if the device changes the domestic production of an imported good, this change is to be valued by the foreign exchange equivalent lost or gained, irrespective of whether or not the change in production leaves domestic supply (domestic production plus imports) unchanged. The UNIDO (Dasgupta, Sen & Marglin) approach holds that if optional trade policies are not being followed, the value of a change in the domestic availability of a commodity (an output or input) is indicated by consumers' willingness to pay for the change (shown by the demand margin, that is the area under the demand function for the amount of the change in supply). Where a quota is being used to support the domestic price, for example, the effect of a device which changes domestic output but leaves the quota unchanged would be valued according to the demand margin lost or gained. If the device altered the quota, however, its effect would be valued according to the foreign exchange lost or gained.

4. THE DECISION-MAKER'S FUNCTION

Decisions on the choice of a device are reached by comparing the present social value of the excess social benefits (social profits) for the prospective period of control under alternative types of devices and under each type with different control provisions. Combinations of devices may also be usefully considered. Although theoretically a cost-effectiveness approach could be utilized, its application is often limited by political constraints. A cost-effectiveness analysis entails the multiplication of 'output'-cost ratios of each objective under alternative devices by the weights attached to these objectives. The optimum device is that yielding the lowest weighted cost for all objectives under consideration. Because an operational statement of objectives is frequently a significant hurdle in commodity negotiations, one can infer that the further specification of the utility function required in weighting objectives would most likely be an insurmountable problem. Being mortal, governments and negotiators come and go, and while present they are inconsistent. Weights they assign to objectives, and the objectives themselves, may be largely arbitrary and unrelated to the compensating variations of society. Negotiators often represent the party in power in their respective countries and, thus, act as politicians. The politician's professional role is to maximize votes or confidence and to stay in office. By its very nature the profession does not allow the stating of weighted objectives, for by doing so those who do not agree are alienated. The assessment of the compensating variations in a careful cost-benefit analysis would already include society's most important objective (consumption maximization); further enumeration and quantification of objectives (national power, autarky, full employment etc.) may not be useful if they are already encompassed by the data, of minor importance, or inconsistent with the consumption objective. The cost-effectiveness approach omits the difficult problem of estimating benefits, since it is an exercise in finding the least cost methods, but it does not indicate which device will provide the greatest excess benefit.

a. THE DISCOUNT RATE

All calculations of a cost-benefit analysis, when quantified in terms of a standard unit of exchange and reduced to a single point in time, are seen as positive or negative contributions to a potential Pareto improvement. The magnitude of the present value when compared to the initial investment is a measure of the extent of the improvement. Given a rate of discount equal to the social rate of time preference for the community under consideration, the present value equivalence of a control device's future net benefit stream will indicate a gain to society if it exceeds the value of using the same investment resources for present consumption. Where there is a single rate of interest for fairly riskless investments on local money markets, reason to believe that this reflects the time preference of those affected by the device (i.e, a perfect capital market) and no externalities, this rate, according to one persuasion, can be used as the social rate of discount in the present value criterion. If different rates of time preference exist among those affected by control, the capitalization of their compensating variations at a uniform rate will result in their present value being different from what the individuals themselves would have assigned. Moreover, the individual's rate of discount may increase with time and with the size of the benefit or loss. The further away the benefit or loss the greater is the preference placed on current welfare, particularly if his income is increasing secularly. The smaller the benefit, the less difference it will make whether it is received now or in the future. The market rate of interest may exceed society's time preference, particularly in developing countries, if financial institutions for mobilizing savings for investment are underdeveloped and if a portion of business gross profits are not invested because business enterprises invest only out of profits net of taxes. Furthermore, the market rate of interest will be influenced by other fiscal and monetary policies and will vary with the level of employment and output. Where market rates of interest are an unreliable indicator of an individual's time preference, it may be ascertained by enquiring as to what present and future sums he views as interchangeable. If he is indifferent between $100 today and $120 in a year's time, his subjective rate of discount is 20 per cent. Should he receive less than $120 in a year's time for $100 of present consumption foregone, he will suffer loss in welfare. The interest rate on loans for consumption purposes would be an indication of the consumption rate of interest (social rate of time preference). The government, as a proxy for the people, may, however, be the most practical indicator of society's intertemporal time preference for a particular project.

Control devices will affect the level of savings since they redistribute income between groups with different marginal propensities to save: smallholders, estates and the government. Owing to the existence of sub-optimal savings in many developing countries and the need to increase savings, it may be useful to identify to whom the benefits of control actually accrue so that separate benefit streams can be constructed for consumption and savings with a higher weight attached to savings as against consumption. If a case is made for differential valuation of savings and consumption benefits, then it is only proper that there be differential valuation of investment funds according to whether the funds are raised from displaced consumption or displaced investment. If the latter, a higher weight should be attached. In the simple case where returns are to be had in perpetuity and all returns are completely consumed, the weight to be attached to displaced investment is given by the ratio of the social rate of return to the social rate of time preference. The social rate of return is the return on the next best alternative investment when the inputs and outputs are valued at shadow prices. One should only consider those control devices with positive net present values after benefits and costs are weighed as suggested here.

When there are no expenses or benefits whose effects are spread over time (as is possible with a progressive export tax, for example) we must nonetheless discount to the present in order to compare the net excess social benefits of alternative devices. Discounting becomes unnecessary only when there are two discrete periods to the analysis and initial period investments are identical for all devices considered. In this case, discounting the second period to the present will have no effect on the outcome since all entries in the second period are affected proportionately. The answer will not remain unambiguous, however, if further periods are considered. (The length of the period, whether a month, year or some other measure, may affect the outcome when more than two periods are considered and values are discounted to the present.) Most devices will have expenses whose effects are not solely concentrated in the period in which they occur. International agreements will have those associated with negotiation if no others. The investment in stocks under stockholding schemes will produce effects which are not realized until the stocks are sold. Moreover, the costs of maintaining administrative facilities and stocks during periods of no control is a form of investment in a future benefit stream.

Discounting future net benefits automatically corrects for future uncertainty; the further into the future the realization of anticipated benefits is, the smaller are the weights attached to these. A premium can be placed on the discount rate where uncertainty is a strictly compounding function of time. This conveniently reduces the need to assign arbitrary cut-off points to the analysis as well as the need to express uncertainty by widening the margin between the probable maximum and minimum excess benefits as these are projected further into the future. A project which may prove worthwhile only in the longer run, such as a buffer stock, may be rejected on the grounds that in the short run for which we have the most reliable predictions it makes a loss on stock held. For this reason it might be unwise to establish a cut-off after two periods, for instance, if it appears, although with greater uncertainty, that the loss could be recouped in the third period. In international agreements the cut-off would, in any case, be three to five years after its inception as this is the accepted duration.

b. Procedures

The procedure in applying the above principles is perhaps best illustrated with an example. Suppose that an exporting country, aware that international agreement on control cannot be reached, is confronted with a choice of the three national devices of Appendix 3 (p. 254), namely the progressive export tax, national buffer fund and national buffer stock, or no control at all. Choice among such national devices conveniently simplifies the analysis since an actual Pareto improvement between communities in international commodity control is not necessary for implementation to occur. The international demand facing the exporting country is ascertained to have an elasticity (N_D) in both periods of the analysis of -0.5 while supply elasticity (N_S) is found to be 0.5. The market is identified as one of supply shift. The analysis is set for two periods on the alternative assumptions that the device chosen is to exist for two periods only, that a very uncertain future necessitates a truncated time horizon, or that the supply shift sequence illustrated will be followed by identical ones in succeeding periods (i.e. the only change in market conditions will be a supply function which alternates with equal probability in consecutive periods between the two positions represented in the appendix). A condensation of benefits and costs of each of the three national devices under these conditions (from Tables A3.2, A3.6, A3.8 and A3.10 of Appendix 3) is given in Table 6.1.

For simplicity of exposition we may further assume that actual changes in export earnings accurately reflect the value of the change to society (in the terms of Section 3b, iii, above, the commodity is a traded good) and that secondary and tertiary effects do not occur or that their likely magnitude does not justify the expense of an estimate. No national weight is assigned here to foreign exchange earnings which would reflect the 'merit want' of independence from the strings that inevitably attach to foreign aid and private foreign investment. No weights reflecting the value placed on income received by the poor or unemployed are assigned to these flows. Losses and gains in producers' income and profits and in government revenue do not enter the calculus since they are already included in export earnings. Because government revenue and money losses or profits to the control authority represent transfer payments they do not enter the analysis as separate costs or benefits. Should for instance, the buffer fund or buffer stock operate through a statutory marketing board or other semi-autonomous body which is taxed, these taxes (as taxes on producer income gains) will not be subtracted from the estimate of social benefits; the value of such taxes is part of the social benefit. The valuation of changes in the fluctuations in these variables are not, however, included in the valuation of changes in export earning fluctuations.

Values of the net percentage changes in percentage fluctuations of the price and income variables can be derived from surveys of individuals affected. Let us assume that a survey of producers and government

TABLE 6.1

COSTS AND BENEFITS FOR THREE NATIONAL DEVICES IN A SUPPLY SHIFT MARKET WITH $N_S = 0.5$ AND $N_D = -0.5$

(From Appendix 3)

Device		World Price % Fluctuation	Producer Price % Fluctuation	Producer Income Level	Producer Income % Fluctuation	Export Earnings Level	Export Earnings % Fluctuation	Profits (Rent) Level	Profits % Fluctuation	Revenue Level	Tax Cost
Uncontrolled Market		40%	40%	20,309	20%	20,309	20%	10,166	40.2%	0	–
Progressive Export Tax	Gross	44%	36%	17,551	13%	21,327	22%	8,328	35%	3,776	0
	Compared to Uncontrolled Market	+10%	-10%	-2,758	-30%	+1,018	+10%	-1,838	-12%	3,776	0
	Valuation	-20	+500	–	+800	+1,018	-200	–	–	–	0
National Buffer Fund	Gross	59%	20%	20,705	10%	20,284	30%	10,430	1%	-421	–
	Compared to Uncontrolled Market	+50%	-50%	+396	-50%	-25	+50%	+364	-96%	-421	–
	Valuation	-100	+2,500	–	+1,333	-25	-1,000	–	–	–	-200
National Buffer Stock	Gross	20%	20%	20,705	10%	20,387	10%	10,430	19%	-319	–
	Compared to Uncontrolled Market	-50%	-50%	+396	-50%	+76	-50%	+364	-96%	-319	–
	Valuation	+100	+2,500	–	+1,333	+76	+1,000	–	–	–	-400

officials enlightened as to the compensating variations of their constituents, where these exist, indicates that in aggregate, society places a value of 20 on each decrease of 10 per cent (or —20 on each increase of 10 per cent) in world price fluctuations. This, then, is the value of decreased price risk to domestic consumers and the subjective present value producers place on the prospects of greater international demand or less search for substitutes and economies in the use of the export. Thus, the valuation of increased world price instability from 40 per cent to 44 per cent due to the progressive export tax is —20, for this change represents a 10 per cent increase in world price instability. Likewise, the producers' compensating variations for a 10 per cent change in their price stability (regardless of what happens to the world price) is assumed to be 500; and a 30 per cent change in income stability 800 (this figure includes the value attached to profit stability). Those who rely on imports for consumption and investment purposes place a further aggregate valuation of 200 on each 10 per cent change in export earnings percentage fluctuations. In making these separate valuations it is assumed, somewhat unrealistically, that they are independent of the effects of joint services or disservices.

Assessment of the buffer fund and buffer stock devices requires the assignment of an additional cost of, say, 200 in those periods where they perform no revenue raising function, on the assumption that the government will have to resort to some other means of raising the revenue that it would have collected under the export tax. This 200 represents the differential between the cheap export tax method of raising revenue and the more expensive alternative methods. Since the buffer fund spends more than it accumulates in supporting the producer price, and the buffer stock accumulates more stock than it can sell, losses are made on fund activities and stockholding.

The present values (shown in Table 6.2) are derived by an application of a hypothetical social rate of discount of 5 per cent to the net benefits of the second period values. Since it affords no choice between future and current consumption, the initial period of investment and/or operation requires no discount. Gains and losses resulting from changes in the percentage fluctuations are assumed to be divided evenly between the two periods. Stock sold by the buffer stock in the first period of ceiling price support is assumed to have been accumulated in the period immediately preceding. The investment in this stock has been compounded forward to the present period (first period) at 5 per cent. If periodical costs or benefits are respectively subtracted from or added to benefits in the period in which they occur, the result is a

TABLE 6.2

PRESENT VALUE OF THREE NATIONAL DEVICES IN A SUPPLY SHIFT MARKET WITH $N_S = 0.5$ AND $N_D = -0.5$

(From Appendix 3 and Table 6.1)

Device	Period	World Price	Producer Price	Producer Income Level	Producer Income Stability	Export Earnings Level	Export Earnings Stability	Profit (Rent) Level	Profit Stability	Revenue	Tax Cost	Excess Social Benefit
Progressive Export Tax	1st	-10	+250	-1,821	+400	+683	-100	-1,214	+50	+2,504	0	1,273
	2nd	-10	+250	-937	+400	+335	-100	-624	+50	+1,272	0	925
	Present Value of 2nd	-9.5	+238	–	+381	+319	-95	–	–	–	0	833
	Valuation	-19.5	+488	–	+781	+1,002	-195	–	–	–	0	2,056
National Buffer Fund	1st	-50	+1,250	-1,368	+666	+497	-500	-912	+400	+1,865	0	2,263
	2nd	-50	+1,250	+1,764	+666	-522	-500	+1,176	+400	-2,286	-200	1,044
	Present Value of 2nd	-48	+1,190	–	+634	-497	-476	–	–	–	-190	613
	Valuation	-98	+2,440	–	+1,300	0	-976	–	–	–	-190	2,476
National Buffer Stock	1st	+50	+1,250	-1,268	+666	-476	+500	-912	+400	-45 +892 (+937)	-200	2,145
	2nd	+50	+1,250	+1,764	+666	+553	+500	+1,176	+400	-1,211	-200	3,219
	Present Value of 2nd	+48	+1,190	–	+634	+527	+476	–	–	–	-190	2,685
	Valuation	+98	+2,400	–	+1,300	+51	+976	–	–	–	-390	4,430

succession of net benefits (shown in the right hand column of Table 6.2) to which investment criteria can be applied. In making a horizontal summation of the net benefit over the two periods figures relating to the level of producer income, government revenue, authority losses or gains or producer profits are not included. Inclusion of these figures would entail double counting. On the basis of the narrow set of considerations applied here and assuming no initial disbursement, the national buffer stock gives the greatest excess social benefit. This outcome can be rejected on considerations of income distribution and would be turned into a near draw between the buffer stock and buffer fund if, for instance, ample foreign exchange reserves meant there was no aggregate valuation on changes in export earnings stability.

In a practical application of this method of analysis, subtractions of the costs of negotiation and surveys, depreciation on warehouses and administrative buildings, administrative expenses and the various costs associated with the storage of stocks would occur before net benefits of the three devices are compared. Both periods one and two net benefits would be discounted to the period preceding period one if investment in negotiation and buildings was incurred before the device became operative in period one. Net benefits of the tax, buffer fund and buffer stock devices discounted to the preceding period, 2,056, 2,476 and 4,430, respectively, should be compared to investment costs to determine the optimum device. If the progressive export tax called for no investment while the buffer fund and buffer stock each entailed investment of 3,000, the progressive export tax would be the optimum device.

The ranking can be altered if money earnings or losses, particularly those accruing to the authority, are considered as investment (or investment foregone) and their returns in perpetuity discounted to the present. Encashed benefits which are reinvested may be assumed to give a rate of return at least as high as the market rate. If the propensity to save out of private income changes under a scheme is known, this procedure can also be applied to the private sector so long as compensating variations are not also estimated. Compensating variations attached to changes in the stability and magnitude of variables will presumably already include the subjective present value of future income streams lost or gained.

Additional cost calculations may be necessary if, after arriving at the greatest excess social benefit device, important unfavourable welfare effects and spillovers remain that must be rectified. Producer income loss in a demand shift market may, for instance, present a formidable political obstacle to the acceptance of a device. Although this loss can be reduced with increases in the controlled price range spread, this itself may seriously impair other aspects of the device. An ancillary scheme could be introduced either to compensate producers for their loss or to induce those who are adversely affected to shift from production of the commodity. The latter course might be considered for high yield risk farmers under a price stabilization scheme. The Pareto improvement is maximized without altering the price range spread if an ancillary device is introduced which spends on income stabilization up to the point at which the costs are equal to the first device's net benefits. This additional intervention in the market would raise society's marginal valuation curve for the device as well as its marginal social cost curve (cf. Figure 6.1). An export quota scheme that stabilizes export earnings might be added to an international buffer stock that destabilizes them. But if, *ceteris paribus*, the resulting control of production brings unemployment, the export quota should not be contemplated as an adjunct unless the loss through unemployment is offset by the gain in export earnings stability. Costs of supplementary efforts may alter the initial ranking so that preference is given to a device that produces a more favourable welfare effect.

In any practical application of cost-benefit analysis, the analysis leading to the construction of Table 6.2 will most likely have to be done for a number of price ranges and market conditions. The net excess benefits under a series of controlled price range spreads are multiplied by the probability of a given market condition occurring and then summed to give a weighted average excess benefit for each device and spread. Table 6.3 illustrates hypothetical excess benefits for a single device and period under three alternative price range spreads and four market conditions. Here, the assumption is that past records indicate a 1/10 probability of a 20 unit horizontal shift in the demand function, a 3/10 probability of a 40 unit demand shift, a 2/10 probability of a 20 unit supply shift, and a 4/10 probability of a 40 unit supply shift. (Price fluctuations can be used instead of shifts to determine costs and benefits in the manner of Appendix 4.) The optimal price range for the device under consideration is seen to be 5 cents. If the probabilities of shifts in functions were unknown, a device with a 5 cents price spread might be rejected because it carries a chance of a 1,500 loss.

An alternative to the above approach is to estimate an upper and lower limit to the most likely outcome for each item under consideration. For example, the most likely demand shift of, say, 35 would be bracketed by estimated extreme limits of 20 and 50. These limits can be

TABLE 6.3

RANKING OF EXCESS BENEFITS WHEN THE PROBABILITY
OF MARKET CONDITIONS IS KNOWN

Controlled Price Spread	Shifts in Functions				Weighted Average Excess Benefit
	Demand Shifts		Supply Shifts		
	20	40	20	40	
5c.	$-300 \times \frac{1}{10}$	$-1,500 \times \frac{3}{10}$	$+\ 300 \times \frac{2}{10}$	$+1,500 \times \frac{4}{10}$	$+180$
10c.	$-600 \times \frac{1}{10}$	$-1,000 \times \frac{3}{10}$	$+600 \times \frac{2}{10}$	$+1,000 \times \frac{4}{10}$	$+160$
15c.	$-1,200 \times \frac{1}{10}$	$-500 \times \frac{3}{10}$	$+1,200 \times \frac{2}{10}$	$+500 \times \frac{4}{10}$	$+170$

widened to accommodate the increased margin of error with the length of the projection. The choice of a device is straightforward if the present values of all the resulting extreme net excess benefits either meet or fail to meet the investment criterion used. If the pessimistic estimate does not meet it, while the others do, the choice will depend on the magnitude of the unfavourable outcome and the likelihood of its occurring. When it is possible to calculate the probability of a given market condition, each period of the analysis will have as many outcomes as there are likely market conditions. Suppose the calculations resulting in Table 6.3, which covers one inter-period comparison only, were to be extended to a second. For any given price range there would be four possible market conditions in each period or 16 possible outcomes over the two periods. If net excess benefits for all price increments from zero to 15 cents. were calculated, there would be 240 outcomes. A comparison of four devices would bring this to 960 outcomes. Sensitivity tests, in which one variable is altered to determine its influence on the outcome, may be used to reduce the manipulation of variables to those most likely to have a significant influence on results.

The probability of any given outcome for a single device will be equal to the product of the separate probabilities of each of the two periods, say $3/10 \times 1/10$ or 3 per cent. For each device and price range spread a probability distribution can be constructed which will indicate the most likely outcome. Since a normal distribution can be expected, calculation of its standard deviation will permit an estimate of the probability of an outcome falling within specified limits. We might estimate, for example, a 97.5 per cent chance of a benefit of at least 3,000 and a 1 per cent chance of a negative benefit of −100 or less with a particular device and price range spread. Needless to say, cost-benefit analysis with even the few variables of this example would require the assistance of a computer.

Cost-benefit analysis along the lines suggested above assumes that each exporting country would exclude consideration of the costs of its action to other countries. The costs to itself of the participation or non-participation of other countries would be taken into consideration, but not the costs to others of its participation or non-participation. Developed countries which wish to aid developing countries would, however, be expected to take into account external effects of their action in their cost-benefit calculations.

c. A POLITICAL QUALIFICATION

Since governments make the decisions as to whether countries will participate in an international commodity agreement or set up a national device, the action adopted may be more the upshot of political conflict than of a considered effort to improve the welfare of society as a whole through the most effective economic means available. As mentioned earlier, a referendum might improve upon the politicians' decision, but even here single votes cannot be weighted to account for the difference in value attached to a device by different voters. A system which allows politicians to determine the quantitative valuations of control is likely to produce results which are inconsistent with those derived through economic analysis. Even when the economist is asked to make a cost-benefit study, the ultimate decision lies with the political machine. If the economist has ignored spillovers that are difficult to measure, in order to present what appears to be firm quantitative results from those effects which can be measured, the latitude for political interpretation is increased. Politicians may use a coherent body of principles in their assessment but in terms of allocative economics these will appear largely arbitrary and the rationale lying behind the choice of a device on the basis of a mixture of both economic and political criteria will be open to no consistent interpretation. Rejected cost-benefit analysis embodying politically determined weights will nevertheless be useful in the long run for it will remind politicians of the existence of rational policies. When confronted with rejection of studies, it is well for the economist to remember that legitimate cost-benefit analysis is made according to independent economic principles, not according to those which rationalize the political process.

5. SUMMARY

Primary commodity control devices have a multitude of often diverging effects on the economic environment, and so it is useful when deciding between devices to employ a system of ordering and summing the effects of single devices in order to facilitate their ranking according to their net contribution to economic welfare. Cost-benefit analysis provides such a method. It allows comparison through the quantification of all effects in terms of a standard unit of measurement and reduction of effects over time to a single point in time. It avoids the troublesome task encountered in cost-effectiveness analysis of specifying operational objectives and their weights; these are implicitly part of the valuation of all significant effects on society in cost-benefit terms.

A common allocative criterion used in such analysis, the potential Pareto improvement, specifies that if the benefits of control could be distributed so as to make some in the community under consideration better off without making anyone worse off, there is an improvement in aggregate welfare. By overlooking the distribution effects of control, however, this criterion can be an inadequate measure of social gain. Results derived by an application of this principle may be considered a first approximation to an optimal control device, to be qualified or rejected by a later consideration of distributional equity. The disparity of results obtained with these two criteria can be small if a redistribution in wealth benefits those to whom it provides the greatest utility or if taxes are sufficiently progressive and competition intense.

Cost-benefit precepts call for an enumeration of all important costs and benefits to the control authority as well as to society in general over the period of the analysis. Aside from the problems of projection of possible market conditions in which the device is to operate, the measurement and valuation of indirect internal and external effects of a device require much of the effort in a cost-benefit analysis, particularly in commodity control where the major effects are external to the unit administering the control device. Where estimates cannot be made through observed price and income elasticities, crop insurance premiums, and costs of hedging, for example, resort must be had to the less 'objective' survey approach. Aggregation of survey information may not be possible, however, if the number of people affected in a certain manner is unknown.

Money costs of commodity control are associated with the negotiation of an agreement, cost-benefit surveys, physical plant, stock accumulation and administration. Costs may be particularly high where the authority attempts to control the trend of prices or to directly control producer income or production on numerous widely scattered producing units. On the other hand, they may be nominal if the administration of the device is placed in the hands of an organization in which the necessary operational machinery already exists. Costs of negotiation represent a significant initial investment to the side which takes the initiative if this entails expensive public relations and other persuasive devices or a comprehensive cost-benefit survey for all parties in order to demonstrate that all sides stand to gain by agreement. Costs of bargaining between producers and consumers and among participants on each side of the market as to the distribution of costs and benefits among themselves enter the calculus as an initial investment for which returns will accrue over the period of the agreement.

In assigning money values to indirect effects it is assumed that an individual made better off on balance would be willing to offer a maximum sum of money rather than go without the benefit. The aggregate value of a favourable effect from a service provided by a control device, such as increased income stability, is the area under the marginal valuation curve of those who benefit by the service. However, their net benefit may be less than this amount if they directly or indirectly pay for the benefit through, for example, reduced profits with price stabilization, reduced income, loss of market share, a freeze on the pattern of trade, export earnings instability or loss on stock held. The optimum degree of control is indicated by the point at which the aggregate marginal valuation of society for a service is equal to the aggregate marginal social cost.

Indirect benefits in the form of increased factor rents accruing to those who switch from alternative outputs to the income stabilized commodity and to those who continue producing the alternative at the higher price which comes with reduced output, enter the enumeration of the device's benefits to society if these are likely to be of significant magnitude. Where perceptible, costs of factor movements as well as reduction in factor prices as the demand for substitutes declines, and gains or losses in consumer surplus are also included. Consumer surplus increases with reductions in the price of the controlled commodity caused by decreases in risk premiums. Consumer surplus for the substitutes both decreases as consumers switch to the controlled commodity and increases as the prices of the substitutes decline with demand. In order to induce the switch, however, consumers must realize a net increase in surpluses. The valuation of these and other effects should enter the analysis when the costs of making the estimates are not out of proportion to the likely significance of the effects. The importance of consumer surplus for a single commodity will be inversely related to the number of close substitutes and the consumer's income. As these rise the consumer will be able to switch between a variety of products and to spend only a portion of his budget on any one type of good; thus, his welfare is unlikely to be severely affected by a pronounced change in the price of a single good. On the other hand, similar changes in factor prices can be of relatively greater importance if the factor can render only one type of service. Primary commodity control devices are apt to have more effect on the prices for the commodity than those of its factors if the prices of factors are determined in a wide national or international market.

Periodical costs and benefits of a device are reduced to a single point in time by discounting them by the preference function of those affected. Where there is a single rate of interest on local money markets and reason to believe that it reflects the time preference of those affected by the device, this rate can be used in the present value criterion. Discrepancies between individual and market discount rates can result from a low level of development of financial institutions, monetary and fiscal policies, and the level of employment and output. Funds raised or earned by the device should be discounted at not less than the market rate in the private sector on the assumption that they would either have been invested in that sector if they had not been raised by the control authority or the authority should invest them there if their investment in the control device cannot earn as high a rate of return. Income accruing to the authority can be considered as worth at least the present value of its returns in perpetuity from investment in the private sector. Likewise, losses to the authority may be considered as equal to the present value of income streams foregone. Few devices will avoid investments in the form of negotiation expenses, accumulation of stock and the maintenance of administrative facilities and stocks during periods of no control.

The government's choice of a device should be reached by comparing the present value of the net excess social benefit resulting from alternative types of devices and each type with different control provisions. Where possible the calculation should be composed of the net benefit of each type of device embodying a specific set of control provisions for each market condition anticipated in any given control period. The net excess benefit of the device under each condition is then multiplied by the probability of the condition occurring and the products for all conditions summed to give a weighted average excess benefit for that period. All possible outcomes for a single device are ranked according to their probability, and statistical methods are used to determine the likelihood that results fall between relevant limits. After arriving at the greatest-excess-social-benefit-device, the government may have to make additional cost calculations if important unfavourable welfare effects and other spillovers remain that have to be rectified. Ancillary schemes bring their own costs, if only those of affecting a redistribution of income, and may increase the cost of a device chosen on a strictly cost-benefit basis.

Readings

Dasgupta, P., Little, I.M.D., *et. al.*, 'Symposium on the Little–Mirrlees Manual of Industrial Project Analysis in Developing Countries', *Bulletin of Oxford University Institute of Economics and Statistics*, Vol. 34, No. 1, February 1972.

————, Sen, A.K., & Marglin, S.A., *Guidelines for Project Evaluation*, UNIDO, Vienna, May 1972.

Hicks, J.R., *A Revision of Demand Theory*, Clarendon Press, Oxford, 1956.

Layard, R. (ed.), *Cost-Benefit Analysis*, Penguin, 1972.

Lipsey, R., & Lancaster, K., 'The General Theory of Second Best,' *Review of Economic Studies*, Vol. 24, No. 1, 1956, pp. 11–32.

Little, I.M.D., & Mirrlees, J., *Social Cost Benefit Analysis*, OECD Development Centre, Paris, 1969.

————, & Tippling, D.G., *A Social Cost Benefit Analysis of the Kulai Oil Palm Estate, West Malaysia*, OECD Development Centre, Paris, 1972.

Marglin, S.A., *Public Investment Criteria*, George Allen & Unwin, London, 1969.

Mishan, E.J., *Cost-Benefit Analysis*, George Allen & Unwin, London, 1971.

————, 'Cost-Benefit Rules for Poorer Countries', *Canadian Journal of Economics*, Vol. 4, No. 1, February 1971, pp. 86–98.

——————, *Elements of Cost-Benefit Analysis*, George Allen & Unwin, London, 1972.

——————, 'The Postwar Literature on Externalities: An Interpretive Essay', *Journal of Economic Literature*, March 1971, pp. 1–28.

——————, 'Survey of Welfare Economics, 1939–1959', *Economic Journal*, Vol. 70, June 1960, pp. 197–256.

——————, *Welfare Economics: An Assessment*, North Holland Publishing Co., Amsterdam, 1969.

Peters, G.H., *Cost-Benefit Analysis and Public Expenditure*, Institute of Economic Affairs, London, 1968.

Pigou, A.C., *Economics of Welfare*, 4th Ed., Macmillan, London, 1946.

Prest, A.R., & Turvey, R., 'Cost-Benefit Analysis: A Survey', *Economic Journal*, Vol. 75, December 1965, pp. 683–735.

Rothenberg, J., *The Measurement of Social Welfare*, Prentice-Hall, 1961.

Stern, N.H., *An Appraisal of Tea Production on Small Holdings in Kenya*, OECD Development Centre, Paris, 1972.

Appendix I
The Development of A Price Model

1. INTRODUCTION

COMMODITY models are a formal representation of a commodity market or industry where the behaviourial relationships selected reflect the underlying economic, political, and social institutions. The econometric equilibrium form of commodity model generally provides a basis for the trade, process, sector and some systems models. In primary commodity control this type of model is useful for determining the market parameters used in a two period analysis (i.e. elasticities of supply and demand and supply and demand shift characteristics) for in estimating parameters it may prove more reliable than the lines of inferential reasoning presented in Chapter 1. Market response studies are necessary for determining where to set the price in order to achieve a given increase in agricultural food output, how much food aid is feasible without being a disincentive to local food output expansion, the effect on prices of given strategic stockpile releases and the like. The equilibrium commodity model can be reduced to a form that allows demand, supply and prices to be explained or predicted on the basis of independent or policy variables. It may be used, for instance, in making the forecasts of market price required for establishing price limits in control schemes or in simulating the effects of a control device over some past or projected period. It can be national, featuring domestic supply and demand, or international including imports and exports.

Contrasting parts of the models for cocoa supply of Bateman, Behrman and the author suggests the diversity of approaches one may take in constructing such a model for a single crop. Space and purpose do not permit a discussion of the viability of these cocoa models nor a presentation and explanation of the results of each when tested; the discussion is intended solely to indicate approaches to the development of a tree crop model. Complex equilibrium commodity models built in this fashion can be tested for the relevant statistics with the prepared multiple regression computer programmes that are available at most computer centres.

2. AN ANNUAL SUPPLY MODEL

An equilibrium commodity model contains one set of relationships representing the demand for a commodity and another for its supply. Both sets are influenced by the level of prices and are equated at the equilibrium price. The multivariate supply model below is composed of a sequence of smaller models which explain facets of the total supply equation. These partial equations are developed in chronological order from the earliest factors influencing current output to the most recent ones. The postulation of a comprehensive supply model is a means of avoiding serial correlation and its unfavourable effects on the degree of bias and consistency in the estimates of parameters in the estimating equation. If the supply model is not well specified so that large systematic variables are not explicitly taken into account in the equation, the residual errors of the sample will be serially correlated rather than random. A widely used test of serial correlation is the Durban-Watson *d* statistic. As the number of supply determinants is increased, however, the chances of multicollinearity are increased. That is, some determinants are so closely correlated with one another that their relative effects on the dependent variable cannot be distinguished. A test of multicollinearity is found in the size of the sampling errors of the regression coefficients. Distributed lag models such as those given below usually suffer from the multicollinearity and general serial correlation problems.

a. PRICE EXPECTATIONS HYPOTHESIS

The price expectations hypothesis explains in recorded variables the producer's expectation of future prices at the time when decisions regarding planting are being made. An equation explaining expected price is necessary when estimating plantings of trees where actual data on planting is not available. Even if figures were available for the number of trees planted or area planted (which is not the case for cocoa in most producing countries) other factors accounting for eventual yield would have to be taken into consideration through a price expectations hypothesis. If area planted is known one would still have to account for trees per acre. The price expectations model can also make allowance for the quality of land used; the number of trees planted may increase but if expectations are not high they may be planted on marginal land. The variety of seedling used and the care taken in planting and tending the plant during the critical early stages of growth are also covered by this model.

Bateman (1965) and Behrman (1965) make two different assumptions about the producer's subjective decision making. They argue that movements in actual prices affect the farmer's expectation of future prices, and that the farmer revises the price he expects to prevail in proportion to the errors in his previous estimate. This hypothesis, the Nerlovian price expectations model, according to Bateman takes the form,

1a)
$$\tilde{P}_t - \tilde{P}_{t-1} = \beta(P_t - \tilde{P}_{t-1}) \qquad 0 \leqslant \beta < 1$$

or

1b)
$$\tilde{P}_t = \tilde{P}_{t-1} + \beta(P_t - \tilde{P}_{t-1})$$

where $\tilde{P}$ is the expected and P the actual farmer price and β the coefficient of expectations. Behrman, on the other hand, assumes that expectations are formed in a slightly different manner,

2)
$$\tilde{P}_t = a_0 + \tilde{P}_{t-1} + a_1(\tilde{P}_{t-1} - P_{t-1}) + u_t$$

where the a's are structural parameters and the 'u' a random disturbance term. Alternatively the expected farmer price could be assumed to be a function of the farmer price last year and the world price this year.

3)
$$P_t = a_0 + a_1 P^f_{t-1} + a_2 P^w_t + u_t$$

where P^f is the fixed producer price and P^w the world price. This third hypothesis saves a degree of freedom and when applied to Bateman's planting assumptions produces a combined model which omits the terms with which he has least success in tests. It is particularly applicable to West Africa where most of the world's cocoa is produced. Farmers there plant in May before the rainy season while the last season's fixed main crop price is still ruling. Although the farmer may base his price expectation in part on the ruling fixed price established by the government buffer fund, he is also likely to look to the world price as an index to future changes in the fixed price. Inclusion of the world price also takes account of changes in governmental decisions regarding the tangible encouragement of production. The structural parameter a_2 is the sum of the parameters as they appear in the farmer and government price expectations.

b. PLANTING MODEL

Bateman's purpose in developing a price expectations model is to explain the number of acres planted in any given period while Behrman is after the desired area in cocoa, T^d_t, at any given time. Farmers' intentions are more readily indicated by the area planted than actual output if inputs other than land can be varied and returns to scale are not diminishing. Bateman maintains that the number of acres planted is a function of the average expected real farmer price for cocoa and the average expected real farmer price of coffee, $\tilde{C}$, an alternative crop. His planting decision model is

4)
$$X_t = a_{10} + a_{11}\tilde{P}_t + a_{12}\tilde{C}_t + u_{1,t.}$$

He assumes that the expected cocoa and coffee prices are determined in the same way and that the adjustment coefficients are equal. Solving for $\tilde{P}_t$ and $\tilde{C}_t$ which are not observable and substituting in this equation gives,

5)
$$X_t = a_{10}\beta + a_{11}\beta P^f_t + a_{12}\beta C^f_t + (1-\beta)X_{t-1} + v_t.$$

where $v_t = u_t - (1-\beta)u_{t-1}$. Use of coffee prices as an indication of opportunity costs would appear to be valid for only one region tested by Bateman since coffee is not grown in the others. (Cf. the article by Ady cited in the Readings for further comment.)

Behrman deduces, in line with the Nerlovian adjustment hypothesis, that producers are able to increase output in any period only to the extent of a fraction a_{21} of the difference between the output they would like to produce and the amount actually produced in the preceding period. This formulation measures farmers' intentions more accurately than No. 5. Using the actual stock of trees, T, and the desired stock of trees, T^d, as proxies for the potential actual output and the potential intended output, gives

6) $$T_t - T_{t-1} = a_{20} + a_{21}(T_t^d - T_{t-1}) + u_{2,t} \qquad 0 \le a_{21} < 1$$

7) $$T_t^d = a_{30} + a_{31}\tilde{P}_t + u_{3,t}$$

where a_{21} is the adjustment coefficient. These two equations may be combined with equation No. 2 to give

8) $$\Delta T_t = [(1 - a_{21}) + (1 - \beta)]\Delta T_{t-1} - (1 - a_{21})(1 - \beta)\Delta T_{t-2}$$
$$+ a_{21}a_{31}\beta\Delta P_{t-1} + v_t$$

where $$v_t = a_{21}\Delta u_{3,t} + \Delta u_{2,t} - (1 - \beta)(a_{21}\Delta u_{3,t-1} + \Delta u_{2,t-1}).$$

The expectations–adjustment model is conceptually the most realistic model available although it does embody a number of statistical problems beyond the scope of this appendix. Moreover, it is inflexible to downward price movements. A further model developed by French and Matthews (see Readings), while being more comprehensive and better specified than the Bateman and Behrman models, continues to suffer from inflexibility. This problem may be overcome by the use of a stock model (e.g. by replacing the lagged planting variable X_{t-1} in No. 5 by the stock of trees, T_{t-1}).

Substituting in No. 6 for T_t^d using equations Nos. 3 and 7 and taking the first difference gives the following alternative estimating equation

9) $$\Delta T_t = (1 - a_{21})\Delta T_{t-1} + a_1 a_{21}a_{31}\Delta P_{t-1}^f + a_1 a_{21}a_{31}\Delta P_t^w + z_t$$

where $$z_t = a_1 a_{21}a_{31}\Delta u_t + \Delta u_{2,t} + a_{21}\Delta u_{3,t}.$$

Construction of an annual crop model might very well end here, with the possible addition of important shift variables such as rainfall and cloud coverage.

c. MEDIUM AND SHORT RUN FACTORS

Although the number of new trees or area newly planted does influence eventual yield, other factors affecting yield may intervene between planting and harvesting a number of years later when the trees begin to bear fruit. Those which are most frequently cited are husbandry, fertilizing, rainfall, and humidity. Husbandry (weeding, pruning etc.) and fertilizers are believed

THE DEVELOPMENT OF A PRICE MODEL 235

to affect yield within two years of application. Since their application can be expected to be related to producer price, producer or world price lagged one or two years is included in the supply equation. Bateman does not consider the possible importance of this term in his region study of Ghana while Behrman does use it but drops it from his published equations. The current price is used to account for the intensity of harvesting, spraying, and care taken in the fermenting and drying process. The total annual production is expressed,

10) $$Q_t = a_{40} + Q_t^* + a_{41}P_t^f + a_{42}P_{t-1}^f + u_{4,t}$$

where Q_t is current production and Q_t^* the potential yield of cocoa in year t based on the estimated stock of trees. Bateman used rainfall and humidity data as additional indices to changes in yield. Rainfall during certain months of the year affects the size and number of pods on the tree. If rainfall continues unabated after the pods have begun to develop, however, they may suffer from blight. To account for the effects of rainfall during this second period a humidity variable was used. Although rainfall data appears to have improved his fit, humidity data produced ambivalent results. Ideally one would also want to account for other cash opportunities at the time of harvest. However, a suitable time-series is not available.

d. THE COMPLETE SUPPLY MODEL

Assuming that for cocoa there is only one spurt in yield 's' years after planting, although there is some evidence that there may be two, the anticipated yield in the current period would be equal to the magnitude of this spurt times the sum of all areas planted 's' and more years ago. That is,

11) $$Q_t^* = b_1\sum_s^\infty X_t = b_1\sum_s^\infty T_t - T_{t-1}$$

where b_1 represents the volume of the spurt. This formulation may oversimplify reality to some extent since the spurt in production 's' years after planting is not the only increase in yield. There is some bearing before the observed spurt, although this may not be economically harvestable, and perhaps increased bearing after it. We may assume as a first approximation that increases in yield in other than spurt years is neutralized by the declining yield of old trees.

Substituting in the previous expression for total production and transforming No. 10 into a first-order difference equation, to overcome the infinite amount of data that equation requires, gives

12) $$\Delta Q_t = b_1\Delta T_{t-s} + a_{41}\Delta P_t^f + a_{42}\Delta P_{t-1}^f + \Delta u_{4,t}.$$

Lagging one year and multiplying through by $(1 - a_{21})$:

13) $$(1-a_{21})\Delta Q_{t-1} = (1-a_{21})b_1\Delta T_{t-s-1} + a_{41}(1-a_{21})\Delta P_{t-1}^f$$
$$+ a_{42}(1-a_{21})\Delta P_{t-2}^f + (1-a_{21})\Delta u_{4,t-1}.$$

Subtracting this equation from the one immediately above it and substituting for ΔT (see equation No. 8):

14)
$$\Delta Q_t = (1-a_{21})\Delta Q_{t-1}$$
$$+ b_1(a_1 a_{21} a_{31}\Delta P^f_{t-s-1} + a_1 a_{21} a_{31}\Delta P^w_{t-s}) + a_{41}\Delta P^f_t$$
$$+ [a_{42} - a_{41}(1-a_{21})]\Delta P^f_{t-1} - a_{42}(1-a_{21})\Delta P^f_{t-2} + w_t$$

where $w_t = \Delta u_{4,t} - (1-a_{21})\Delta u_{4,t-1} + b_1 z_t.$

If $a_{21} = 1$, then:

15)
$$\Delta Q_t = b_1 a_1 a_{31}\Delta P^f_{t-s-1} + b_1 a_1 a_{31}\Delta P^w_{t-}$$
$$+ a_{41}\Delta P^f_t + a_{42}\Delta P^f_{t-1} + w_t.$$

A time trend variable can be added to this formulation as a proxy for the gradual effects of extension education, research on higher yielding varieties, land fragmentation and the like. Although the trend variable will not explain a secular change in output, it may help explain planting decisions if knowledge of a secular trend enters into the farmer's forecast of the future. Long run price elasticity of supply is obtained by dividing the regression coefficient $b_1 a_1 a_{21} a_{31}$ of the first price variable by the adjustment coefficient a_{21} and multiplying the result by the arithmetic mean of the price-series data for P^f divided by the arithmetic mean of the output-series data for Q. Short run elasticity is obtained in like manner except that the coefficient is not divided by a_{21}. When the relationship is logarithmic, the elasticity is given directly by the regression coefficient of the price variable.

e. EXPORT FUNCTION

In order to transform the production model into a market supply model account must be taken of speculative stock accumulation in the exporting country. Generally, stocks on the demand and supply sides of the market will influence price increasingly as the elasticities of demand and supply decrease. The ability and motivation to speculate will depend on the size of the harvest, the world prime, and forecasts of demand and supply. That is, changes in exports are given by

16)
$$\Delta E_t = \Delta Q_t + a_{51}\Delta P^w_t + a_{52}\Delta F^g_t + a_{53}\Delta F^s_t + \Delta u_{5,t}$$

where F^g is the forecast of grindings and F^s that of supply. ΔQ_t may be replaced with the production model above. Substituting Equation No. 15 for ΔQ_t gives an export function (the combined planting-decision model, planting-output relationship and speculation model) in terms of recorded variables.

17)
$$\Delta E_t = b_1 a_1 a_{31}\Delta P^f_{t-s-1} + b_1 a_1 a_{31}\Delta P^w_{t-s} + a_{42}\Delta P^f_{t-1}$$
$$a_{41}\Delta P^f_t + a_{51}\Delta P^w_t + a_{52}\Delta F^g_t + a_{53}\Delta F^s_t + x_t$$

where $x_t = w_t + \Delta u_{5,t}.$

3. A DEMAND MODEL

a. MARKET DEMAND

Market demand is determined by the volume of raw cocoa the fabricator desires for processing and by his and the speculator's demand for stocks. In its simplest form (omitting use of the neater adjustment relationship shown in No. 6) the demand function is,

18) $$D_t = a_{60} + a_{61}G_t + a_{62}S_t + u_{6,t}$$

where D_t is the current net market demand (i.e. demand for new exports from producing countries), G_t the rate at which raw cocoa is being processed into cocoa products expressed in terms of grindings, and S_t the desired level of stocks held for precautionary or speculative reasons. If this model is applied globally, sales of semi-processed cocoa between manufacturers and between consuming countries do not have to be considered.

b. CONSUMER DEMAND

Grindings of cocoa are, in turn, the product of numerous recorded and unrecorded variables. The pattern of consumer demand reaction to changes in the world market prices for raw cocoa tends to be complex and prolonged. The manufacturer normally possesses three to six months of stocks and at certain times of year may have more because of the seasonal nature of production. Thus it might be three to six months before moderate price changes are passed on to the consumer and, even then, these may be disguised in various ways, particularly through weight and content changes. A year or more may pass before the retail price changes or before the consumer realizes he is not purchasing the same product as before, longer still before he changes his buying habits. Thus, grindings may reflect the influence of prices on the world market up to two years previously. In order to account for these lagged responses, world price P^w_{t-2} is used in the following equations. More rapid changes in retail demand can, as a first approximation, be given by retail prices P^r_t or $P^r_{t-\frac{1}{2}}$. When annual data is used, $P^r_{t-\frac{1}{2}}$ would be the annual average retail price of the twelve months ending six months before the end of year t. Consumer income, Y, will also influence the level of demand. Grindings will be influenced by the relative prices of sugar and coconut palm oil. The latter is a popular substitute for cocoa fat in confectionary. Sugar proportions in confectionery may vary about 20 per cent with relative price changes since sugar is both a substitute and complement to cocoa in its main uses. Taking into account the accumulation of cocoa stocks at past prices and the time necessary to change chocolate confectionery formulae, grindings are likely to react to sugar and palm oil prices only after half a year. The influence of these variables is accounted for by $P^s_{t-\frac{1}{2}}$, and $P^v_{t-\frac{1}{2}}$, the manufacturer's price of sugar and coconut palm oil, respectively. From these recorded variables a grindings function emerges:

19) $$G_t = a_{70} + a_{71}P^r_t + a_{72}Y_{t-\frac{1}{2}} + a_{73}P^s_{t-\frac{1}{2}} + a_{74}P^v_{t-\frac{1}{2}} + a_{75}P^w_{t-2} + u_{7,t}.$$

238 PRIMARY COMMODITY CONTROL

c. STOCKS

Stocks desired by manufacturers and others are a function of the level of grindings and expectations regarding the short term future price of cocoa. Manufacturers are believed to maintain stocks in a given proportion to grindings. This proportion will vary, however, as the manufacturer attempts to buy at the most favourable price in the spectrum of current and expected prices. Price develops during the year not in relation to ultimate production and grindings, since these are unknown, but according to the expectation of these. Expectations are built upon forecasts of supply and of grindings and estimates of stocks in the hands of manufacturers and traders. Thus, the short term price expectation may be expressed,

20) $$\tilde{P}_t = a_{80} + a_{81}F_t^s + a_{82}F_t^g + a_{83}S_t^{est} + u_{8,t}$$

where F^s and F^g are short term forecasts of supply and grindings, respectively, and S_t^{est} is the stock estimate. No quarterly estimate of stocks is published in the most widely circulated market reports. Some circulars do publish an end-year estimate based on the difference between imports and grindings with adjustment for loss in weight. However, in the absence of reliable estimates, S_t^{est} may have to be dropped. The level of stocks can be expressed,

21) $$S_t = a_{90} + a_{91}G_t + a_{92}\tilde{P}_t + u_{9,t}.$$

Substituting equation No. 20 for $\tilde{P}_t$ gives an expression which can be used in equation No. 18 for S_t:

22) $$S_t = a_{90} + a_{91}G_t + a_{81}a_{92}F_t^s + a_{82}a_{92}F_t^g + a_{83}a_{92}S_t^{est} + a_{92}u_{8,t}$$
$$+ u_{9,t} + a_{80}a_{92}.$$

The development of this stock model illustrates the common problem that theoretical formulations do not always result in relationships between variables which can be observed directly. This is circumvented by specifying further relationships between the non-observable and observable variables.

d. THE COMPLETE DEMAND MODEL

Equations 18, 19 and 22 may be manipulated in the following manner to give a comprehensive demand model:

23) $$D_t = a_{60} + a_{61}\left[a_{70} + a_{71}P_t^r + a_{72}Y_{t-\frac{1}{2}} + a_{73}P_{t-\frac{1}{2}}^s\right.$$
$$+ a_{74}P_{t-\frac{1}{2}}^v + a_{75}P_{t-2}^w + u_{7,t}\right] + a_{62}\left[a_{90}\right.$$
$$+ a_{91}(a_{70} + a_{71}P_t^r + a_{72}Y_{t-\frac{1}{2}} + a_{73}P_{t-\frac{1}{2}}^s$$
$$+ a_{74}P_{t-\frac{1}{2}}^v + a_{75}P_{t-2}^w + u_{7,t}) + a_{81}a_{92}F_t^s$$
$$+ a_{82}a_{92}F_t^g + a_{83}a_{92}S_t^{est} + a_{92}u_{8,t} + u_{9,t} + a_{80}a_{92}\right] + u_{6,t}.$$

24) $$D_t = a + a_{71}(a_{61} + a_{62}a_{91})P_t^r + a_{72}(a_{61} + a_{62}a_{91})Y_{t-\frac{1}{2}}$$
$$+ a_{73}(a_{61} + a_{62}a_{91})P_{t-\frac{1}{2}}^s + a_{74}(a_{61} + a_{62}a_{91})P_{t-\frac{1}{2}}^v$$
$$+ a_{75}(a_{61} + a_{62}a_{91})P_{t-2}^w + a_{62}a_{81}a_{92}F_t^s$$
$$+ a_{62}a_{82}a_{92}F_t^g + a_{62}a_{83}a_{92}S_t^{est} + v_t$$

where $a = a_{60} + a_{61}a_{70} + a_{62}a_{90} + a_{62}a_{70}a_{91} + a_{62}a_{80}a_{92}$

$v_t = a_{61}u_{7,t} + a_{61}a_{91}u_{7,t} + a_{62}a_{92}u_{8,t} + a_{62}u_{9,t}.$

4. MARKET CLEARING EQUATION AND PRICE MODEL

Changes in the supply and demand for cocoa can be equated to arrive at changes in the world price. Taking the first order difference of equation No. 24, placing the solution equal to No. 17 and solving for the change in world price will give,

25) $$a_{51}\Delta P_t^w = -b_1a_1a_{31}\Delta P_{t-s-1}^f - b_1a_1a_{31}\Delta P_{t-s}^w$$
$$- a_{41}\Delta P_t^f - a_{42}\Delta P_{t-1}^f + a_{71}(a_{61} + a_{62}a_{91})\Delta P_t^r$$
$$+ a_{72}(a_{61} + a_{62}a_{91})\Delta Y_{t-\frac{1}{2}} + a_{73}(a_{61} + a_{62}a_{91})\Delta P_{t-\frac{1}{2}}^s$$
$$+ a_{74}(a_{61} + a_{62}a_{91})\Delta P_{t-\frac{1}{2}}^v + a_{75}(a_{61} + a_{62}a_{91})\Delta P_{t-2}^w$$
$$+ (a_{62}a_{81}a_{92} - a_{52})\Delta F_t^g + (a_{62}a_{83}a_{92} - a_{53})\Delta F_t^s$$
$$+ a_{62}a_{83}a_{92}\Delta S_t^{est} + y_t$$

where $y_t = v_t + x_t.$

If preliminary tests show the coefficients of some of the variables are insignificant or very close to zero, a somewhat simpler formulation might be used.

Readings

Ady, P.H., 'Supply Functions in Tropical Agriculture,' *Bulletin of the University of Oxford Institute of Statistics*, Vol. 31, 1968, pp. 157–88.

Agarwala, R., 'A Simulation Approach to the Analysis of Stabilization Policies in Agricultural Markets; A Case Study', *Journal of Agricultural Economics*, Vol. 22, No. 1, January 1971, pp. 13–28.

Arak, M., 'Estimation of Asymetric Long Run Supply Functions: The Case of Coffee', *Canadian Journal of Agricultural Economics*, Vol. 17, No. 1, February 1969, pp. 15–22.

Bateman, M.J., 'Aggregate & Regional Supply Functions for Ghanaian Cocoa', *Journal of Farm Economics*, Vol. 47, No. 2, May 1965, pp. 384–401.

Bates, T.H., & Schmitz, A., 'A Spatial Equilibrium Analysis of the World Sugar Economy', *Giannini Foundation Monograph No. 23*, Berkeley, May 1969.

Behrman, J.R., 'Cocoa, a Study of Demand Elasticities in Five Leading Consuming Countries, 1950–1961', *Journal of Farm Economics*, Vol. 47, No. 2, May 1965, pp. 410–7.

——————— 'Econometric Model Simulations of the World Rubber Markets, 1950–1980', in Klein, L.R., (ed.), *Essays in Industrial Economics*, Vol. 3, University of Pennsylvania, 1969.

——————— 'Monopolistic Cocoa Pricing', *American Journal of Agricultural Economics*, Vol. 50, No. 3, August 1968, pp. 702–19.

——————— *Supply Response in Underdeveloped Agriculture, A Case Study of Four Major Annual Crops in Thailand, 1937–1962*, North-Holland Publishing Co., Amsterdam, 1968.

Bell, P.F., & Tai, J., 'Markets, Middlemen and Technology: Agricultural Supply Response in the Dualistic Economies of Southeast Asia', *Malayan Economic Review*, Vol. 14, No. 1, April 1969, pp. 29–43.

Brown, C.P., *Analytical Aspects of Control of Trade with Special Reference to Cocoa*, D. Phil. dissertation for the University of Oxford, England, August 1968.

Chan, F., 'A Preliminary Study of the Supply Response of Estates between 1948 and 1959', *Malayan Economic Review*, Vol. 7, No. 2, October 1962, pp. 77–94.

Clark, R., 'The Economic Determinants of Jute Production', *Monthly Bulletin of Agricultural Economics*, F.A.O., Vol. 6, No. 9, Sept. 1957, pp. 1–10.

Dean, E., *The Supply Responses of African Farmers: Theory and Measurement in Malawi*, North-Holland Publishing Company, Amsterdam, 1966.

Desai, M.J., 'An Econometric Model of the World Tin Economy, 1948–1961', *Econometrica*, Vol. 34, No. 1, January 1966, pp. 105–134.

Falcon, W.P., 'Farmer Response to Price in a Subsistence Economy; the Case of West Pakistan', *American Economic Review* (P & P), Vol. 59, No. 3, May 1964, pp. 580–91.

French, B.C., & Matthews, J.L., 'A Supply Response Model for Perennial Crops', *American Journal of Agricultural Economics*, Vol. 53, No. 3, August 1971, pp. 478–90.

——————— & Bressler, R.G., 'The Lemon Cycle', *Journal of Farm Economics*, Vol. 44, November 1962, pp. 1021–36.

Khan, A.R., & Chowdhury, A.H.M.N. 'Marketed Surplus Function: A Study of the Behavior of West Pakistan Farmers', *Pakistan Development Review*, Vol. 2, No. 3, 1962, pp. 34–76.

Krishna, R., 'Farm Supply Response in India–Pakistan, A Case Study of the Punjab Region', *Economic Journal*, Vol. 73, Sept. 1963, pp. 477–87.

Labys, W.C., *Dynamic Commodity Models, Specification, Estimation, and Simulation*, Heath & Co., Lexington, 1973.

Lim, D., *Supply Responses of Primary Producers*, University of Malaya Press, Kuala Lumpur, forthcoming.

Mangahas, M., *et. al.*, 'Price and Market Relationships for Rice and Corn in the Philippines', *Journal of Farm Economics*, Vol. 48, No. 3, August 1966, pp. 685–703.

Meadows, D.L., *Dynamics of Commodity Production Cycles*, Wright-Allen Press, 1970.

Nerlove, M., *The Dynamics of Supply: Estimates of Farmers' Response to Price*, Baltimore, Johns Hopkins Press, 1958.

Parikh, A., 'Market Responsiveness of Peasant Cultivators: Some Evidence from Pre-War India', *Journal of Development Studies*, Vol. 8, No. 2, January 1972.

Rojko, A.S., Urban, F.S., & Naive, J.J., 'World Demand Prospects for Grain in 1980 with Emphasis on Trade by the Less Developed Countries', *Foreign Agricultural Economic Report No. 75*, U.S. Department of Agriculture, December, 1971.

Working, H., 'The Theory of Price of Storage', *American Economic Review*, Vol. 39, December 1949, pp. 1254–62.

Wymar, F.H., 'The Supply of Storage Revisited', *American Economic Review*, Vol. 56, December 1966, pp. 1226–34.

Appendix II
Mathematical Approaches
to Two-Period Analysis

1. INTRODUCTION

APPENDIX 2 illustrates how the geometric analysis in the text may be duplicated and refined with mathematics. In the literature of commodity control, market functions frequently assume a linear form in which postulated elasticities are expressed at one point only. Below, alternative approaches are offered in increasing order of plausibility; these serve to illustrate the variability in results due to the method of analysis adopted. The approaches may be readily adopted to all manner of control devices, although the discussion here relates to the buffer fund, export quota, buffer stock and fixed *ad valorem* export tax devices.

2. LINEAR FUNCTIONS WITH PARALLEL SHIFTS (CASE I)

a. THE UNCONTROLLED MARKET

If the point at which linear demand function D_1 intersects the horizontal axis in Figure 4.1a in Chapter 4 (p. 121), is designated $a - c$ and the reciprocal of the negative slope of the function b, demand may be expressed algebraically,

1) $D_1 = (a - c) - bP$

where P is price and c is the deviation of D_1 from the norm. Similarly D_2 may be given by

2) $D_2 = (a + c) - bP.$

That is, D_1 and D_2 are seen to be parallel and to lie equal horizontal distances from a mean function $D = a - bP$. Supply is given by,

3) $S = d + eP$ and remains fixed over the two periods.

Price in either period is derived by equating the supply and demand functions for that period. Thus, in period one

4) $(a - c) - bP = d + eP.$

Therefore

5) $P = \dfrac{a - c - d}{e + b}$.

Substituting for P in equation No. 3,

6) $S = d + e \left[\dfrac{a - c - d}{e + b} \right]$.

Total earnings in the first period is then

7) $d \left[\dfrac{a - c - d}{e + b} \right] + e \left[\dfrac{a - c - d}{e + b} \right]^2$.

Similarly, total earnings in the second period is

8) $d \left[\dfrac{(a + c) - d}{e + b} \right] + e \left[\dfrac{(a + c) - d}{e + b} \right]^2$

and over the two periods,

9) $\dfrac{2(ad - d^2)}{e + b} + 2e \left[\dfrac{a^2 + c^2 - 2ad + d^2}{(e + b)^2} \right]$.

b. BUFFER FUND EFFECTS

Under a buffer fund using a single fixed producer price over the two periods, world price in the first period is given by

10) $a - c - bP = d + eP^*$

where P^* is the fixed producer price. Combined earnings under the fund is

11) $2\dfrac{d + eP^*}{b} [a - d - eP^*]$.

i. Breakeven Price

The buffer fund will break even over the two periods if producer income is equal to export earnings. Producer income over the two periods is

12) $2P^*(d + eP^*)$.

This must equal No. 11 above. Setting the two expressions equal to one another gives

13) $2P^* = 2\dfrac{(a - d - eP^*)}{b}$.

Solving for P^*,

14) $P^* = \dfrac{a - d}{e + b}$.

This is the mean of the two uncontrolled market prices, for in adding the two uncontrolled market prices and dividing by two we get,

15) $\text{Mean} = \dfrac{a - d}{e + b}$.

ii. Net Income Loss

Total producer income under a buffer fund that breaks even is,

16) $\dfrac{2(ad - d^2)}{e + b} + 2e\left[\dfrac{a - d}{e + b}\right]^2.$

The left hand expression is identical to the left hand expression of No. 9. The right hand expression may be expanded,

17) $\dfrac{2e(a^2 - 2ad + d^2)}{(e + b)^2}.$

This must be smaller than the right hand expression of No. 9 if a break-even policy will realize a net income loss. That is,

18) $\dfrac{2e(a^2 - 2ad + d^2)}{(e + b)^2} < \dfrac{2e(a^2 + c^2 - 2ad + d^2)}{(e + b)^2}.$

Cancelling like terms,

19) $0 < c^2.$

Therefore, there is a net income loss.

iii. Optimum Producer Price

The export earnings maximizing producer price is found by differentiating the combined revenue under the buffer fund, No. 11, with respect to the fixed producer price, P^*, and comparing gross earnings under this fixed price with that under an uncontrolled market.

20) $\dfrac{dR}{dP^*} = 2\dfrac{e}{b}[(a - d)] - \dfrac{4e^2P^*}{b} - \dfrac{2de}{b}.$

Setting this equal to zero,

21) Optimum $P^* = \dfrac{a - 2d}{2e}.$

This is positive if $a > 2d$ and $\dfrac{d^2R}{dP^2}$ is negative. This optimum price is below the mean price of No. 15 for $e \geqslant b$. It is also below the mean when 'b' is slightly larger than 'e' but not much larger. The maximum export earnings under the buffer fund is given by substituting the optimum fixed producer price of No. 21 into equation No. 11. The result decreases with 'b' and is independent of 'e'.

iv. Buffer Funds and Buffer Stocks

If the buffer fund fixes producer price, short run supply to the world market will be perfectly inelastic. In a supply shift market, supply in the first period is given by,

22) $S = (d - f) + \dfrac{P}{\infty} = d - f$

and in the second period,

23) $S = (d+f) + \dfrac{P}{\infty} = d+f.$

World price for each period would be $\dfrac{a-d-f}{b}$ and $\dfrac{a-d+f}{b}$, respectively. With an international buffer stock which attempts to dampen the price fluctuation, price limits will be

24) $\dfrac{a-d-f-g}{b}$ and $\dfrac{a-d+f-h}{b}$

respectively, where 'g' is an addition to or subtraction from the world price in the first period and 'h' an addition to or subtraction from the world price in the second period. Whether an addition or subtraction occurs will depend on the world price in the second period relative to that in the first period. In a demand shift market, for instance, 'g' will be an addition and 'h' a subtraction. If there is a static supply and 'g–h' is positive, then exporters gain by the buffer stock agreement. If there is no ceiling price, exporters will also gain with shifts in supply. Possible gains are limited to $h(d+f)$. If $g < h$ and $f > c$, there will be a gain.

c. BUFFER STOCKS, EXPORT QUOTAS AND EXPORT TAXES

If the international buffer stock operates in a market with a price responsive supply, export earnings in a first period of low price in a supply shift market will be

25) Earnings $= (d - f + eP_B)P_B$

where P_B is the buffer stock floor or ceiling price. This equation may also take the form

26) Earnings $= e\left(P_B + \dfrac{d-f}{2e}\right)^2 - \dfrac{(d-f)^2}{4e^2}$

where for positive values for earnings and P_B, earnings will increase as P_B increases.

Export earnings under an export quota will be determined by demand at the price limits. For instance earnings will be given by,

27) Earnings $= (a - c - bP_E)P_E$

in a low price year in a demand shift market, where P_E is the export quota floor price. At that price $d + eP_E$ will be produced and the difference between this and No. 27 will be stored.

In applying these formulae to a particular situation actual values must be assigned to the alphabetical letters 'a' through 'h'. Tin control under the 1971 Tin Agreement and the typical export tax on tin, of roughly 15 percent, provides a particular situation which permits illustration of the possible effects of three devices currently being used. Normal world tin output and price may be placed at 150,000 tons (150) and £1,500 per ton (15), respectively. Demand is postulated to shift in two hypothetical exceptional years by 12,500 (12.5) tons either side of the normal absorption. The slope and horizontal axis intercept for the normal demand may be derived in the following manner:

28)   Assumed supply elasticity $= 0.1 = \dfrac{\Delta Q}{\Delta P} \cdot \dfrac{P}{Q}$.

29)   Since $\dfrac{\Delta Q}{\Delta P} = e$, $e \left[\dfrac{P}{d + eP} \right] = 0.1$ and $\dfrac{1}{e}$ or the slope, L, $= \dfrac{9P}{d}$,

therefore,

30) $Q = d + \dfrac{\delta}{9}$.

If $Q = 150$, then $d = 135$; therefore $L = \dfrac{9P}{135}$. If $P = 12.75$, $L = 0.85$ and $e = 1.18$. $P = 12.75$ has been chosen to give an equilibrium price of 15 at demand 150 when an export tax of 15 per cent is imposed, i.e. 12.75 is 85 per cent of base price 15. Deriving the other slopes and intercepts in like fashion and applying them to the Case I formulations of Table A2.1 gives results shown in Table A2.2. Profits are derived from the area of the trapezium formed by the origin, the supply function intercept on the horizontal axis, the point of equilibrium and the producer price on the vertical axis. Total profits are not given by this area since an aggregate marginal cost function would join the vertical axis at a positive price. Comparison of areas does, however, give a rough estimate of relative profits. The devices are assumed, in line with experience, to operate in a demand shift market which is characterized by a short run supply elasticity of 0.1 and demand elasticity of -0.1 or -0.5. The buffer stock price range is 24 per cent of the free market price fluctuation. This figure was chosen to give a price range of 13.5 — 16.5 under the export tax, Column 8, with a mean of 15.0. This approximates the current Fourth International Tin Agreement range of £1,340—£1,650 per ton.

In Table A2.2 the 15 per cent export tax is shown to have no effect on world market price, Column 2, or producer price, Column 4, percentage fluctuations. Export earnings are increased because of an inelastic demand, Column 3, and producer income decreased, Column 5, while percentage fluctuations in export earnings and producer income remain unchanged. Producer 'profits' decrease with the tax and percentage fluctuations in 'profits' are unaffected, Column 6.

The use of buffer stock control reduces the percentage fluctuation in producer income and export earnings, Column 9, compared to the uncontrolled market, Column 3. There is a lesser reduction in the absolute level of producer income. 'Profits' and tax revenue are similarly stabilized and reduced over the two periods, Columns 10 v. 6 and 11 v. 7.

TABLE A2.1

EQUATIONS USED TO DETERMINE EXPORT EARNINGS

Without Export Tax	*With Export Tax*

(FREE MARKET)

Cases I & II

$$d\left[\frac{a\pm c-d}{a+b}\right]+e\left[\frac{a\pm c-d}{c+b}\right]^2 \qquad d\left[\frac{a\pm c-d-e\dfrac{a\pm c-d}{b}}{e+\dfrac{x}{b}}\right]+ex\left[\frac{a\pm c-d-e\dfrac{a\pm c-d}{b}}{e+\dfrac{x}{b}}\right]^2$$

Case III

Case I world prices and quantities are assumed given.

$$\frac{Q_{1;2}\left[\dfrac{S_E P_{1;2}-xD_E P_{1;2}}{xS_E-xD_E}\right]^2}{D_E\left[P_{1;2}-\dfrac{S_E P_{1;2}-xD_E P_{1;2}}{xS_E-xD_E}\right]+1}$$

Case IV

$$\left[d+e\frac{k^n}{Q_{1;2}^n}\right]\frac{k^n}{Q_{1;2}^n} \qquad\qquad \left[d+xe\frac{k^n}{Q_{1;2}^n}\right]\frac{k^n}{Q_{1;2}^n}$$

Case V

$$(d+eP_{1;2})\,P_{1;2} \qquad\qquad (d+xeP_{1;2})\,P_{1;2}$$

where P is given by:

$$d+eP_{1;2}=a_0+a_1P_{1;2}+a_2P_{1;2}^2+a_3P_{1;2}^3=Q_{1;2} \qquad d+xeP_{1;2}=a_0+a_1P_{1;2}+a_2P_{1;2}^2+a_3P_{1;2}^3=Q_{1;2}$$

(CONTROLLED MARKET WITH BUFFER STOCK)

Cases I, II, IV & V

$$(d+eP_{F;C})P_{F;C} \qquad\qquad (d+xeP_{F;C})P_{F;C}$$

Case III

$$\left[\frac{Q_{1;2}P_{F;C}}{S_E(P_{1;2}-P_{F;C})+P_{F;C}}\right]P_{F;C} \qquad \left[\frac{xQ_{1;2}P_{F;C}}{S_E(P_{1;2}-xP_{F;C})+xP_{F;C}}\right]P_{F;C}$$

(CONTROLLED MARKET WITH EXPORT QUOTA

Cases I & II

$$(a\pm c-bP_{F;C})P_{F;C} \qquad\qquad (a\pm c-bP_{F;C})P_{F;C}$$

Case III

$$\left[\frac{Q_{1;2}\,P_{F;C}}{D_E(P_{1;2}-P_{F;C})+P_{F;C}}\right]P_{F;C} \qquad \left[\frac{Q_{1;2}P_{F;C}}{D_E(P_{1;2}-P_{F;C})+P_{F;C}}\right]P_{F;C}$$

Case IV

$$\left[\frac{K}{P_{F;C}^n}\right]P_{F;C} \qquad\qquad \left[\frac{K}{P_{F;C}^n}\right]P_{F;C}$$

Case V

$$[a_0+a_1P_{F;C}+a_2P_{F;C}^2+a_3P_{F;C}^3]P_{F;C} \qquad [a_0+a_1P_{F;C}+a_2P_{F;C}^2+a_3P_{F;C}^3]P_{F;C}$$

Key: $a\pm c=a-c$ in period 1 and $a+c$ in period 2.

$P_{1;2}=P_1$, world price in period 1 and, P_2, world price in period 2.

$P_{F;C}=P_F$, floor price in period 1 and, P_C, ceiling price in period 2.

TABLE A2.2
POSSIBLE CONTROL EFFECTS WITH LINEAR ANALYSIS*

(1) Period	(2) World Price without Control Cases: I	II	III	(3) Export Earnings without Control Cases: I	II	III	(4) Producer Price without Control	(5) Producer Income without Control	(6) Producer "Profits" without Control	(7) Tax Revenue (3-5)	(8) Price Limits	(9) Export Earnings with Buffer Stock Cases: I	II	III
Elasticity														
							(WITHOUT EXPORT TAX)							
$S_E = 0.1$, $D_E = -0.1$														
2nd	19.5	19.5	19.5	3,085	3,056	3,085	19.5	3,085	2,861	–	15.2	2,318	2,282	2,328
1st	8.0	7.8	8.0	1,162	1,119	1,162	8.0	1,162	1,124	–	12.4	1,856	1,818	1,859
Difference	11.5	11.6	11.5	1,923	1,936	1,923	11.5	1,923	1,737	–	2.8	416	465	470
% Fluctuation	(83.3)	(85.5)	(83.3)	(90.6)	(92.8)	(90.6)	(83.3)	(90.6)	(87.0)	–	(20.0)	(22.1)	(22.7)	(22.5)
Total	–	–	–	4,247	4,175	4,247	–	4,247	3,985	–	–	4,174	4,100	4,186
$S_E = 0.1$, $D_E = -0.5$														
2nd	16.6	16.5	16.6	2,564	2,547	2,564	16.6	2,564	2,404	–	15.0	2,299	2,278	2,303
1st	13.0	12.4	13.0	1,879	1,850	1,897	13.0	1,879	1,786	–	14.1	2,135	2,110	2,134
Difference	4.0	4.1	4.0	685	696	685	4.0	685	615	–	1.0	164	167	170
% Fluctuation	(27.8)	(28.6)	(27.8)	(30.8)	(31.7)	(30.8)	(27.8)	(30.8)	(29.4)	–	(6.7)	(7.4)	(7.6)	(7.7)
Total	–	–	–	4,443	4,397	4,444	–	4,444	4,189	–	–	4,434	4,388	4,436
							(WITH EXPORT TAX)							
$S_E = 0.1$, $D_E = -0.1$														
2nd	21.3	21.0	21.2	3,320	3,277	3,330	18.1	2,823	2,631	497	16.5	2,500	2,457	2,508
1st	8.3	8.5	8.8	1,258	1,216	1,254	7.4	1,069	1,037	188	13.3	2,005	1,962	2,010
Difference	13.0	12.5	12.5	2,062	2,060	2,076	10.6	1,754	1,594	308	3.0	495	494	498
% Fluctuation	(83.3)	(85.0)	(83.3)	(90.6)	(91.7)	(90.6)	(83.3)	(90.1)	(87.0)	(90.1)	(20.0)	(22.1)	(22.3)	(22.0)
Total	–	–	–	4,578	4,493	4,584	–	3,893	3,668	685	–	4,504	4,419	4,519
$S_E = 0.1$, $D_E = -0.5$														
2nd	17.1	16.9	17.1	2,598	2,575	2,602	14.5	2,209	2,085	389	15.5	2,333	2,309	2,334
1st	12.9	12.8	12.9	1,910	1,886	1,907	11.0	1,624	1,554	286	14.5	2,168	2,144	2,168
Difference	4.2	4.2	4.2	688	689	696	3.5	585	532	103	1.0	165	165	167
% Fluctuation	(27.8)	(28.2)	(27.8)	(30.8)	(30.9)	(30.8)	(27.8)	(30.8)	(29.4)	(30.8)	(6.7)	(7.4)	(7.4)	(7.4)
Total	–	–	–	4,508	4,460	4,509	–	3,834	3,639	675	–	4,500	4,453	4,502

Key: S_E = Supply Elasticity   Case II = Columns No. 2, 3, 9 & 12 only
D_E = Demand Elasticity   Case III = Columns No. 2, 3, 9 & 12 only

*Calculations were carried out to the third decimal place and rounded for the table.

(Continued)

TABLE A2.2

POSSIBLE CONTROL EFFECTS WITH LINEAR ANALYSIS (CONTINUED)

(10) Producer 'Profits' with Buffer Stock	(11) Tax Revenue with Buffer Stock	(12) Export Earnings with Quotas and Producer Stocks Cases: I	(12) II	(12) III	(13) Tax Revenue with Quotas and Producer Stocks	(14) Export Earnings with Quotas and no Stocks	(15) Producer 'Profits' with Quotas and no Stocks	(16) Tax Revenue with Quotas and no Stocks	(17) Earnings Maximizing Producer Price	(18) World Price under (17)	(19) Profit Maximizing Producer Price	(20) World Price under (19)
					(WITHOUT EXPORT TAX)							
2,182	—	2,462	2,431	2,466	—	3,085	2,861	—	−39.3	76.2	13.41	26.8
1,766	—	1,738	1,705	1,732	—	1,738	1,727	—	−49.9	88.8	5.5	11.0
417	—	723	726	735	—	1,347	1,134	—	10.6	12.5	7.8	15.7
(21.1)	—	(34.4)	(35.1)	(35.0)	—	(55.8)	(49.4)	—	(23.8)	(15.2)	(83.3)	(83.3)
3,947	—	4,200	4,137	4,198	—	4,824	4,588	—	—	—	—	—
2,166	—	2,442	2,432	2,452	—	2,564	2,402	—	−13.8	21.2	9.2	18.3
2,018	—	2,001	1,984	2,000	—	2,001	1,980	—	−24.4	23.8	7.0	13.9
148	—	441	447	452	—	563	422	—	10.6	2.5	2.2	4.5
(7.1)	—	(19.9)	(20.2)	(20.3)	—	(24.7)	(19.3)	—	(55.5)	(11.1)	(27.8)	(27.8)
4,184	—	4,444	4,416	4,452	—	4,566	4,382	—	—	—	—	—
					(WITH EXPORT TAX)							
2,009	375	2,656	2,618	2,656	398	3,320	2,631	497	−39.3	76.2	13.4	26.8
1,626	301	1,876	1,842	1,875	281	1,876	1,588	281	−49.9	88.8	5.5	11.0
382	74	780	776	78	117	1,444	1,043	215	10.6	12.5	8.1	15.7
(22.7)	(22.0)	(34.4)	(34.8)	(34.5)	(34.4)	(55.8)	(49.4)	(55.8)	(23.8)	(15.2)	(83.3)	(83.3)
3,636	676	4,533	4,459	4,530	680	5,197	4,220	778	—	—	—	—
1,881	350	2,480	2,466	2,483	372	2,598	2,085	389	−13.8	21.2	9.2	18.3
1,766	325	2,030	2,016	2,034	304	2,030	1,715	304	−24.4	23.8	7.0	13.9
130	24	450	450	448	68	568	370	84	10.6	2.5	2.2	4.5
(7.1)	(7.3)	(19.9)	(20.1)	(19.8)	(17.9)	(24.7)	(19.3)	(24.7)	(55.5)	(11.1)	(27.8)	(27.8)
3,634	675	4,510	4,482	4,517	677	4,628	3,800	693	—	—	—	—

An export quota scheme using the same price limits increases export earnings and producer income, Column 12, over the buffer stock, with the disadvantage of greater instability. Compared to the uncontrolled market, quotas reduce (for $D_E = -0.1$) and stabilize proceeds. Tax revenue, Column 13, is stabilized in relation to that under the uncontrolled market, Column 7, and destabilized in relation to that under the buffer stock, Column 11. If stocks are held by national governments under export quota control, the absolute level of producer income and percentage fluctuations will be the same as under a buffer stock. If, as under the post-war tin agreements, no stocks are held by producers and their governments, producer and national proceeds, Column 14, are considerably increased while stabilized compared to the uncontrolled market, Column 3. Tax revenue and 'profits', Columns 15 and 16, are likewise increased and stabilized.

The optimum device or combination of devices is determined by what is to be maximized. Work effort is increased with price and, subject to the constraint that the producer price does not exceed the ceiling price, is maximized by limiting control to period one. On the other hand, producer profits (and savings) are maximized at the marginal-cost-equals-marginal-revenue price, Column 19, reducing work effort while having no effect on world price or producer price stability, Columns 19 and 20 v. 2. This price is given by,

$$31) \quad \frac{a \pm c - d}{c + 2d}.$$

Under our assumptions, export earnings are maximized at the lowest possible producer price since the point of unitary demand elasticity is only reached by a negative producer price, Column 17. This price is given by,

$$32) \quad \frac{a - \frac{1}{2}(a \pm c)}{b}.$$

A rough compromise between the maximization of work effort and export earnings objectives would be a producer price which approaches the profit maximizing price. A step in this direction, although for other reasons, has been made by some producing countries through the export tax, Column 19 v. 4.

3. LINEAR FUNCTIONS WITH CONSTANT ELASTICITY AT A BASE PRICE (CASE II)

The use of parallel shifts in the linear demand function of Case I requires the unnecessary assumption that for a given price the elasticity of demand decreases as demand shifts to the right. This may be avoided by a demand function which retains constant elasticity, in this case of -0.1 or -0.5 at price 15, for all quantities. When using the derivation of terms suggested in the discussion surrounding equations Nos. 28–30 above, the quantities involved become 137.5 and 162.5. Table A2.2, Case II, illustrates, however, that for small shifts in demand with the market parameters postulated, Case I observations are not appreciably altered. Percentage fluctuations in export earnings and producer income are increased slightly.

4. LINEAR FUNCTIONS WITH ARC ELASTICITIES (CASE III)

Cases I and II have implicitly assumed that demand becomes more elastic as price increases. The use of arc elasticities is one means of relaxing this assumption. Postulated arc elasticities may be used to determine the location of a point on a plane in relation to a given point. In relation to the given uncontrolled market equilibrium prices and quantities of Case I, world prices after the imposition of an export tax are found in the following manner:

33) Demand elasticity, $D_E = \dfrac{Q - \bar{Q}}{P - \bar{P}} \cdot \dfrac{\bar{P}}{\bar{Q}}$ where P and Q are the Case

I uncontrolled market equilibrium price and quantity, respectively, and $\bar{P}$ and $\bar{Q}$ the equilibrium price and quantity, respectively, after the imposition of an export tax. Therefore,

34) $Q = \dfrac{D_E(P - \bar{P})\bar{Q}}{P} + \bar{Q}.$

Similarly,

35) supply elasticity, $S_E = \dfrac{Q - \bar{Q}}{P - x\bar{P}} \cdot \dfrac{x\bar{P}}{\bar{Q}}$ where $(1 - x)$ is the rate of ex-

port tax. Therefore,

36) $Q = \dfrac{S_E(P - \bar{P})\bar{Q} + \bar{Q}}{x\bar{P}}.$

Setting equations Nos. 34 and 35 equal to one another and solving for $\bar{P}$ gives,

37) $\bar{P} = \dfrac{P(S_E - x D_E)}{x(S_E - D_E)}.$

The arc elasticities of demand under control are those between the uncontrolled market price as given in Case I and the ceiling price of the control device. Those of supply take as points the world price and the floor price when no export tax is used and the producer price and floor when a tax is used. The main limitation of this approach is the dependence of the results on the predetermination of uncontrolled market prices by one of the other four methods. The derived export earnings equations are given in Table A2.1. The solutions, Table A2.2 Columns 2, 3, 9 and 12, show that this line of analysis used with our market parameters largely confirms the results of Cases I and II. One notable difference between the three cases is the amount of buffer stock purchases and sales and export quota restrictions and releases needed to defend the price limits. Case I purchases and sales (restrictions and releases) balance over the two periods. This will always hold where shifts in a normal demand function are parallel and the price range is symmetrically distributed within the uncontrolled market equilibrium prices. Under Case II more is sold or released at the ceiling than bought or restricted at the floor price. On the other hand, the converse occurs in Case III, demand elasticity -0.1. Tin control experience has on occasion demonstrated this latter possibility. In Case III the difficulty may be overcome by raising the floor and/or ceiling price (we have assumed throughout that $P_F - P_1 = P_2 - P_C$). When, in practice, more is needed to defend the ceiling than is accumulated at the floor, it would suggest that the mean of the price range is below the mean of the free market prices or that quota restrictions are so large at the floor that buffer stock purchases needed to defend the floor are small and insufficient to support the ceiling price. It is interesting to note that the export tax does not affect the volume of purchases and sales in Case I nor the difference between them in Case II.

5. LOGARITHMIC-LINEAR FUNCTIONS (CASE IV)

Use of logarithmic functions avoids the linear assumptions of Cases I and II and the limitations of the arc elasticity formulation, Case III. Market functions assume the general form

38) $\quad Q = KP^n$

where 'K' is an arbitrary constant and 'n' the price elasticity of demand. Functions take the given elasticities at all quantities, i.e. demand parabola D_2 will not be equidistant at all points from D_1. A constant elasticity of demand greater than -1 (in particular between 0 and -1) leads automatically to a loss in export earnings in a supply shift market under a buffer stock or export quota without tax. The convexity and the direction of the convexity of the total revenue curve depends on the second derivative of the total revenue function:

39) $\quad \dfrac{d^2R}{dQ^2} = \dfrac{d^2QP}{dQ^2} = \dfrac{P}{Q} \cdot \dfrac{1}{n}\left(1 + \dfrac{1}{n}\right) - \dfrac{P}{n^2} \cdot \dfrac{dn}{dQ},$

the sign of which depends on $\dfrac{dn}{dQ}$ (See Chapter 4, Section 2b, p. 142). If the elasticity 'n' is constant,

$\dfrac{dn}{dQ} = 0,\ \dfrac{d^2R}{dQ^2} = \dfrac{P}{Q} \cdot \dfrac{1}{n}\left(1 + \dfrac{1}{n}\right)$ which is positive for $n > -1$ since

$\dfrac{P}{Q} > 0$. When a logarithmic function is applied to the assumptions regarding tin control made above, the absolute levels of earnings in the uncontrolled market are above comparable figures of Case I for demand elasticity

−0.1 and below for −0.5, while percentage fluctuations are less in both instances. Export earnings percentage fluctuations under a buffer stock are more than for Case I. A further application of this method of analysis is given in Appendix 3.

6. CUBIC FUNCTIONS (CASE V)

Where it is likely, for the reasons cited in Chapter 1, that demand may be more or less elastic at price extremes than within the range of normal price fluctuations, cubic demand functions can be used. A third degree demand function is given by the general formulation,

40) $Q = a_0 + a_1 P + a_2 P^2 + a_3 P^3$

and the first derivative,

41) $\dfrac{dQ}{dP} = a_1 + 2a_2 P + 3a_3 P^2.$

Therefore, the price elasticity of demand is,

42) $D_E = \dfrac{dQ}{dP} \cdot \dfrac{P}{Q} = \dfrac{(a_1 + 2a_2 P + 3a_3 P^2)P}{a_0 + a_1 P + a_2 P^2 + a_3 P^3}.$

If $P = 15$ and $Q = 150$, as would be the case for a demand function midway between D_1 and D_2 at price 1, then $150 = a_0 + a_1 15 + a_2 15^2 + a_3 15^3$. At price 15, $D_E = -0.1$. Therefore $31.15^3 a_3 + 21.15^2 a_2 + 11.15 a_1 + a_0 = 0$. If $D_E = -0.5$ at $P = 10$, then $7.10^3 a_3 + 5.10^2 a_2 + 3.10 a_1 + a_0 = 0$. Similarly, when $D_E = -0.5$ at $P = 20$, $7.20^3 a_3 + 5.20^2 a_2 + 3.20 a_1 + a_0 = 0$. The simultaneous solution of the last four equations gives $Q = 445.95 - 53.55P - 3.258P^2 - 0.06996P^3$, the cubic demand function. Results are similar to those reached in previous cases with noticeable differences in percentage fluctuations and optimum prices. Uncontrolled market percentage fluctuations in producer incomes and export earnings are nearly halved when compared to Case I under demand elasticity −0.1. Export earnings percentage fluctuations under buffer stock and export quotas are increased about 50 per cent with demand elasticity −0.5 and greatly reduced with demand elasticity −0.1 in relation to Case I. The advantage of control from the standpoint of stabilization appears to be less when compared to Case I demand elasticity −0.1 and more when compared to −0.5. The export earnings maximizing producer price is considerably increased while the profit maximizing price is reduced compared to Case I. The latter is not, however, as low as in Case IV.

Readings
Further elaborations on the above approach are given in articles by Duloy (1966), Massell (1969), Porter (1964), Tisdell (1963), Zucker (1965) and the author (1970 & 1972) cited in the Readings to Chapters 3 and 4.

Appendix III
Tables Illustrating Effects of Control
with Logarithmic Functions

THE following tables illustrate the effects of control by export taxes, buffer funds, buffer stocks and export quotas when supply and demand functions are assumed to have constant elasticity within the range of prices considered. Functions assume the form $Q = KP^n$, where Q is the quantity demanded or supplied, K an arbitrary constant, P price and n the price elasticity of demand or supply. Shifts in functions are by 40 units of output at price 100 and functions retain the given elasticity at both positions. Shifts are centred at output 100. 'Profits' are given by the area bounded by price 40, the logarithmic supply function, the producer price and the vertical axis. Price 40 is an arbitrary cut-off point below which prices are assumed not to cover costs. Profit results will generally reflect the effect of control on the level of profits and their fluctuation, but will not show the exact magnitude in a given period for this would depend on the cut-off point chosen. Percentage fluctuations are derived by a division of the actual change by the mean of the two observations. The progressive export tax percentage increases proportionately with price such that at price 100 it is 15 per cent and at 200, 30 per cent. Buffer fund, buffer stock and export quota price limits are placed symmetrically within the uncontrolled market prices and reduce the absolute difference in uncontrolled market prices by 50 per cent. When more extreme supply and demand elasticities than those illustrated are used deviations from the uncontrolled market will be larger in the direction indicated by those illustrated. Larger shifts in the functions will create different absolute changes while the general effects of control will remain the same. Likewise, as the controlled prices approach the uncontrolled market prices, or the export tax becomes less progressive or of a lower percentage, the effects of control will diminish. If one drops the assumption that current demand and supply elasticities are unaffected by control, the figures in the following tables will give a rough idea of how results are influenced when one takes one set of elasticities for the uncontrolled market and another set for the controlled market. The same procedure can be applied to the analysis of Appendix 4 which provides results under a range of demand elasticities.

TABLE A3.1
UNCONTROLLED DEMAND SHIFT MARKET

(1) Supply Elasticity	(2) Period	(3) World and Producer Price				(4) Export and Producer Earnings				(5) Producer 'Profits'			
		\- \- \- \- Demand Elasticity \- \- \- \-											
		0.0	−0.5	−1.0	−5.0	0.0	−0.5	−1.0	−5.0	0.0	−0.5	−1.0	−5.0
−1.0	1st	125	156	–	94	10,000	10,000	–	10,000	11,394	13,625	–	8,605
	2nd	83	69	–	104	10,000	10,000	–	10,000	7,340	5,515	–	9,618
	% Fluctuation	40	77	–	10	0	0	–	0	43	85	–	11
	Total	–	–	–	–	20,000	20,000	–	20,000	18,734	19,140	–	18,223
−0.5	1st	156	–	64	95	12,500	–	8,000	9,754	12,351	–	3,350	6,858
	2nd	69	–	144	104	8,333	–	12,000	10,204	4,017	–	11,350	7,760
	% Fluctuation	77	–	77	9	77	–	40	5	102	–	109	12
	Total	–	–	–	–	20,833	–	20,000	19,958	16,368	–	14,700	14,618
0.0	1st	–	64	80	96	–	6,400	8,000	9,564	–	2,400	4,000	5,563
	2nd	–	144	120	104	–	14,400	12,000	10,371	–	10,400	8,000	6,371
	% Fluctuation	–	77	40	8	–	77	40	8	–	125	67	13
	Total	–	–	–	–	–	20,800	20,000	19,935	–	12,800	12,000	11,934
0.5	1st	64	80	86	96	5,120	7,155	8,000	9,408	1,727	3,084	3,647	4,585
	2nd	144	120	113	103	17,280	13,145	12,000	10,510	9,833	7,077	6,313	5,320
	% Fluctuation	77	40	27	7	108	59	40	11	140	79	53	15
	Total	–	–	–	–	22,400	23,300	20,000	19,918	11,560	10,161	9,960	9,905
1.0	1st	80	86	89	96	6,400	7,426	8,000	9,282	2,400	2,913	3,200	3,841
	2nd	120	113	110	103	14,400	12,751	12,000	10,626	6,400	5,576	5,200	4,513
	% Fluctuation	40	27	20	7	77	53	40	14	91	63	48	16
	Total	–	–	–	–	20,800	20,177	20,000	19,908	8,800	8,489	8,400	8,354
5.0	1st	96	96	96	98	7,651	7,839	8,000	8,747	1,268	1,300	1,326	1,451
	2nd	104	103	103	102	12,446	12,200	12,000	11,156	2,067	2,027	1,994	1,852
	% Fluctuation	8	7	7	4	48	44	40	24	48	44	40	24
	Total	–	–	–	–	20,097	20,039	20,000	19,903	3,336	3,326	3,320	3,303

TABLE A3.2
UNCONTROLLED SUPPLY SHIFT MARKET

(1) Supply Elasticity	(2) Period	(3) World and Producer Price				(4) Export and Producer Earnings — Demand Elasticity				(5) Producer 'Profits'			
		0.0	−0.5	−1.0	−5.0	0.0	−0.5	−1.0	−5.0	0.0	−0.5	−1.0	−5.0
−1.0	1st	80	64	—	106	8,000	8,000	—	8,000	5,545	3,760	—	7,770
	2nd	120	144	—	96	12,000	12,000	—	12,000	13,183	15,370	—	10,448
	% Fluctuation	40	77	—	10	40	40	—	40	82	121	—	29
	Total	—	—	—	—	20,000	20,000	—	20,000	18,728	19,130	—	18,224
−0.5	1st	64	—	156	105	6,400	—	10,000	8,202	2,681	—	9,880	6,282
	2nd	144	—	69	96	14,400	—	10,000	11,759	13,621	—	4,820	8,340
	% Fluctuation	77	—	77	9	77	—	0	36	134	—	69	28
	Total	—	—	—	—	20,800	—	20,000	19,961	16,302	—	14,700	14,622
0.0	1st	—	156	125	104	—	12,500	10,000	8,365	—	9,300	9,800	5,165
	2nd	—	69	83	96	—	8,333	10,000	11,570	—	3,533	5,200	6,770
	% Fluctuation	—	77	40	8	—	40	0	32	—	90	52	27
	Total	—	—	—	—	—	20,833	20,000	19,935	—	12,833	12,000	11,935
0.5	1st	156	125	116	104	15,625	11,180	10,000	8,502	9,067	6,104	5,317	4,319
	2nd	69	83	89	97	6,944	9,129	10,000	11,425	2,606	4,062	4,643	5,586
	% Fluctuation	77	40	27	7	77	20	0	29	111	40.2	27	26
	Total	—	—	—	—	22,569	20,309	20,000	19,927	11,673	10,166	9,960	9,905
1.0	1st	125	116	112	104	12,500	10,772	10,000	8,618	5,610	4,746	5,360	3,689
	2nd	83	88	91	97	8,333	9,410	10,000	11,297	3,207	3,745	4,040	4,685
	% Fluctuation	40	27	20	7	40	13	0	27	55	24	8	24
	Total	—	—	—	—	20,833	20,182	20,000	19,915	8,817	8,491	8,400	8,354
5.0	1st	105	104	104	102	10,456	10,205	10,000	9,146	1,737	1,695	1,662	1,519
	2nd	96	97	97	98	9,642	9,836	10,000	10,757	1,599	1,631	1,658	1,785
	% Fluctuation	8	7	7	4	8	36	0	16	8.3	3.9	0	16
	Total	—	—	—	—	20,098	20,041	20,000	19,903	3,336	3,326	3,320	3,304

TABLE A3.3
15% EXPORT TAX IN A DEMAND SHIFT MARKET

All sub-columns are labelled by **Demand Elasticity** (0.0, -0.5, -1.0, -5.0).

(1) Supply Elasticity	(2) Period	(3) World Price				(4) Export Earnings				(5) Producer 'Profits'				(6) Export Tax Revenue			
		0.0	-0.5	-1.0	-5.0	0.0	-0.5	-1.0	-5.0	0.0	-0.5	-1.0	-5.0	0.0	-0.5	-1.0	-5.0
-1.0	1st	144	216	—	91	11,500	11,764	—	11,766	11,394	15,250	—	6,572	1,500	1,764	—	1,760
	2nd	96	96	—	100	11,500	11,764	—	11,766	7,340	7,140	—	7,586	1,500	1,764	—	1,766
	% Fluctuation	40	77	—	10	0	0	—	0	43	72	—	14	0	0	—	0
	Total	—	—	—	—	23,000	23,528	—	23,532	18,734	22,390	—	14,158	3,000	3,528	—	3,532
-0.5	1st	180	—	54	93	14,375	—	8,000	10,488	12,351	—	950	5,172	1,875	—	1,200	1,578
	2nd	80	—	122	102	9,583	—	12,000	10,969	4,018	—	7,750	5,998	1,250	—	1,800	1,645
	% Fluctuation	77	—	77	9	40	—	40	5	102	—	156	15	40	—	40	4
	Total	—	—	—	—	23,958	—	20,000	21,457	16,368	—	8,700	11,170	3,125	—	3,000	3,223
0.0	1st	—	64	80	96	—	6,400	8,000	9,564	—	1,440	2,800	4,129	—	960	1,200	1,434
	2nd	—	144	120	104	—	14,400	12,000	10,371	—	8,240	6,200	4,816	—	2,160	1,800	1,556
	% Fluctuation	—	77	40	8	—	77	40	8	—	140	76	15	—	77	40	8
	Total	—	—	—	—	—	20,800	20,000	19,934	—	9,680	9,000	8,945	—	3,120	3,000	2,990
0.5	1st	74	87	91	97	5,888	7,452	8,000	8,869	1,726	2,536	2,846	3,338	768	1,118	1,200	1,331
	2nd	166	130	119	105	19,872	13,690	12,000	9,907	9,833	6,071	5,114	3,927	2,592	2,054	1,800	1,486
	% Fluctuation	77	40	27	7	108	59	40	11	140	82	57	16	108	59	40	11
	Total	—	—	—	—	25,760	21,142	20,000	18,776	11,560	8,607	7,960	7,265	3,360	3,172	3,000	2,817
1.0	1st	92	96	97	99	7,360	7,840	8,000	8,329	2,400	2,532	2,600	2,740	960	1,176	1,200	1,250
	2nd	138	125	119	106	16,560	13,462	12,000	9,535	6,400	4,921	4,300	3,252	2,160	2,020	1,800	1,430
	% Fluctuation	40	27	20	7	77	53	40	14	91	64	49	17	77	53	40	14
	Total	—	—	—	—	23,920	21,302	20,000	17,864	8,800	7,453	6,900	5,992	3,120	3,196	3,000	2,680
5.0	1st	110	111	110	106	8,798	8,440	8,000	6,319	1,268	1,189	1,126	888	1,148	1,266	1,200	948
	2nd	119	120	118	110	14,312	13,136	12,000	8,060	2,067	1,854	1,694	1,135	1,867	1,970	1,795	1,209
	% Fluctuation	8	7	7	4	48	44	40	24	48	44	40	24	48	44	40	24
	Total	—	—	—	—	23,110	21,576	20,000	14,379	3,335	3,043	2,820	2,023	3,014	3,236	2,995	2,157

TABLE A3.4

15% EXPORT TAX IN A SUPPLY SHIFT MARKET

(1) Supply Elasticity	(2) Period	(3) World Price				(4) Export Earnings				(5) Producer 'Profits'				(6) Export Tax Revenue			
		Demand Elasticity															
		0.0	−0.5	−1.0	−5.0	−5.0	−1.0	−0.5	0.0	0.0	−0.5	−1.0	−5.0	0.0	−0.5	−1.0	−5.0
−1.0	1st	92	89	—	102	9,412	10,000	9,412	9,200	5,545	5,060	—	6,251	1,200	1,412	1,500	1,412
	2nd	138	199	—	92	14,120	10,000	14,118	13,800	13,183	17,321	—	8,008	1,800	2,118	1,500	2,120
	% Fluctuation	40	77	—	10	40	0	40	40	82	110	—	26	40	40	0	40
	Total	—	—	—	—	23,532	20,000	23,529	23,000	18,728	22,381	—	14,159	3,000	3,530	3,000	3,532
−0.5	1st	74	—	133	103	8,815	10,000	—	7,366	2,680	—	6,881	4,866	960	—	1,500	1,322
	2nd	166	—	59	94	12,642	10,000	—	16,560	13,621	—	1,821	6,306	2,160	—	1,500	1,899
	% Fluctuation	77	—	77	9	36	0	—	77	134	—	116	26	77	—	0	36
	Total	—	—	—	—	21,457	20,000	—	23,920	16,301	—	8,702	11,172	3,120	—	3,000	3,221
0.0	1st	—	156	124	104	8,365	10,000	12,500	—	—	7,425	5,300	3,910	—	1,875	1,500	1,255
	2nd	—	69	83	96	11,570	10,000	8,333	—	—	2,283	3,700	5,035	—	1,250	1,500	1,736
	% Fluctuation	—	77	40	8	32	0	40	—	—	106	36	25	—	40	0	32
	Total	—	—	—	—	19,935	20,000	20,833	—	—	9,708	9,000	8,945	—	3,125	3,000	2,991
0.5	1st	180	136	122	106	8,014	10,000	11,644	17,969	9,067	5,249	4,317	3,192	2,344	1,746	1,500	1,202
	2nd	80	90	93	98	10,763	10,000	9,507	7,986	2,666	3,364	3,643	4,075	1,042	1,426	1,500	1,614
	% Fluctuation	77	40	27	7	29	0	20	77	111	44	17	24	77	20	0	29
	Total	—	—	—	—	18,777	20,000	21,151	25,955	11,673	8,613	7,960	7,267	3,386	3,172	3,000	2,816
1.0	1st	143	129	121	107	7,733	10,000	11,372	14,375	5,610	4,193	3,610	2,646	1,875	1,706	1,500	1,160
	2nd	96	99	99	100	10,133	10,000	9,934	9,583	3,207	3,262	3,290	3,346	1,250	1,490	1,500	1,520
	% Fluctuation	40	27	20	7	27	0	13	40	55	25	9	23	40	13	0	27
	Total	—	—	—	—	17,866	20,000	21,306	23,958	8,817	7,455	6,900	5,992	3,125	3,196	3,000	2,680
5.0	1st	120	121	119	111	6,608	10,000	10,987	12,025	1,737	1,551	1,411	931	1,568	1,648	1,500	991
	2nd	111	112	111	107	7,771	10,000	10,590	11,088	1,599	1,492	1,409	1,093	1,446	1,588	1,500	1,166
	% Fluctuation	8	7	7	4	16	0	3.6	8	8.3	3.9	0	16	8	3.6	0	16
	Total	—	—	—	—	14,379	20,000	21,577	23,113	3,336	3,043	2,820	2,024	3,014	3,236	3,000	2,157

TABLE A3.5

PROGRESSIVE EXPORT TAX IN A DEMAND SHIFT MARKET

Demand Elasticity (sub-columns: 0.0, -0.5, -1.0, -5.0)

(1) Supply Elasticity	(2) Period	(3) World Price (Producer Price)				(4) Export Earnings[a]				(5) Producer 'Profits'[a]				(6) Export Tax Revenue			
		0.0	-0.5	-1.0	-5.0	0.0	-0.5	-1.0	-5.0	0.0	-0.5	-1.0	-5.0	0.0	-0.5	-1.0	-5.0
-1.0	1st	248(125)	b	—	91(79)	11,875	b	—	11,584	11,394	b	—	6,767	1,875	b	—	1,584
	2nd	94(83)	—	—	100(85)	11,250	—	—	11,775	7,340	—	—	7,576	1,250	—	—	1,775
	% Fluctuation	45(40)	—	—	10(8)	5.4(0)	—	—	2(0)	43	—	—	11	40	—	—	11
	Total	—	—	—	—	23,125	—	—	23,359	18,734	—	—	14,343	3,125	—	—	3,359
-0.5	1st	193(156)	—	b	94(80)	15,430	—	b	10,433	12,350	—	b	5,289	2,930	—	b	1,464
	2nd	77(69)	—	—	102(87)	9,201	—	—	10,988	4,018	—	—	5,957	868	—	—	1,686
	% Fluctuation	86(77)	—	—	9(7)	51(40)	—	—	5(4)	102	—	—	12	109	—	—	—
	Total	—	—	—	—	24,631	—	—	21,421	16,368	—	—	11,246	3,798	—	—	3,150
0.0	1st	—	64(58)	80(70)	96(82)	—	6,400	8,000	9,564	—	1,786	3,040	4,192	—	614	960	1,372
	2nd	—	144(113)	120(98)	104(88)	—	14,400	12,000	10,071	—	7,290	5,840	4,758	—	3,110	2,160	1,613
	% Fluctuation	—	77(64)	40(33)	8(7)	—	77(64)	40(33)	8(6.6)	—	121	63	12.6	—	134	77	16
	Total	—	—	—	—	—	20,800	20,000	19,935	—	9,076	8,880	8,950	—	3,725	3,120	2,985
0.5	1st	70(64)	86(75)	90(78)	97(83)	5,612	7,405	8,000	8,884	1,727	2,616	2,923	3,371	492	952	1,086	1,298
	2nd	175(144)	134(107)	121(99)	105(98)	21,012	13,906	12,000	9,875	9,833	5,717	4,865	3,859	3,732	2,801	2,173	1,556
	% Fluctuation	86(77)	44(36)	29(23)	7(6)	116(108)	61(53)	40(35)	10(9)	140	74	50	13.5	153	99	67	18
	Total	—	—	—	—	26,624	21,311	20,000	18,759	11,560	8,333	7,788	7,230	4,224	3,753	3,259	2,854
1.0	1st	90(80)	96(82)	97(83)	99(84)	7,168	7,819	8,000	8,340	2,400	2,549	2,619	2,751	768	1,121	1,161	1,238
	2nd	142(120)	131(105)	121(99)	106(89)	16,992	13,713	12,000	9,466	6,400	4,713	4,110	3,180	2,592	2,686	2,180	1,507
	% Fluctuation	45(40)	31(25)	22(18)	7(5.7)	81(77)	55(49)	40(36)	13(11)	91	60	44	14	109	82	61	20
	Total	—	—	—	—	24,160	21,532	20,000	17,806	8,800	7,262	6,729	5,931	3,360	3,807	3,341	2745
5.0	1st	109(95)	114(94)	112(93)	107(90)	8,748	8,536	8,000	6,171	1,268	1,173	1,102	856	1,098	1,458	1,348	988
	2nd	120(104)	125(101)	122(100)	112(93)	14,382	13,398	12,000	7,733	2,067	1,810	1,628	1,066	1,936	2,494	2,191	1,295
	% Fluctuation	9(8)	9(7)	8(6)	4.5(3.6)	49(48)	44(42)	40(38)	22(21)	48	43	39	22	55	52	48	30
	Total	—	—	—	—	23,130	21,934	20,000	13,904	3,336	2,983	2,730	1,923	3,334	3,952	3,539	2,283

[a] Bracketed figures refer to producers' income stability.
[b] Double roots are obtained with the quadratic functions used and equilibrium positions are extreme.

TABLE A3.6

PROGRESSIVE EXPORT TAX IN A SUPPLY SHIFT MARKET

(1) Supply Elasticity	(2) Period	(3) World Price (Producer Price)				(4) Export Earnings[a]					(5) Producer 'Profits'				(6) Export Tax Revenue			
								Demand Elasticity										
		0.0	-0.5	-1.0	-5.0	0.0	-0.5	-1.0	-5.0	-5.0	0.0	-0.5	-1.0	-5.0	0.0	-0.5	-1.0	-5.0
-1.0	1st	90(80)	b	—	101(86)	8,960	b	—	9,437	5,545	b	—	—	6,125	960	b	—	1,437
	2nd	142(120)	—	—	92(79)	14,160	—	—	13,922	13,183	—	—	—	8,219	2,160	—	—	1,923
	% Fluctuation	45(40)	—	—	10(8)	45(40)	—	—	38(40)	82	—	—	—	29.2	77	—	—	28.9
	Total	—	—	—	—	23,120	—	—	23,359	18,728	—	—	—	14,344	3,120	—	—	3,360
-0.5	1st	70(64)	—	b	103(87)	7,014	—	b	8,837	2,681	b	—	—	4,819	614	—	b	1,368
	2nd	175(144)	—	—	94(81)	7,510	—	—	12,585	13,621	—	—	—	6,427	3,110	—	—	1,782
	% Fluctuation	86(77)	—	—	9(7)	86(77)	—	—	35(36.5)	134	—	—	—	29	134	—	—	26
	Total	—	—	—	—	14,524	—	—	21,422	16,302	—	—	—	11,246	3,724	—	—	3,150
0.0	1st	—	156(119)	125(102)	105(88)	—	12,500	10,000	8,365	—	—	6,370	4,925	3,853	—	2,930	1,875	1,312
	2nd	—	69(62)	83(73)	96(82)	—	8,333	10,000	11,570	—	—	2,665	3,950	5,097	—	868	1,250	1,673
	% Fluctuation	—	77(65)	40(33)	8(6.6)	—	40(25)	0(7)	32(34)	—	—	82	22	28	—	109	40	24
	Total	—	—	—	—	—	20,833	20,000	19,935	—	—	9,035	8,875	8,950	—	3,798	3,125	2,985
0.5	1st	193(156)	141(111)	124(101)	106(89)	19,287	11,863	10,000	7,984	9,067	—	4,890	4,074	3,128	3,662	2,504	1,864	1,268
	2nd	77(69)	90(78)	93(80)	98(84)	7,668	9,464	10,000	10,775	2,606	—	3,438	3,711	4,102	723	1,272	1,397	1,586
	% Fluctuation	86(77)	44(36)	29(23)	7(6)	86(77)	22(13)	0(6)	30(31)	111	—	35	9	27	134	65	29	22
	Total	—	—	—	—	26,955	21,327	20,000	18,759	11,673	—	8,328	7,785	7,230	4,385	3,776	3,261	2,854
1.0	1st	148(125)	135(108)	124(101)	107(90)	14,844	11,616	10,000	7,670	5,610	—	3,992	3,431	2,580	2,344	2,351	1,859	1,230
	2nd	94(83)	99(84)	99(84)	100(85)	9,375	9,926	10,000	10,137	3,207	—	3,269	3,298	3,351	1,042	1,467	1,485	1,515
	% Fluctuation	45(40)	31(25)	22(18)	7(6)	45(40)	16(9)	0(4)	28(29)	55	—	20	4	26	77	46	22	21
	Total	—	—	—	—	24,219	21,152	20,000	17,807	8,817	—	7,261	6,729	5,931	3,385	3,818	3,344	2,745
5.0	1st	121(105)	126(102)	123(100)	112(93)	12,096	11,218	10,000	6,328	1,737	—	1,513	1,355	872	1,640	2,109	1,840	1,064
	2nd	110(96)	115(95)	113(94)	107(90)	11,036	10,719	10,000	7,576	1,599	—	1,470	1,375	1,051	1,394	1,847	1,699	1,218
	% Fluctuation	9(8)	9(7)	8(6)	4.4(3.6)	9(9)	5(2.6)	0(2)	17.9(18.8)	8.3	—	2.8	1.5	18.6	16	13	8	13
	Total	—	—	—	—	23,132	21,936	20,000	13,904	3,336	—	2,983	2,730	1,923	3,034	3,936	3,539	2,282

[a] Bracketed figures refer to producers' income stability.
[b] Double roots are obtained with the quadratic functions used and equilibrium positions are extreme.

TABLE A3.7
BUFFER FUND IN A DEMAND SHIFT MARKET

(1) Supply Elasticity	(2) Period	(3) World Price[b]			(4) Export Earnings (Producer Income)			(5) Producer 'Profits'			(6) Buffer Fund Account		
		−0.5	−1.0	−5.0	−0.5	−1.0	−5.0	−0.5	−1.0	−5.0	−0.5	−1.0	−5.0
−1.0	1st	115	—	95	18,610(10,000)	—	10,208(10,000)	12,130	—	8,868	−1,380	—	−208
	2nd	120	—	104	13,134(10,000)	—	9,803(10,000)	8,235	—	9,374	−3,126	—	197
	% Fluctuation	13(38)	—	9(5)	41(0)	—	4(0)	38	—	6	—	—	—
	Total	—	—	—	21,734(20,000)	—	19,989(20,000)	20,365	—	18,242	−1,734	—	−11
−0.5	1st	—	73	95	—	8,000(9,165)	9,665(9,868)	—	5,681	7,087	—	−1,165	−203
	2nd	—	134	104	—	12,000(11,135)	10,294(10,094)	—	9,622	7,538	—	865	200
	% Fluctuation	—	58(38)	9(4)	—	40(19)	6(2)	—	52	6	—	—	—
	Total	—	—	—	—	20,000(20,300)	19,960(19,962)	—	15,303	14,626	—	−300	−3
0.0	1st	64	80	96	6,400(8,400)	8,000(9,000)	9,563(9,765)	4,400	5,000	5,765	−2,000	−1,000	−202
	2nd	144	120	104	14,400(12,400)	12,000(11,000)	10,372(10,170)	8,400	7,000	6,169	2,000	1,000	202
	% Fluctuation	77(38)	40(20)	8(4)	77(38)	40(20)	8(4)	62	33	7	—	—	—
	Total	—	—	—	20,800(20,800)	20,000(20,000)	19,935(19,935)	12,800	12,000	11,934	0	0	0
0.15	1st	71	83	96	6,846(8,538)	8,000(8,949)	9,480(9,679)	4,005	4,279	4,766	−1,792	−949	−199
	2nd	131	116	104	13,730(11,537)	12,000(10,950)	10,435(10,230)	6,005	5,613	5,134	2,193	1,050	204
	% Fluctuation	59(20)	34(13)	8(4)	68(30)	40(20)	10(6)	40	27	7	401	101	5
	Total	—	—	—	20,476(20,075)	20,000(19,999)	19,915(19,910)	10,010	9,892	9,900	401	101	5
1.0	1st	74	85	96	6,892(8,624)	8,000(8,924)	9,412(9,609)	3,512	3,662	4,005	−1,732	−924	−197
	2nd	128	115	103	13,554(11,286)	12,000(10,924)	10,488(10,282)	4,843	4,662	4,341	2,269	1,076	205
	% Fluctuation	53(13)	30(10)	7(3)	65(27)	40(20)	11(7)	32	24	8	537	150	8
	Total	—	—	—	20,446(19,910)	20,000(19,848)	19,900(19,891)	8,355	8,324	8,346	537	150	8
5.0	1st	79	88	97	7,131(8,783)	8,000(8,877)	9,114(9,304)	1,457	1,473	1,544	−1,652	−877	−190
	2nd	124	112	103	13,344(10,956)	12,000(10,874)	10,720(10,507)	1,819	1,806	1,744	2,388	1,126	212
	% Fluctuation	44(4)	24(3)	6(2)	61(22)	40(20)	16(12)	22	20	12	736	248	22
	Total	—	—	—	20,475(19,739)	20,000(19,751)	19,834(19,811)	3,276	3,279	3,288	736	248	22

[a] Demand elasticity 0.0 has been omitted because it does not produce meaningful results. Results are extreme in the direction indicated by the other demand elasticities.

[b] Bracketed figures refer to producer price stability.

TABLE A3.8
BUFFER FUND IN A SUPPLY SHIFT MARKET

(1) Supply Elasticity	(2) Period	(3) World Price[b]			(4) Export Earnings (Producer Income)			(5) Producer 'Profits'			(6) Buffer Fund Account		
		Demand Elasticity[a]											
		-0.5	-1.0	-5.0	-0.5	-1.0	-5.0	-0.5	-1.0	-5.0	-0.5	-1.0	-5.0
-1.0	1st	110	–	105	10,500(8,000)	–	8,158(8,000)	5,935	–	7,581	-2,500	–	158
	2nd	107	–	96	10,333(12,000)	–	11,750(12,000)	13,576	–	10,764	1,666	–	-250
	% Fluctuation	3(38)	–	9(5)	2(40)	–	36(40)	78	–	35	–	–	–
	Total	–	–	–	20,833(20,000)	–	19,908(20,000)	19,511	–	18,345	-834	–	-92
-0.5	1st	–	145	105	–	10,000(9,279)	8,273(8,112)	–	8,439	6,105	–	720	161
	2nd	–	80	96	–	10,000(11,456)	11,650(11,897)	–	7,733	8,615	–	-1,456	-247
	% Fluctuation	–	58(38)	9(4)	–	0(20)	34(38)	–	9	34	–	–	–
	Total	–	–	–	–	20,000(20,735)	19,923(20,000)	–	16,172	14,720	–	-734	-86
0.0	1st	156	125	104	12,500(10,764)	10,000(9,167)	8,365(8,202)	7,564	5,967	5,002	1,736	833	162
	2nd	69	83	96	8,333(10,937)	10,000(11,250)	11,570(11,815)	6,137	6,450	7,015	-2,604	-1,250	-244
	% Fluctuation	77(38)	40(20)	8(4)	40(16)	0(20)	32(36)	21	8	33	–	–	–
	Total	–	–	–	20,833(21,701)	20,000(20,417)	19,935(20,017)	13,701	12,417	12,016	-868	-417	-81
0.5	1st	136	120	104	11,677(9,812)	10,000(9,125)	8,441(8,276)	5,192	4,734	4,168	1,865	875	165
	2nd	74	85	97	8,607(10,893)	10,000(11,186)	11,504(11,745)	5,238	5,434	5,806	-2,286	-1,186	-240
	% Fluctuation	59(20)	33(13)	7.7(3.7)	30(10)	0(20)	31(35)	1	14	33	–	–	–
	Total	–	–	–	20,284(20,705)	20,000(20,311)	19,945(20,021)	10,430	10,168	9,974	-421	-311	-75
1.0	1st	131	117	104	11,450(9,534)	10,000(9,104)	8,505(8,338)	4,126	3,912	3,529	1,916	896	167
	2nd	76	86	97	8,733(10,927)	10,000(11,155)	11,449(11,689)	4,503	4,618	4,884	-2,194	-1,155	-240
	% Fluctuation	53(13)	30(10)	7.4(3.4)	27(14)	0(20)	30(33)	9	17	32	–	–	–
	Total	–	–	–	20,183(20,461)	20,000(20,259)	19,954(20,027)	8,630	8,530	8,413	-278	-259	-73
5.0	1st	125	113	103	11,162(9,164)	10,000(9,063)	8,788(8,614)	1,522	1,505	1,430	1,998	937	174
	2nd	80	89	97	8,947(11,020)	10,000(11,097)	11,208(11,442)	1,828	1,841	1,899	-2,073	-1,097	-233
	% Fluctuation	44(4)	24(3)	6(2)	22(18)	0(20)	24(28)	18	20	28	–	–	–
	Total	–	–	–	20,109(20,184)	20,000(20,160)	19,996(20,056)	3,350	3,346	3,329	-75	-160	-59

a Demand elasticity 0.0 has been omitted because it does not produce meaningful results. Results are extreme in the direction indicated by the other demand elasticities.
b Bracketed figures refer to producer price stability.

TABLE A3.9

INTERNATIONAL BUFFER STOCK AND EXPORT QUOTA (NATIONAL BUFFER STOCK) IN A DEMAND SHIFT MARKET

(1) Supply Elasticity	(2) Period	(3) World and Producer Price				(4) Export Earnings with Export Quota (National Buffer Stock)				(5) Producer Income with Export Quota and Buffer Stock. Export Earnings with Buffer Stock				(6) Producer 'Profits'				(7) Export Quota (National Buffer Stock Fund)			
		Demand Elasticity																			
		0.0	−0.5	−1.0	−5.0	0.0	−0.5	−1.0	−5.0	0.0	−0.5	−1.0	−5.0	0.0	−0.5	−1.0	−5.0	0.0	−0.5	−1.0	−5.0
−1.0	1st	114	134	—	97	9,167	9,279	—	9,001	10,000	13,000	—	10,000	10,524	12,130	—	8,868	−833	−721	—	−999
	2nd	94	91	—	102	11,250	11,456	—	11,027	10,000	13,000	—	10,000	8,518	8,235	—	9,374	1,250	1,456	—	1,027
	% Fluctuation	20	38	—	5	204	21	—	20	0	0	—	0	21	38	—	6	—	—	—	—
	Total	—	—	—	—	20,417	20,735	—	20,028	20,000	23,000	—	20,000	19,042	20,365	—	18,242	417	735	—	28
−0.5	1st	134	—	84	97	10,720	—	8,000	8,895	11,524	—	9,165	9,868	10,550	—	5,681	7,087	−804	—	−1,165	−973
	2nd	91	—	124	102	10,920	—	12,000	11,137	9,464	—	11,135	10,094	6,445	—	9,622	7,538	1,454	—	865	1,043
	% Fluctuation	38	—	38	4	—	—	40	22	—	—	19	2	48	—	51	6	—	—	—	—
	Total	—	—	—	—	21,640	—	20,000	20,022	20,988	—	20,300	19,962	16,995	—	15,303	14,625	650	—	−300	70
0.0	1st	—	84	90	98	—	7,332	8,000	8,797	—	8,400	9,000	9,765	—	4,400	5,000	5,765	—	−1,068	−1,000	−968
	2nd	—	124	110	102	—	13,361	12,000	11,220	—	12,400	11,000	10,169	—	8,400	7,000	6,169	—	963	1,000	1,051
	% Fluctuation	—	38	20	4	—	58	40	24	—	38	20	4	—	62	33	7	—	—	—	—
	Total	—	—	—	—	—	20,695	20,000	20,017	—	20,800	20,000	19,934	—	12,800	12,000	11,934	—	−105	0	−83
0.5	1st	84	90	93	98	6,720	7,589	8,000	8,726	7,699	3,538	8,949	9,679	3,446	4,006	4,279	4,776	−979	−949	−949	−953
	2nd	124	110	106	102	14,880	12,386	12,000	11,292	13,808	11,537	10,950	10,230	7,519	6,005	5,613	5,134	1,072	1,049	1,050	1,062
	% Fluctuation	38	20	13	4	76	50	40	26	57	30	20	6	74	40	27	7	—	—	—	—
	Total	—	—	—	—	21,600	20,175	20,000	20,018	21,507	20,075	19,899	19,909	10,965	10,011	9,892	9,900	93	100	101	109
1.0	1st	90	93	94	98	7,200	7,709	8,000	8,664	8,100	8,624	8,924	9,609	3,250	3,512	3,662	4,005	−900	−915	−924	−945
	2nd	110	106	104	101	13,200	12,368	12,000	11,351	12,100	11,286	10,924	10,282	5,250	4,843	4,662	4,341	1,100	1,082	1,076	1,069
	% Fluctuation	20	13	10	3	59	46	40	27	40	27	20	7	47	32	24	8	—	—	—	—
	Total	—	—	—	—	20,400	20,077	20,000	20,015	20,200	19,910	19,848	19,891	8,500	8,355	8,324	8,346	200	167	152	124
5.0	1st	98	98	98	99	7,812	7,914	8,000	8,394	8,672	8,783	8,877	9,304	1,439	1,457	1,473	1,544	−860	−869	−877	−910
	2nd	109	102	101	101	12,203	12,092	12,000	11,610	11,060	10,956	10,874	10,507	1,837	1,819	1,806	1,744	1,143	1,136	1,126	1,103
	% Fluctuation	4	4	3	2	44	42	40	32	24	22	20	12	25	22	20	12	—	—	—	—
	Total	—	—	—	—	20,015	20,006	20,000	20,004	19,733	19,739	19,751	19,811	3,276	3,276	3,279	3,288	283	267	249	193

TABLE A3.10

INTERNATIONAL BUFFER STOCK AND EXPORT QUOTA (NATIONAL BUFFER STOCK) IN A SUPPLY SHIFT MARKET

(1) Supply Elasticity	(2) Period	(3) World and Producer Price				(4) Export Earnings with Export Quota (National Buffer Stock)				(5) Producer Income with Buffer Stock and Export Quota. Export Earnings with Buffer Stock				(6) Producer Profits'				(7) Export Quota (National Buffer Stock) Fund			
		Demand Elasticity																			
		0.0	-0.5	-1.0	-5.0	0.0	-0.5	-1.0	-5.0	0.0	-0.5	-1.0	-5.0	0.0	-0.5	-1.0	-5.0	0.0	-0.5	-1.0	-5.0
-1.0	1st	90	84	—	103	9,000	9,165	—	8,822	8,000	8,000	—	8,000	6,487	5,935	—	7,581	1,000	1,165	—	822
	2nd	110	124	—	98	11,000	11,135	—	10,812	12,000	12,000	—	12,000	12,139	13,576	—	10,764	-1,000	-865	—	-1,188
	% Fluctuation	20	38	—	5	20	20	—	20	40	40	—	40	61	78	—	35	—	—	—	—
	Total	—	—	—	—	20,000	20,300	—	19,624	20,000	20,000	—	20,000	18,626	19,511	—	18,345	0	300	—	-366
-0.5	1st	84	—	135	103	8,400	10,000	10,000	8,948	7,332	—	9,279	8,112	4,545	—	8,439	6,105	1,068	—	721	836
	2nd	124	—	91	98	12,400	10,000	10,000	10,713	13,362	—	11,456	11,897	11,546	—	7,733	8,615	-962	—	-1,456	-1,897
	% Fluctuation	38	—	38	4	—	0	0	18	58	—	21	38	87	—	9	34	—	—	—	—
	Total	—	—	—	—	20,800	20,000	20,000	19,661	20,694	—	20,735	20,009	16,091	—	16,172	14,720	106	—	-735	-1,061
0.0	1st	—	135	115	103	—	11,600	10,000	9,050	—	10,764	9,167	8,202	—	7,564	5,967	5,002	—	836	833	848
	2nd	—	91	94	98	—	9,547	10,000	10,643	—	10,937	11,250	11,815	—	6,137	6,450	7,015	—	-1,309	-1,250	-1,172
	% Fluctuation	—	38	20	4	—	19	0	16	—	2	20	36	—	21	8	33	—	—	—	—
	Total	—	—	—	—	—	21,147	20,000	19,693	—	21,701	20,417	20,017	—	13,701	12,417	12,017	—	-544	-417	-324
0.5	1st	135	115	109	102	13,455	10,704	10,000	9,136	12,486	9,812	9,124	8,276	6,974	5,292	4,734	4,268	969	892	876	860
	2nd	91	94	95	99	9,114	9,682	10,000	10,590	10,442	10,893	11,185	11,745	4,938	5,238	5,343	5,806	-1,328	-1,211	-1,186	-1,155
	% Fluctuation	38	20	13	4	38	10	0	15	18	10.4	20	35	34	1	14	33	—	—	—	—
	Total	—	—	—	—	22,569	20,387	20,000	19,726	22,928	20,705	20,311	20,021	11,912	10,430	10,168	9,974	-359	-319	-310	-295
1.0	1st	115	109	107	102	11,458	10,448	10,000	9,206	10,503	9,534	9,104	8,338	4,612	4,127	3,912	3,529	955	914	896	868
	2nd	94	95	96	99	9,375	9,769	10,000	10,539	10,547	10,927	11,155	11,689	4,313	4,504	4,618	4,884	-1,172	-1,158	-1,155	-1,150
	% Fluctuation	20	13	10	3	20	7	0	14	0.4	14	20	33	7	9	17	32	—	—	—	—
	Total	—	—	—	—	20,833	20,217	20,000	19,745	21,050	20,461	20,259	20,027	8,925	8,631	8,530	8,413	-217	-244	-259	-282
5.0	1st	102	102	102	101	10,253	10,114	10,000	9,519	9,293	9,164	9,063	8,614	1,543	1,522	1,505	1,430	960	950	937	905
	2nd	98	98	99	99	9,846	9,929	10,000	10,323	10,930	11,020	11,097	11,442	1,813	1,828	1,841	1,899	-1,084	-1,091	-1,097	-1,119
	% Fluctuation	4	4	3	2	4	2	0	8	16	18	20	28	16	18	20	28	—	—	—	—
	Total	—	—	—	—	20,099	20,043	20,000	19,842	20,223	20,184	20,160	20,056	3,357	3,350	3,346	3,329	-124	-141	-160	-214

Appendix IV
Price Control Simulation

1. INTRODUCTION

THE two period analysis presented in the text and Appendices 2 and 3 can be applied to a series of two period situations in a representative past period using actual market prices in order to arrive at probable net control effects over a long period of time. The usefulness of such simulation of control over a past period is dependent upon the extent to which the period will be representative of the future. Although the approach suggested below is most straightforward for commodities which have experienced no significant control in the recent past, such as rubber and cocoa, it may also be applied to analysing possible control effects on commodities which are controlled. If the volume of quota or buffer stock restrictions and releases is known for all periods in the simulation, postulated supply and demand elasticities can be used to derive the uncontrolled market prices. Once these are obtained, the procedure is the same as presented here. Where reliable forecasting models exist, the procedure can also be applied to projected market conditions.

This appendix demonstrates the application of simulation techniques to rubber market control by the Malaysian national rubber buffer stock from 1961 through 1970. The national buffer stock authority enters the market when the Kuala Lumpur price touches the established floor or ceiling price. Ribbed Smoked Sheet grades 1–5 are purchased, with most purchases being weighted toward the higher grades. Price limits are given a $M0.10–0.15 per pound spread and reviewed as frequently as once a month in the light of possible trend developments. No attempt is made to influence the trend. During periods of floor price support rubber is purchased by the authority in Kuala Lumpur from local dealers and brokers, and transported to the nearest large port, Port Klang, where it is stored in private commercial and port authority godowns until sold at the f.o.b. price during a period of ceiling price support. Funds for financing the stock are obtained interest free from the Government and there is no overt policy of profit making on operations.

An important factor indicated by the simulation is the large amount of

TABLE A4.1
BUFFER STOCK MONTHLY OPERATING EXPENSES PER LONG TON*
—$M—

Items of Expenditure	Fees upon Purchase	Monthly Costs	Turnover Costs	Fees upon Sale
Brokerage	2.85	–	5.69	2.85
Transport to Port	5.08	–	5.08	–
Handing (Unloading)	0.91	–	1.83	0.91
Internal Haulage	–	–	2.03	2.03
Storage	–	15.24	–	–
Interest at 8% p.a.	–	9.90	–	–
Insurance	–	0.07	–	–
Loss in Grade	–	–	11.20	–
TOTAL COST	8.85	25.21	25.83	5.79

*$M1=$US0.36

funds operators may expect to spend to cover the cost of even a modest buffer stock programme. In compiling a schedule of costs, it was assumed that the authority would operate, as they do, through the private commercial trade in Kuala Lumpur. Table A4.1 enumerates these fees. Should the authority sell shortly after purchase, the price differential between the Kuala Lumpur and f.o.b. prices may be recovered in part or in whole. However, margins might not permit recovery of purchasing and/or selling fees since the authority is entering the market as an additional middleman. Because of the lapse of time between purchase and sale, all buffer stock expenses are seen as speculative investment which may not be recouped at a later date. The debatable aspects of this assumption are circumvented by the authority's assumed unlimited access to capital. The magnitude of brokerage and handling expenses will marginally affect capital requirements but leave control unaffected. Although purchases are financed by an interest-free Government advance, an opportunity cost of 8 per cent per annum, comparable to that obtainable on the local financial market for this purpose, has been imputed to the value of stock held. Simulated sales are on a first-in-first-out basis and stock turnover occurs after twelve months of storage. (Loss in grade may be avoided by turnover after six months, involving approximately identical costs.) Difficulties in estimation precluded the use of other administrative expenses.

The method adopted here for establishing the monthly price range assumes frequent review of the price range and the avoidance of trend control in accordance with the authority's policy. The authority is assumed to make an exact prediction of the ten year linear trend which becomes the mean of alternative price spreads. In comparison, results obtained with a price range mean equal to the weighted moving average of the uncontrolled market weighted average price during the previous twelve months produced only marginal changes over those effects presented here. Although there is no acknowledged set procedure for determining the mean of the price range used by the authority, either of these may provide a likely approximation to actual practice.

2. SIMULATION MODEL

Formulations used in the 120 monthly iterations of each test are given in Table A4.2 where:

P the uncontrolled market price, Kuala Lumpur, derived from Malaysian Statistics Department data.

$P_{f;c}$ the floor or ceiling price limit.

P_r the price obtaining under buffer stock control. Where the authority has insufficient resources to defend the price limits, P_r will not coincide with P_f or P_c.

Q the uncontrolled export volume from Malaysia, derived from Statistics Department data.

Q_a the quantity which appears on the control-influenced market. Q_a does not necessarily equal Q_d.

Q_b stocks or funds available to defend a price limit.

Q_d the quantity needed (demanded) on the market to support a price limit.

$Q_{f;c}$ the quantity bought by the authority at the floor or sold at the ceiling during a month of price support.

Q_1 the largest quantity the authority can buy or sell if it uses all its capital or stocks in a given month.

Q_s the quantity supplied at the control-influenced price by sellers other than the authority.

B fees per ton incurred upon purchase.

E the total operating expenses (excluding the cost of stock purchased) of the authority for the month.

H the storage cost per ton per month.

J the balance of capital in the buffer stock at the end of the month.

$K_{d;s}$ the constant term in the logarithmic-linear demand or supply function.

$n_{f;c;s}$ the price elasticity of demand in a month of floor, n_f, or ceiling, n_c, price support, or the price elasticity of supply.

R the rubber stock on hand at the end of the month.

R_e the twelve month old rubber stock.

T the turnover cost per ton.

V the selling expenses per ton.

X the export earnings, and

Y the producer earnings.

Under assumptions of constant supply and demand elasticity, market functions assume the form $Q = KP^n$. The quantity supplied to the market in a given month of floor or ceiling price support, Q_s, is given by

$K_s P_{f;c}^{n_s}$ and that demanded by the market, Q_d, by $K_d P_{f;c}^{n_{f;c}}$.

The quantity which appears on the control-influenced market, $Q_s \pm Q_{f;c}$, will equal the quantity demanded, Q_d, only if stocks, R, or funds,

$\dfrac{J - RH - R_e T}{P_f + H + B}$, are at least as large as $Q_s \pm Q_d$. The funds formulation

indicates that resources available to defend a floor price limit are dependent upon the balance of capital in the stock, J, less storage costs of rubber held, RH, and costs of turning over twelve month old stock, $R_e T$. Assuming that storage costs must be paid in the month of purchase, the volume that can be purchased with the funds indicated in the numerator of the formulation is given by the sum of the floor price, P_f, unit fees incurred upon purchase, B, and monthly unit storage costs, H. Should either stocks or funds be inadequate for complete price support, the partially controlled world price will not correspond to the price limit being supported. That is, P_r will differ

from the limit and is given by $\left[\dfrac{Q_a}{K_a}\right]^{\frac{1}{n_{f;c}}}$. Export earnings under control

are $P_r Q_a$ during a month of floor price support and the sum of $Q_s P_r$ and $Q_c P_c$, producer income plus authority income, during a month of ceiling price support.

Operating expenses of the authority given in Table A4.1 will be a function of stock held, turnover of old stock, and fees associated with market support activities. In a month of no price support expenses will be those incurred in storage, RH, and turnover of old stock, $R_e T$. In a month of floor price support expenses will also include storage costs, $Q_f H$, and fees, $Q_f B$, associated with the purchases. In periods of ceiling price support, stock is sold on a first-in-first-out basis to reduce loss in grade through quality deterioration. Thus, if old stock, R_e, is less than the volume to be sold at the ceiling, Q_e, operating expenses will be $(R - Q_e)H + (Q_e - R_e)V + R_e V$ assuming that old stock, R_e, is sold before it loses value during its twelfth month of storage. At the end of a given month, the balance of capital in the buffer stock to be carried forward, J, is determined by the balance at the end of the previous month, J_{t-1}, less operating expenses incurred during the month, E, plus the value of stock sold, $Q_c P_c$, or less the value of stock purchased, $Q_f P_f$.

In addition to those already cited, the analysis uses a variety of other assumptions, the principal ones being: producer price variations which reflect current nominal world market price changes; a derivation of producer in-

TABLE A4.2

FORMULATIONS USED TO DETERMINE MONTHLY VARIABLES

Free Market Price Position	Variables										
	Q_s	Q_d	Q_a	Q_b	$Q_{f;c}$	P_r	X	Y	R	E	J
$P_f \leqslant P \leqslant P_c$	Q	Q	Q	—	R_{t-1} and $J_{t-1}-RH-R_eT$	P	PQ	QP	R_{t-1}	$RH+R_eT$	$J_{t-1}-E$
$P_f > P$	$K_s P_f^{n_s}$	$K_d P_f^{n_f}$	Q_s-Q_f	$\dfrac{J-RH-R_eT}{P_f+H+B}$	If $(Q_s-Q_d) \leqslant Q_b$ then $Q_f=(Q_s-Q_d)$; If $(Q_s-Q_d) > Q_b$ then $Q_f=Q_b$	$\left[\dfrac{Q_a}{K_d}\right]^{\frac{1}{n_f}}$ (see note)	$Q_a P_r$	$X+Q_f P_f$	$R_{t-1}+Q_f$	$(R+Q_f)H+Q_f B+R_e T$	$J_{t-1}-E-Q_f P_f$
$P > P_c$	$K_s P_c^{n_s}$	$K_d P_c^{n_c}$	Q_s+Q_c	R	If $(Q_d-Q_s) \leqslant Q_b$ then $Q_c=(Q_d-Q_s)$; If $(Q_d-Q_s) > Q_b$ then $Q_c=Q_b$	$\left[\dfrac{Q_a}{K_d}\right]^{\frac{1}{n_c}}$ (see note)	$Q_s P_r+Q_c P_c$	$Q_s P_r$	$R_{t-1}-Q_c$	If $Q_c > R_e$ then $E=(R-Q_c)H+(Q_c-R_e)V+R_eV$; If $Q_c \leqslant R_e$ then $E=(R-Q_c)H+Q_c V+(R_e-Q_c)T$	$J_{t-1}-E+Q_c P_c$

Note: Mueller's iteration scheme of successive bi-section and inverse parabolic interpolation was used to determine market price, P_r, when $Q_b < Q_d$. In our case, Mueller's $f(P_r) = 0$ becomes $Q_b - K_s P^{n_s} + K_d P^{n_d} = 0$. Iterations were continued until an accuracy to the nearest dollar was obtained.

CHART A4.1

SIMULATION FLOW CHART

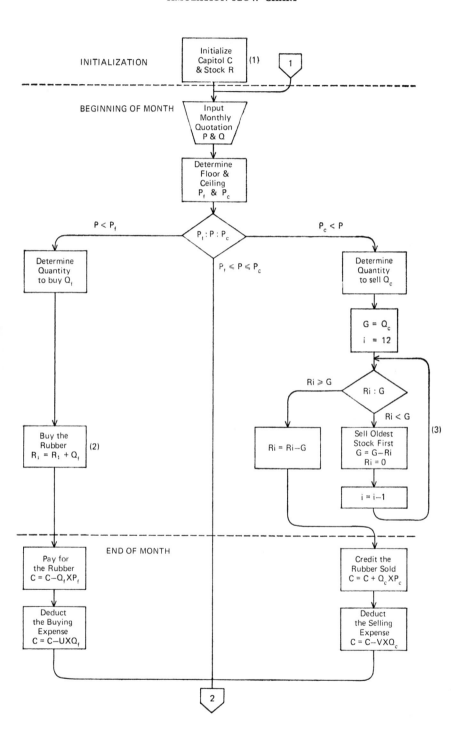

CHART A4.1 (Continued)

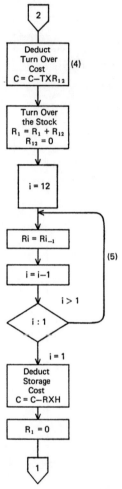

2

Deduct
Turn Over
Cost
$C = C - TXR_{12}$ (4)

Turn Over
the Stock
$R_1 = R_1 + R_{12}$
$R_{12} = 0$

$i = 12$

$Ri = Ri_{-1}$

(5)

$i = i-1$

$i > 1$

$i : 1$

$i = 1$

Deduct
Storage
Cost
$C = C - RXH$

$R_1 = 0$

1

Key: (1) C is set equal either to the initial funds of the authority or to zero if the authority is assumed to have unlimited capital, in which case negative C is permitted. (2) Rubber which is bought always enters the queue at R_1. (3) Rubber is always sold from R_{12} (the oldest stock) first. If that is insufficient then it is sold from R_{11}, R_{10} etc. (4) Twelve month old rubber is turned over (if not sold) and placed in R_1. (5) The entire queue is rotated one place at the end of the month.

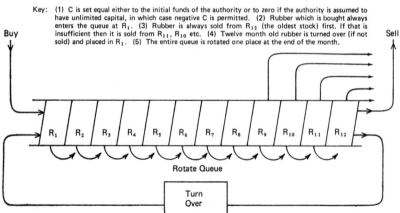

come which disregards marketing expenses, export taxes, and the small proportion of sales for the domestic market; market supply and demand functions which exhibit constant elasticity in any given period and over time and remain unaffected by control; and an authority which looks only at the weighted average price of exported rubber in setting price limits and either stocks all grades in weighted proportion or, through purchasing one or a few grades, has an identical effect on the spectrum of rubber prices.

The most recent decade, 1961–70, has been selected for the simulation because it is most likely to approximate future periods. With the discovery of stereo regular polymers in 1959, the 1960's is a period, like future periods, in which natural rubber enjoys no significant technical advantage over synthetic rubber. 1955 marked the end of the United States Government's control and subsidy of synthetic production and research and 1959, the end of the Malaysian insurgency which affected estate production through physical destruction and cost inflation. During the simulation period two notable changes occured in the production and marketing of rubber: a) 'super clones' were introduced which appreciably raised productivity and, to a lesser extent (because of declining prices), incomes in the rubber industry and b) rubber 'block', embodying improvements in grading and processing, was marketed. Improved clones, however, have accompanied every decade of production since the turn of the century and those currently on trial suggest that the 1970's will be no exception. To the extent that they increase producer incomes they reduce the urgency of income stabilization and possibly affect work effort response to price. By raising demand, improved grading and processing could be expected to show a similar effect. An extension of the simulation period would be difficult because of the official secrecy surrounding national buffer stock activities in 1971. The 1967–69 support is known not to have exceeded 20,000 tons.

Partial runs of the simulation over the period of price support during 1967–69, using as a capital constraint the $M17 million spent on stock purchased, had no significant effect on the monthly price and volume series. Effective control, with unlimited access to capital and a 15 cent price spread, required the purchase of 136,000 tons at a cost of $M222 million. The latter figure approaches an UNCTAD estimate of $M229.

3. SIMULATED CONTROL EFFECTS

A synthesis of the results of empirical tests and inferential reasoning of other studies suggests monthly supply and demand elasticities of 0.2 and −0.2, respectively. A rough estimate of the demand elasticity facing Malaysia may be obtained from the formulation:

$$n_d \text{Malaysia} = \frac{1}{\text{Proportion of world demand supplied by Malaysia}} \cdot n_d \text{world}$$

$$- \frac{\text{Proportion of world demand supplied by others}}{\text{Proportion supplied by Malaysia}} \cdot n_s$$

As a means of making accurate estimates of export demand elasticities for single countries this formulation is lacking in its disregard of tariff and transport barriers and other market impediments. Its advantage here lies in its use of a limited number of variables for which we have approximate magnitudes. With Malaysia exporting about 35 per cent of world natural rubber during the period of simulation, her short run demand elasticity is −0.95.

Table A4.3 presents the simulated control effects. By varying the demand elasticity and the controlled price spread about the mean of the price range, producer income is shown to increase with demand elasticity and decrease with a widening of the price spread. At low demand elasticities, including those most probable for Malaysia, and price spreads of 10–15 cents used by the buffer stock managers, producers suffer a loss over income earned in an uncontrolled market. Possible reasons for such a loss have been suggested in Chapter 4. The loss, however, amounts to less than one per cent of producer income and is premised on the assumption that price stabilization has no impact on the medium-long range demand function, a debatable assumption for a natural product with a close synthetic substitute. (To accommodate this effect in the model's terms, it would be necessary to make the demand function for a given period dependent upon prices and quantities in the preceding periods.) The effect of reduced price risk on demand would not have to be strong in order to make the device beneficial. Within the range of demand elasticities and price spreads appropriate for Malaysia, there is possibly a negligible increase in producer income instability measured by the logarithmic variance of the series. That is,

$$V_{log} = \Sigma \left[\frac{\log \frac{X_{t+1}}{X_t} - m}{N} \right]^2$$

where X_t is price, export earnings or producer income in month t; $N=120$ months of the simulation period minus 1; and m the arithmetic mean of the differences between the logs of X_t and X_{t+1} and X_{t+2}, etc. The instability index is

$$= [(\text{antilog } \sqrt{V_{log}}) - 1] \, 100,$$

and is roughly comparable to percentage fluctuations between periods.

The figures of Table A4.3 show export earnings generally decreasing with the width of the price range spread for low and increasing for high demand elasticities. The change over the uncontrolled market is less than one per cent for the postulated demand elasticity. Instability of export earnings is increased with control, particularly under high demand elasticities. The un-

TABLE A4.3

SIMULATED CONTROL EFFECTS WITH LINEAR PRICE MEAN AND $n_8 = 0.2$*

$M000,000

Demand Elasticity		Controlled Price Spread			
		0 cents lb.	5 cents lb.	10 cents lb.	15 cents lb.
No Control	Free Price	(3.16)	(3.16)	(3.16)	(3.16)
	Export Earnings	13,700 (15.2)	13,700 (15.2)	13,700 (15.2)	13,700 (15.2)
	Producer Income	13,700 (15.2)	13,700 (15.2)	13,700 (15.2)	13,700 (15.2)
−0.25	Controlled Price	(1.42)	(1.92)	(2.45)	(2.52)
	Export Earnings	13,717 (15.6)	13,674 (15.6)	13,670 (15.0)	13,674 (15.2)
	Producer Income	13,764 (16.0)	13,680 (15.8)	13,664 (15.0)	13,671 (15.2)
	Capital	f155 m267 h107	f70 m172 h64	f28 m99 h35	f12 m56 h20
	Control Periods	c98 p3 i19	c52 p0 i15	c31 p1 i8	c20 p1 i5
−0.50	Controlled Price	(1.42)	(1.97)	(2.42)	(2.56)
	Export Earnings	13,702 (15.5)	13,680 (15.4)	13,680 (15.1)	13,686 (15.2)
	Producer Income	13,764 (16.0)	13,686 (15.9)	13,671 (15.1)	13,674 (15.2)
	Capital	f222 m407 h160	f102 m263 h96	f43 m152 h53	f18 m87 h30
	Control Periods	c98 p3 i19	c50 p1 i16	c30 p1 i9	c20 p1 i5
−1.00	Controlled Price	(1.61)	(2.07)	(2.38)	(2.55)
	Export Earnings	13,700 (15.2)	13,700 (15.2)	13,700 (15.2)	13,700 (15.2)
	Producer Income	13,783 (16.1)	13,700 (16.1)	13,684 (15.4)	13,680 (15.2)
	Capital	f337 m671 h254	f166 m436 h156	f71 m253 h87	f30 m146 h50
	Control Periods	c95 p4 i21	c48 p1 i18	c29 p1 i10	c19 p1 i6
−1.50	Controlled Price	(1.73)	(2.44)	(2.34)	(2.58)
	Export Earnings	13,707 (15.1)	13,720 (15.5)	13,719 (15.4)	13,713 (15.3)
	Producer Income	13,821 (16.3)	13,733 (15.0)	13,696 (15.3)	13,686 (15.2)
	Capital	f451 m915 h338	f224 m598 h211	f96 m349 h119	f42 m202 h69
	Control Periods	c93 p4 i23	c46 p1 i20	c28 p1 i11	c19 p1 i6
−2.00	Controlled Price	(2.26)	(2.32)	(2.46)	(2.66)
	Export Earnings	13,715 (16.0)	13,739 (15.4)	13,738 (15.6)	13,726 (15.4)
	Producer Income	13,856 (15.1)	13,755 (15.6)	13,709 (15.3)	13,692 (15.3)
	Capital	f555 m1139 h414	f277 m749 h261	f119 m438 h148	f53 m256 h87
	Control Periods	c91 p4 i25	c46 p1 i20	c27 p1 i12	c19 p1 i6
−3.00	Controlled Price	(1.90)	(2.44)	(2.56)	(2.84)
	Export Earnings	13,729 (16.7)	13,775 (16.9)	13,769 (16.1)	13,751 (15.9)
	Producer Income	13,921 (15.7)	13,797 (15.5)	13,729 (15.5)	13,703 (15.4)
	Capital	f738 m1538 h545	f372 m1025 h350	f162 m603 h202	f73 m357 h120
	Control Periods	c89 p4 i27	c43 p1 i23	c27 p1 i12	c18 p1 i7

*Key: Bracketed figures in rows relating to price, export earnings and producer income indicate variance.
   f Outstanding deficit at end of simulation period.
   m Maximum amount of capital needed to support the floor price and cover costs.
   h Total operating expenses (excludes cost of rubber purchased).
   c Periods of complete control at the price limits.
   p Periods of partial control at the ceiling due to insufficient stocks.
   i Periods of no control at the ceiling due to lack of stocks.

favourable effect of the national buffer stock on the balance of payments may be averted if an overseas lender finances stocks held. Alternatively, a national buffer fund could be expected to reduce fluctuations in both producer incomes and export earnings. (See Table 4.1 in Chapter 4, p. 125).

In all cases, as may be expected, control has reduced price instability, but only marginally at the higher demand elasticities. If we relax our unrealistic assumption of unlimited capital, price support would not be as successful as demonstrated. As the capital constraint is made increasingly limiting, results would approach those obtained in the uncontrolled market unless the frequent depletion of resources during a period of price support caused precipitous changes in producer prices which more than neutralized the favourable effects of control. This occurred in the partial run mentioned above. For effective control (i.e. successful defence of the price limits) the amount of capital required under even the most favourable conditions is far in excess of the $M22 million at the disposal of the buffer stock managers in 1967–69 and increases appreciably with demand elasticity and the narrowness of the price range spread. The 'deficit' of the buffer stock at the end of the simulation (f) is dependent largely on the terminal period and does not include the value of stocks held. Although terminal period prices cannot be imputed to the value of stocks held since disposal of stocks would alter the price, an 'opportunity cost' of stabilizing prices in the future could be. For price spreads of 10–15 cents in Table A4.3 there are no terminal stocks and very low stock balances for the 0–5 cents spreads. If the analysis were continued into 1971, the 'deficit' would have increased greatly, but might subsequently have been eliminated by a rise in rubber prices above the ceiling. With a widening of the price spread, the period over which stocks must be held increases. Since the ceiling price is in secular decline over the period of the simulation, the longer stocks are held the less likely it is that costs will be covered by buying at low prices and selling at high. A wide price range reduces control and cost of rubber purchased and increases the period of storage while a narrow price range has the opposite effect. It should be noted that the model assumes the buffer stock is managed with atypical unsophistication. Making use of reliable forecasts and economic computations, the manager could sell rubber before the price reached the ceiling if the quantity in the stock appears excessive, so long as the amount sold does not drive the price below the floor. Conversely, he could buy rubber before the price reached the floor if the quantity in stock appears insufficient for the device to stabilize price effectively in the future.

With the model as it stands and within the range of likely elasticities and controlled price spreads ($M0.10–0.15), operating expenses on the one hand and the deficit at the end of the period on the other do not reach one per cent of export earnings or producer income. The required capital itself is only about 2.5 per cent of these last magnitudes. Consequently a buffer stock financed by Malaysia alone would be beneficial for the country if the stock succeeded in increasing the price of rubber (through reduced price risk) by roughly three per cent. The benefit would be larger and the cost in terms of proportion of producer income and export earnings would be smaller if all rubber producing countries were considered. The quantities to be bought or sold by an international device are the same as the quantities to be bought or sold by a national buffer stock for the same price range. If unit costs are the same, operating costs, deficit and capital requirements would also be the same. But the benefit or detriment will be distributed differently depending on whether the stock is operated by a given country, any other country, or at the international level. Likewise, the optimal patterns of price stabilization may differ between countries, especially if the supply functions are dissimilar and if the aim of the price stabilization is to maximize producers' income or export earnings.

Readings

Brown, C.P., 'International Commodity Control Through National Buffer Stocks: A Case Study of Natural Rubber', *Journal of Development Studies*, Vol. 10, No. 2, 1974 of which this appendix is an extract printed with permission.

Duloy, J.H., 'On the Variance Effects of a Buffer Stock Scheme: A Simulation Study of a Floor Price Plan for Wool', *Australian Economic Papers*, Vol. 4, 1965, pp. 79–92.

Kofi, T.A., 'International Commodity Agreements & Export Earnings: Simulation of the 1968 "Draft International Cocoa Agreement"', *Food Research Institute Studies in Agricultural Economics, Trade, & Development*, Vol. 11, No. 2, 1972, pp. 178–201.

Index

DATE DUE
